JOURNAL FOR THE STUDY OF THE OLD TESTAMENT
SUPPLEMENT SERIES
205

Editors
David J.A. Clines
Philip R. Davies

Executive Editor
John Jarick

GENDER, CULTURE, THEORY
1

Editor
J. Cheryl Exum

Sheffield Academic Press

Interested Parties

The Ideology of Writers and Readers
of the Hebrew Bible

David J.A. Clines

Journal for the Study of the Old Testament
Supplement Series 205

Gender, Culture, Theory 1

Copyright © 1995 Sheffield Academic Press

Published by Sheffield Academic Press Ltd
Mansion House
19 Kingfield Road
Sheffield, S11 9AS
England

Printed on acid-free paper in Great Britain
by Bookcraft Ltd
Midsomer Norton, Bath

British Library Cataloguing in Publication Data

A catalogue record for this book is available
from the British Library

ISBN 1-85075-570-1
ISBN 1-85075-748-8 pbk

for Heather

אשת חיל   אשה כנגדי

CONTENTS

ABBREVIATIONS

AV	Authorised Version (King James Version)
EVV	English versions
GNB	Good News Bible
JB	Jerusalem Bible
NAB	New American Bible
NEB	New English Bible
NIV	New International Version
NJB	New Jerusalem Bible
NJPS	New Jewish Publication Society Version
NRSV	New Revised Standard Version
REB	Revised English Bible
RSV	Revised Standard Version
RV	Revised Version

1

The Ideology of Writers and Readers of the Hebrew Bible

This book is about ideology, and the impact of various ideologies upon the formation of the Hebrew Bible (Old Testament) by its writers and upon its reception by its readers. It is not a systematic analysis of the ideologies of writers and readers of the Hebrew Bible, and it is far from presenting a unified and organized profile of ideologies ancient or modern. Rather, this collection of essays is a series of probes into issues of ideology, a set of studies of particular biblical texts and their interpretation in which I have found ideological questions coming to the surface. I did not set out to write a book about ideology, but I find that is what I seem to have done, even when I thought I was writing on Amos or Job or the Psalms.

Ideological criticism is something relatively new among biblical scholars,[1] so an introduction to what I understand by it may be of value. In this Chapter, I shall consider in turn, 1. the term 'ideology', 2. the import of the phrase 'writers and readers of the Hebrew Bible', 3. what I intend to examine under the heading of 'the ideology of writers and readers of the Hebrew Bible', and 4. how the ideology of writers and readers makes them 'interested parties'.

1. Ideology

The meaning of the word 'ideology' is something it is notoriously difficult to get agreement about. As I see it, there are

---

1.   At least in its more systematic and theoretical mode; two key works have been Fernando Belo's *A Materialist Reading of the Gospel of Mark* (trans. Matthew J. O'Connell; Maryknoll: Orbis Books, 1981) and issue 59 of *Semeia, Ideological Criticism of Biblical Texts* (ed. David Jobling; Guest Editor, Tina Pippin; Atlanta: Scholars Press, 1992).

several equally good denotations of the word, and even more connotations. Since the word appears in the subtitle of this book, I had better try to make clear how I am using it, and what I do not mean by it.[2]

I would arrange the *denotations* of 'ideology' according to their 'weakness' or 'strength', that is, their degree of generality or specificity. 'Ideology' can mean

1. a more or less connected group of ideas
2. a relatively coherent set of ideas amounting to a world-view, or outlook on life
3. a set of such ideas special to a particular social class or group
4. the set of ideas held by the dominant group in a society

Among the *connotations* of the term 'ideology' are the following:

1. ideas that are shared with others
2. ideas serving the interests of a particular group, especially a dominant group
3. ideas that are wrongly passed off as natural, obvious or commonsensical
4. ideas that are assumed rather than argued for

2. Here are some of the works (in alphabetical order of their authors' names) I have consulted on the concept 'ideology': Louis Althusser, 'Ideology and Ideological State Apparatuses', in his *Lenin and Philosophy and Other Essays* (trans. Ben Brewster; London: New Left Books, 2nd edn, 1971), pp. 121-73 (reprinted in *Mapping Ideology*, pp. 100-40 [see Žižek below); Maurice Cranston, 'Ideology', in *The New Encyclopedia Britannica: Macropaedia*, XX (Chicago, 1974), pp. 768-72; Terry Eagleton, *Ideology: An Introduction* (London: Verso, 1991); Eagleton, *Criticism and Ideology: A Study in Marxist Literary Theory* (London: Verso, 1978 [original edition, 1976]); Christopher Hampton, *The Ideology of the Text* (Milton Keynes: Open University Press, 1990); Fredric Jameson, *The Political Unconscious: Narrative as a Socially Symbolic Act* (Ithaca: Cornell University Press, 1981); James H. Kavanagh, 'Ideology', in *Critical Terms for Literary Study* (ed. Frank Lentricchia and Thomas McLaughlin; Chicago: University of Chicago Press, 1990), pp. 306-20; George Lichtheim, *The Concept of Ideology and Other Essays* (New York: Random House, 1967), pp. 3-46; Slavoj Žižek (ed.), *Mapping Ideology* (London: Verso, 1994).

5.   ideas that are often unexpressed and unrecognized by those who hold them
6.   ideas oriented toward action, ideas controlling or influencing actions
7.   'a representation of the imaginary relationship of individuals to their real conditions of existence'[3]
8.   false ideas
9.   ideas, different from our own, that other people have
10. rationalistic or metaphysical ideas, as distinct from practical politics
11. a romantic view of the world, idolizing the ideal and scorning the actual
12. a totalitarian attitude
13. a pseudo-scientific attitude to history and social realities.

For myself, and for the purposes of this book, I am operating for the most part with denotations 2 and 3. That is, by 'ideology' I do not mean just any group of ideas on any subject whatever; I am interested in the kind of large-scale ideas that influence and determine the whole outlook of groups of people. Sometimes, if I think I can, I try to relate such ideologies to identifiable groups or classes; but sometimes, lacking the evidence, I stop short of suggesting a particular social location for the ideology I am considering. I am not claiming that what I identify as 'ideologies' are necessarily the ideology of the ruling class of their time, whether ancient or modern, but I am usually conscious of the will to power expressed in ideologies, whether it is, for instance, the royal ideology of ancient Israel or the religious ideology of the guild of modern biblical scholars.

As for the connotations of the term, when I say 'ideology' I usually have in mind some of the first seven connotations I have mentioned above, but not the last six. I do not assume, for example, that ideologies are false, partly because I too have ideology and I hold to my ideology with conviction, thinking it 'true'. I don't believe that ideologies are private affairs, however, and I accept that most of 'my' ideology is inherited or acquired

3.   Althusser, 'Ideology and Ideological State Apparatuses', in *Mapping Ideology*, p. 123.

from others (from some group or other), that my ideology serves
my own interests and the interests of my group or groups, that I
tend to think of my ideology as natural and obvious, and that I
am not always fully aware of what and how much I am taking
for granted. So while I am not ashamed of having an ideology, I
am abashed at taking so much at second-hand, so much for
granted. Nor am I unhappy that other people have ideologies of
their own, but only that they also too often think that their ideologies are obviously right and (especially) that they try to tell me
that I should be adopting their ideologies.

Since ideologies are, in my opinion, very often simply
assumed, even without their adherents even knowing quite what
they are assuming, it is my purpose in this book to do a lot of
uncovering of ideologies, ideologies adhered to both by writers
and by readers of the Hebrew Bible. I think it is bad when we
assert things on the basis of some hidden agenda or presuppositions, worse in a way when we don't even know that that is what
we are doing, and worse still when we influence or control other
people with our ideology-led assertions, especially when their
ideology may be quite different. So I suppose it has become
something of a crusade for me to try to reach beneath the surface
of the text of the Hebrew Bible and the texts of biblical scholars
and to expose what it is I think is 'really' going on underneath
the claims and commands and statements of the biblical and the
scholarly texts—at the level of big ideas, I mean, of ideology.

The term 'ideology' is by no means unknown in biblical
criticism, I must say. Not a few people use it in one of the
'weaker' (though perfectly valid) senses, as when they write
about the ideology of kingship in ancient Israel,[4] meaning the

4. For example, Antti Laato, 'Psalm 132 and the Development of the
Jerusalemite/Israelite Royal Ideology', *Catholic Biblical Quarterly* 54 (1992),
pp. 49-66; Robert P. Carroll, 'Textual Strategies and Ideology in the Second
Temple Period', in *Second Temple Studies: 1. Persian Period* (ed. Philip R.
Davies; Journal for the Study of the Old Testament Supplement Series, 117;
Sheffield: JSOT Press, 1991), pp. 108-24; Carroll, 'Ideology', in *A Dictionary
of Biblical Interpretation* (ed. R.J. Coggins and J.L. Houlden; London: SCM
Press, 1990), pp. 309-11; J. Cheryl Exum, 'Murder They Wrote: Ideology and
the Manipulation of Female Presence in Biblical Narrative', in *Telling Queen
Michal's Story: An Experiment in Comparative Interpretation* (ed. David J.A.

views people (especially writers of the biblical books) held about kingship, or when they speak of a biblical writer's 'ideological point of view', meaning 'the set of assumptions and convictions against which everything in the story...is evaluated'.[5] But the term 'ideology' is not the most frequently used term for sets of ideas in the biblical writings: much more often, they are called 'theology'. This terminology makes sense, of course, since many of the ideas in the Bible are directly about God and most others have at least a theological element in them. But I prefer to speak of 'ideology' and to regard theology as a subset of ideology, just as I would regard cosmology or politics or law.

Some biblical scholars indeed use 'ideology' in the more pejorative sense of 'false consciousness'. Thus, for example, Walter Brueggemann in his book, *Israel's Praise: Doxology against Idolatry and Ideology*, understands 'ideology' as 'vested interest which is passed off as truth, partial truth which counterfeits as whole truth, theological claim functioning as a mode of social control'.[6] I am very sympathetic to this definition and especially to his

Clines and Tamara C. Eskenazi; Journal for the Study of the Old Testament Supplement Series, 119; Sheffield: JSOT Press, 1991), pp. 176-98 (previously published in *Union Seminary Quarterly Review* 43 [1989], pp. 19-39, and in *The Pleasure of her Text: Feminist Readings of Biblical and Historical Texts* [ed. Alice Bach; Philadelphia: Trinity Press International, 1990], pp. 45-68); Michael V. Fox, *Character and Ideology in the Book of Esther* (Studies on Personalities of the Old Testament; Columbia: University of South Carolina Press, 1992); Sara Japhet, *The Ideology of the Book of Chronicles and Its Place in Biblical Thought* (trans. Anna Barber; Frankfurt am Main: Peter Lang, 1989); Seth Schwartz, 'A Note on the Social Type and Political Ideology of the Hasmonean Family', *Journal of Biblical Literature* 112 (1993), pp. 305-309; A.G. van Aarde, 'Narrative Point of View: An Ideological Reading of Luke 12:35-48', *Neotestamentica* 22 (1988), pp. 235-52; S. van Tilborg, 'Ideology and Text: John 15 in the Context of the Farewell Discourse', in *Text and Interpretation: New Approaches to the Criticism of the New Testament* (ed. P.J. Hartin and J.H. Petzer; New Testament Tools and Studies, 15; Leiden: E.J. Brill, 1991), pp. 259-70; W.J. Wessels, 'Jeremiah 22, 24-30: A Proposed Ideological Reading', *Zeitschrift für die altestamentliche Wissenschaft* 101 (1989), pp. 232-49.

5.   So Stephen D. Moore, *Literary Criticism and the Gospels: The Theoretical Challenge* (New Haven: Yale University Press, 1989), p. 56.

6.   Walter Brueggemann, *Israel's Praise: Doxology against Idolatry and Ideology* (Philadelphia: Fortress Press, 1988), p. 111.

identification and evaluation of the royal, statist, cultic ideology
in ancient Israel. But I would rather say that those who opposed
that 'bad' ideology were themselves caught up in some ideology
or another, and the fault with the royal ideology is not that it is
ideology but that it deceptively promotes the interests of those in
power—which Brueggemann (and I) do not approve of.

For Brueggemann, the false consciousness he terms ideology is
the ideology of certain *writers* of the Hebrew Bible: he finds their
ideology inscribed in certain texts, and he finds other texts, such
as those of the prophets, to be in opposition to their ideology.
For Giovanni Garbini, on the other hand, in his book *History and
Ideology in Ancient Israel*, the ideology that distorts reality is the
ideology of certain *readers* of the Hebrew Bible, namely theologians who masquerade as historians.[7] To be sure, as Garbini
observes, the writers of the biblical histories themselves had 'an
ideological motivation which controls the exposition of events',[8]
but in this respect they were no different from historians everywhere, and it is not *their* ideological formation that is the
problem. The real problem is created by those modern readers
who are so susceptible to the biblical ideology that they themselves cannot allow 'a history writing which leaves theological
preoccupations out of account'.[9] I am entirely in sympathy with
Garbini's position, and applaud his unmasking of an uncritical
historiographical ideology. But the way I would express my
agreement would be to say that I accept Garbini's ideology in
preference to that of his opponents—rather than saying that I am
against ideology (as if to imply that he and I have none of our
own).

Now by some accounts, what I have said so far about ideology
will have sounded very limited, not to say shallow. For a fuller
understanding of the concept 'ideology' will acknowledge that it
is not only in words written in texts that ideology inscribes itself,
but also in speech and in customs and in images. Hollywood is
as much embroiled in ideology as any Marxist text, and the prac-

---

7.   Giovanni Garbini, *History and Ideology in Ancient Israel* (trans. John
Bowden; London: SCM Press, 1988), pp. 2-3; cf. also p. 174, where he speaks
of the 'false problems created by theology'.

8.   Garbini, *History and Ideology*, p. 14.

9.   Garbini, *History and Ideology*, p. 14.

tices of the democratic political system, of education, of the media, as well as the customary behaviour in families, and at formal meetings and informal social events, create and transmit the ideological systems in which we are all implicated, and which we most of the time take for granted as normal and natural.[10] All of these institutions can be regarded, from the standpoint of ideology and its propagation, as 'ideological state apparatuses',[11] which function to reproduce the dominant ideology in successive generations of citizens. And all their practices that convey ideology can be termed 'signifying practices', the different institutions generating their own sets of signifying practices or 'discourses'.[12]

This fuller sense of 'ideology' is one that I entirely accept, but it is not the sense in which I use the term in this book. For I find it hard to conceive how a detailed ideological analysis—in the fuller sense—could be made of ancient Israel, given the extreme paucity of the data we have for the reconstruction of social reality in that culture. I have no doubt that more could be done than has been attempted in the present book, the scope of which is very definitely texts, ancient and modern. I think that both Norman Gottwald and David Jobling, as well as other contributors to the Society of Biblical Literature Consultation on Ideological Criticism of Biblical Texts (originating in 1990), have given more theoretical attention to the social realities of ancient Israel as the matrix of biblical ideologies than I have been able to

---

10. So ideology may be defined as 'a system of representations, perceptions, and images that precisely encourages men and women to "see" their specific place in a historically peculiar social formation as inevitable, natural, a necessary function of the "real" itself' (Kavanagh, 'Ideology', in *Critical Terms for Literary Study*, p. 310).

11. The term is Louis Althusser's; the institutions he identifies as 'ideological state apparatuses' can be found in 'Ideology and Ideological State Apparatuses', in *Mapping Ideology*, pp. 100-40 (110-11) (originally in his *Lenin and Philosophy and Other Essays* [trans. Ben Brewster; London: New Left Books, 1977]).

12. This sense of the term 'discourse' comes from Michel Foucault; see especially his work, *The Archaeology of Knowledge* (trans. A.M. Sheridan Smith; London: Tavistock, 1972 [first published, 1969]). Cf. also Paul A. Bové, 'Discourse', in *Critical Terms for Literary Study*, pp. 50-65.

do in this book; but I stick to my last, and hope (to continue the metaphor) to leave my readers well shod.[13]

2. *Writers and Readers of the Hebrew Bible*

Wwriters and readers of the Hebrew Bible are equally the focus of this book. That fact makes the book rather unusual, I believe, because the tendency of biblical criticism has been to attend only—or at least primarily—to the writing, the composition, of the texts. Pick up any Introduction to the Old Testament, and you will find an almost exclusive concentration on how the texts came into being, who their authors were and what their intentions in writing them were. The *readers* of the Hebrew Bible, on the other hand, those for whom these very Introductions are being written, and who are expected to lay out good money for them, are invisible. They are never profiled or differentiated; their interests or needs are not referred to.[14] Even that reader of the Hebrew Bible who is the author of an Introduction to it keeps himself (or herself?) hidden; except in the preface, where it is apparently *de rigueur* to divulge details of the author's domestic life, the author goes underground, implicitly representing the contents of his (or her?) book as impersonal, objective, normative scholarship.

With the advent of rhetorical criticism in biblical studies, attention shifted, in some circles at least, away from the writers of the biblical texts to 'the texts themselves', to 'intrinsic

13. I am referring especially to issue 59 of *Semeia, Ideological Criticism of Biblical Texts* (ed. David Jobling; Guest Editor, Tina Pippin; Atlanta: Scholars Press, 1992). Norman Gottwald has been the pioneer in ideological studies of the Hebrew Bible, especially with his groundbreaking work *The Tribes of Yahweh: A Sociology of the Religion of Liberated Israel 1250–1050 B.C.E.* (London: SCM Press, 1980). See also *The Bible and Liberation: Political and Social Hermeneutics* (ed. Norman K. Gottwald; Maryknoll, NY: Orbis Books, 1983). A precursor whose work should not be forgotten is Morton Smith, *Palestinian Parties and Politics That Shaped the Old Testament* (Lectures on the History of Religions, ns 9; New York: Columbia University Press, 1971).

14. I don't mean to deny that certain assumptions about them are made by the authors, especially about their religious beliefs and about the nature of their interest in biblical criticism; it is just that these assumptions are not expressed in the text of their books.

criticism', and so on.[15] And with reader response criticism, the existence of actual readers of texts was at last given some formal and theoretical acknowledgment within the praxis of biblical scholarship.[16] It will be a long day, nevertheless, before the presence of readers, in their varying forms and manifestations, are adequately recognized in the discipline, where authors are still the major focus for scholarship. The present book, with its concern to examine the ideologies of writers as well as readers of the Hebrew Bible, might perhaps be thought to be something of a concession to the traditional biblical criticism, so I should stress that in no way do I abjure the rights of readers to feature in scholarly works about the Hebrew Bible. I simply do not want to concentrate all my attention on readers, and I think that, in the matter of ideology, there are worthwhile things to be said about writers as well as readers. I should also add that by enquiring after authors I do not mean to subscribe to the older questions about date and authorship and composition. I am asking about authors as producers of texts, about their social, class and gender locations, and not usually about 'real' authors, but about 'implied' authors—the authors whom the extant texts presuppose.[17]

So, as I say, I am interested here in the ideologies both of writers and of readers of the Hebrew Bible. I make no claim to a

15. On rhetorical criticism, see, for example, Jared J. Jackson and Martin Kessler (eds.), *Rhetorical Criticism: Essays in Honor of James Muilenburg* (Pittsburgh Theological Monograph Series, 1; Pittsburgh: Pickwick Press, 1974); David J.A. Clines, David M. Gunn and Alan J. Hauser, *Art and Meaning: Rhetoric in Biblical Literature* (Journal for the Study of the Old Testament Supplement Series, 19; Sheffield: JSOT Press, 1982).

16. See, for example, Robert Detweiler (ed.), *Reader Response Approaches to Biblical and Secular Texts, Semeia* 31 (1985); David J.A. Clines, *What Does Eve Do to Help? and Other Readerly Questions to the Old Testament* (Journal for the Study of the Old Testament Supplement Series, 94; Sheffield: JSOT Press, 1990).

17. I shall try not to speak of the ideology of the texts, since, as Stephen Fowl has rightly pointed out, texts do not 'have' ideologies, any more than they 'have' meanings ('Texts Don't Have Ideologies', *Biblical Interpretation* 3 [1995], pp. 15-34). For that matter, I should probably not speak of *writers* having ideologies, but rather of ideologies having writers. But I shall not promise to resist the way of the world on either count.

generalizing analysis of the ideologies of either group. On the Hebrew Bible front, what I am undertaking in this book is to examine certain key texts, like the Decalogue or Job or Amos, in order to uncover the ideologies that lie beneath the surface. And on the readers' front, I am mainly interested in the ideology of scholarly interpreters of those texts, especially the ways in which they either uncritically adopt the ideology of the text they are commenting on or impose the values of their own ideology upon the biblical text. There are of course more biblical texts, and a much greater variety of readers, than I have paid attention to in these essays. They are essays that are meant to be exemplary rather than comprehensive.

3. *The Ideology of Writers and Readers of the Hebrew Bible*

The essays contained in this volume do not all follow the same method. Some of them concentrate more upon the writers, some more upon the readers of the Hebrew Bible. Some of them suggest it is a good idea to read the Hebrew Bible from the standpoint of our own ideologies, some of them try to point out how foolish doing that can be. Some of them attempt to expose the uncritical complicity of modern readers with the ideology of the ancient texts, and some, contrariwise, take issue with the colonization of the ancient texts by alien modern ideologies. In short, I find, looking back over these essays, that in the four years I have been writing them I have been experimenting with questions about the clash of ideologies, and even now am only beginning to understand what the tendencies of these studies may be.

Deep down, I think these essays are operating with a fundamental distinction I want to make between *understanding* and *critique*.[18] In the project known as 'understanding' (which is the

18. I first outlined this distinction, and briefly argued for the foregrounding of the project of critique, in 'Possibilities and Priorities of Biblical Interpretation in an International Perspective', *Biblical Interpretation. A Journal of Contemporary Approaches* 1 (1993), pp. 67-87; see, for example, pp. 86-87: 'If we are not all the time making *judgments* on what we read and what we see, what claim can we have to be intellectual or ethical? Perhaps

Enlightenment project to which most scholars of the present day still subscribe), we aim at a fair-minded, patient and sympathetic re-creation of the meaning, significance and intentions of the ancient text in its own time.[19] Now that I am more alert than I used to be to the pervasive effects of ideology, both in the ancient and in the modern world, I am all the time looking for evidence of the ways ideologies threaten to hinder or skew this project of understanding the texts—which I continue to regard as part of my proper business. The project of understanding is always at risk when one of the three following facts is ignored: that the biblical text is an ideological production, that the interpreter is reading the text from within a particular ideological formation, and that the ideologies of ancient Israel are historically and culturally far removed from the ideologies of our own day. Now, there is no procrustean procedure that must be followed willy-nilly in order to ensure that the question of ideology is brought to the forefront, but in one way or another it is essential, so I have come to believe, that we recognize the ideologies of writers and readers and the inevitable distance between the ideologies in which both writers and readers are embedded.

It is possible to believe that the scholarly study of the Bible has reached its goal when it has attained an 'understanding' of the texts. Most biblical scholars indeed regard it as the whole of their task to understand, exegete, explain, and comment on their texts. There is, however, yet another distinct project in which I think that we ought to be engaged as readers of the biblical texts: that of 'critique' or evaluation. It is a measure of our commitment to our own standards and values that we register disappointment, dismay or disgust when we encounter in the texts of ancient Israel ideologies that we judge to be inferior to ours. And it is a

in fact the almost unchallenged assumption that the task of biblical scholars is essentially to *interpret* the text represents a systematic repression of our ethical instincts.'

19. I am aware of the problems associated with concepts like 'meaning' and 'intention', and in another, more purist, frame of mind would be denying that texts 'have' meanings, that texts can 'intend' anything, that texts should be regarded as the expression of authorial intentions, and so on. In everyday life, however, I act and speak 'as if' such sentences were unproblematic, just as I generally say without embarrassment that the sun 'rises' though I know that strictly speaking it does no such thing.

measure of our open-mindedness and eagerness to learn and do better that we remark with pleasure, respect and envy values and ideologies within the biblical texts that we judge to be superior to our own. 'Critique' does not of course imply *negative* evaluation, but it does imply evaluation of the texts by a standard of reference outside themselves—which usually means, for practical purposes, by the standards to which we ourselves are committed. For the task of critique, it is not *distance* between the ideology of the text and our own that we want (as for the project of understanding), but a close confrontation. To evaluate the text according to our own best values, we have to read it as the people we are, to collapse the historical distance between the text and ourselves, to treat the Bible as a book existing in the modern world, in competition to be heard alongside all the other ideological productions that surround us.[20] We have a responsibility, I believe, to evaluate the Bible's claims and assumptions, and if we abdicate that responsibility, whether as scholars or as readers-in-general of the Bible, we are in my opinion guilty of an ethical fault.

To my programme of reading the biblical texts according to my own cultural and ethical values I give the name, 'reading from left to right'.[21] If we are to read a Hebrew text, there is a cultural convention that our eyes must move from right to left; try to read a Hebrew sentence from left to right and it will be gibberish. The control exercised by this ancient cultural convention, even over modern readers who read everything else

20. A recent work that is taking seriously social and thus ideological location of interpreters is *Reading from this Place: Social Location and Biblical Interpretation in the United States* (ed. Fernando F. Segovia and Mary Ann Tolbert; Minneapolis: Fortress Press, 1995), with a sequel announced that addresses the wider world.

21. In my first paper using this phrase, 'Reading Esther from Left to Right: Contemporary Strategies for Reading a Biblical Text', in *The Bible in Three Dimensions: Essays in Celebration of Forty Years of Biblical Studies in the University of Sheffield* (ed. David J.A. Clines, Stephen E. Fowl and Stanley E. Porter; Journal for the Study of the Old Testament Supplement Series, 87; Sheffield: JSOT Press, 1990), pp. 22-42, I used 'left to right' to mean in our own cultural context and using the reading strategies of our own time. In the present book, however, the phrase has taken an ethical turn, and it means rather: according to the values of our culture.

from left to right, is an absolute one. Now this orthographic control is what I use as a symbol for the control the texts try to assert (and are often successful in asserting) over their readers. Readers who are not wide awake to the designs that texts have on them (to speak anthropomorphically) find themselves succumbing to the ideology of the texts, adopting that ideology as their own, and finding it obvious and natural and common-sensical. That is the default mode for commentators on biblical texts, for they rarely, if ever, offer a critique of the text; in confining themselves to 'understanding' and 'explaining' the text they typically screen out or suppress questions of value—and so leave half their proper task unattempted.

In this book, the various chapters present differing ways of critiquing ideology. In *The Ten Commandments* (Chapter 2) my aim is to uncover the class and gender ideology of a text that is usually regarded as purely of general theological import. I call the programme of reading biblical texts according to our own values a 'reading from left to right'—which is to say, subjecting the ancient text to a critique from (what I perceive to be) our own ideological position. The focus here is on readers. In *Haggai's Temple* (Chapter 3) the issue is the ideology of the writer who conceives of the Jerusalem temple as a treasury (rather than simply as a place of worship), with obvious implications for eschatology and Jewish–Gentile relationships in the writer's own day; the ideology of scholarly readers of Haggai, who make a theological and apolitical reading of an essentially political text, are considered only coincidentally. In *Why Is There a Song of Songs, and What Does It Do to You If You Read It?* (Chapter 5) and in the parallel essay on the Book of Job (Chapter 6), the accent is strongly on the influence that the ideology of the ancient text continues to exert upon modern readers, with an implicit message to modern readers that they should resist any uncritical adoption of the ideology of the text. In *Metacommentating Amos* (Chapter 4) the accent is upon discerning the ideological identity of the text by counterposing to it our own ideological stances about God and about crime and punishment, for example; without a counterpoint from an alien ideology, it has proved difficult for readers to recognize ideology in the book of Amos, and, for the most part, Amos has been thought to be transmitting some truth that is beyond cultural relativity. It is much the same with *A World Founded on Water (Psalm 24)* (Chapter 8): the deconstructive approach to the ancient poem highlights the ideology about holiness and war on which the text depends and invites modern readers to critique it according to the standards of their own ideology rather than simply adopt it as their own. In *God in the Pentateuch* (Chapter 9) the difficulties in identifying the ideology of the ancient author come to the fore: to what extent does the Pentateuch proffer an ideology of the divine that is harmonious and comfortable, and to what extent is it troublesome, inconsistent or subversive? No doubt the ideology of the reader who is also the author of this study has a powerful effect in shaping the way he constructs the ideology of the writer of the text. *David the Man: The Construction of Masculinity in the Hebrew Bible* (Chapter 10) begins from an analysis of the modern ideology of masculinity, and asks whether the biblical text matches the elements of that ideology at any point. What comes to light through such an analysis is that modern representations of the character David operate with the ideology of the present day rather than that of ancient Israel. So the implicit message of the essay is that the biblical narrative is distorted if it is read uncritically out of the constructions of masculinity prevalent in our own time. In *Job and the Spirituality of the Reformation* (Chapter 7) it is the ideology of the sixteenth century that is under investigation, with the intention of showing the distinctive contours of readings by Luther and Calvin that uncritically superimposed their own ideology upon the ancient text. I am not arguing that they (or we) should not use our own values when reading a text, but simply that they (and we) should not assume that there is no difference between the values inscribed in the biblical texts and those of interpreters from another culture. *Psalm 2 and the MLF (Moabite Liberation Front)* (Chapter 11), the last of the chapters, returns to the theme of *The Ten Commandments* in inviting readers to distance themselves from the ideology of the text by bringing to bear upon the text what I assume to be their own modern ideological convictions; it brings the book to a conclusion by emphasizing what I perceive to be the ethical dimension in this controversy of ideologies and by launching what I call a 'Bible readers' liberation movement'—a liberation from false ideologies (as I would call them) of certain biblical texts and especially of commentators.

4. *Interested Parties*

The final question for this introductory chapter is: How does the ideology of writers and readers of the Hebrew Bible make them 'interested parties'?[22]

At the simplest level, what I mean by that term is that writers and readers alike have some ideological investments.[23] Writers do not, on the whole, write their texts just for the fun of it; they have a case to put, an argument to advance, or an opponent to overcome. And since the name for their case, their argument, their position, is their 'ideology', I say that their text is a realization of their ideology, a performance of their investment in their ideology; one could say that ideology is 'inscribed' in their texts, meaning that the texts are themselves ways of thinking and speaking ideologically.[24] Readers too have ideological invest-

---

22. This is the place where I should thank my colleague Philip Davies for suggesting that the title of this book should be *Interested Parties*. It is not the first time that he suggested the *mots justes*.

23. It was a different world in the university system of the nineteenth century (a system that many academics think is still in operation), where a fundamental principle, not only in Germany, was the '[s]eparation of ideas from vested interests, the search for truth without extraneous influence' (Christian Simon, 'Hitory as a Case-Study of the Relations between University Professors and the State in Germany', in *Biblical Studies and the Shifting of Paradigms, 1850–1914* [ed. Henning Graf Reventlow and William Farmer; Journal for the Study of the Old Testament Supplement Series, 192; Sheffield: Sheffield Academic Press, 1995], pp. 168-96 [174]).

24. See Catherine Belsey, *Critical Practice* (New Accents; London: Methuen, 1980), p. 5: 'Ideology...is not a separate element which exists independently in some free-floating realm of "ideas" and is subsequently embodied in words, but a way of thinking, speaking, experiencing'. Bernard Sharratt has drawn our attention to the way anonymous texts (like those of the Hebrew Bible, we might say) have a special capacity for imposing their ideology on readers through the absence of an author; there is no author to stand over against the reader as an Other, just a text that readers are tempted to call their own (*Reading Relations: Structures of Literary Production. A Dialectical Textbook* [Brighton: Harvester Press, 1982], pp. 118-19).

ments—in what they choose to read, how they incorporate or fail to incorporate what they read into their own structure of opinions, how they report on what they have read and how they recommend or insist to others that they read the same works. Writers and readers alike are, on the whole, not casual, disinterested bystanders to their own activity, but promoters of their own ideological causes as they write and as they read.

There is another sense of 'interested parties' that is perhaps more important. It depends on the fact that ideologies are not just sets of mental ideas, but ideas that influence people's actions,[25] and so the relations among people, in the world. Since there is almost always a dissymmetry of power in relations between people and groups of people, an ideology tends to support and enhance the power of its adherents. In some streams of modern thought, indeed, ideology has been defined as the set of ideas that legitimate a dominant political power—as if ideology had to do only with social structures. I do not see the need to be so exclusive about the forms of ideology that can be encountered, but I agree that ideology is an important element within power relations. All those with ideological positions—which means all of us—are interested parties in the sense that our power, our control, and our significance are upheld by our ideology, and a challenge to our ideology is a threat to our importance.

There is yet a further sense I have in mind when I use the phrase 'interested parties' as the title of this book. I am thinking of the tendency to concealment (deliberate or unconscious) by ideologues of the motivation or rationale (in part or whole) for what they are saying. On the surface, their texts lay claim to coherence and rationality, and they give the appearance of sincerity and either moral fervour or objectivity. But beneath the surface there are issues of power, of self-identity and security, of group solidarity, of fear and desire, of need and greed, that have also played a role in the production of the text, sometimes a leading role. These are the kinds of interests that writers and readers of the Hebrew Bible are serving. We all do this kind of concealment of our motivations, and perhaps there is nothing wrong in it. Perhaps you do not even want to know what un-

25. 'Action-oriented sets of beliefs' (Eagleton, *Ideology*, p. 2).

expressed reasons I have for writing this book,[26] and perhaps I could not tell you the most of them even if I wanted to. Perhaps you do not know for what hidden reasons you are reading it. But texts and readers are fair game for ideological critics, and especially when texts are used by their readers in the service of power and of social control—which is often how the Bible is used—the temptation on the part of those who feel they are being controlled to search out what has been concealed becomes overwhelming. So this is not an innocent book, any more than the texts and the readers it discusses are innocent of vested interests. It does not lay claim to a calm neutrality or a distanced objectivity—not as a whole, that is. There is, I should hope, a good deal of scholarly rigour within it, but I would be deceiving myself if I thought that I (or any of us) were capable of disinterested scholarship. This book too is an ideological production. *Caveat lector.*

26. Part of the pleasure of reading is that authors never tell us the whole truth; reticence and partial concealment have their own special charm, as connoisseurs of the erotic know well enough. Analogically, Freud recognized that day-dreamers, even if they were to communicate their fantasies, 'could give us no pleasure by [their] disclosures'. But when a creative writer transforms his or her personal day-dreams into literature, 'we experience a great pleasure' ('Creative Writers and Day-Dreaming', in *The Standard Edition of the Complete Psychological Works of Sigmund Freud*, IX [trans. and ed. James Strachey, in collaboration with Anna Freud; London: Hogarth Press and the Institute of Psycho-Analysis, 1959], pp. 143-53 [152-53]). In Chapter 4 and elsewhere in this book, it may seem that I take a higher moral tone with commentators who conceal what they are doing from their readers; but I hope that my pleasure (not *Schadenfreude*, I insist) in the game of hide and seek is evident. See too Peter Hutchinson, *Games Authors Play* (London: Methuen, 1983), esp. pp. 21-23, on reading the 'unwritten' as a game in which authors and readers collaborate.

2

The Ten Commandments, Reading from Left to Right[*]

1. *Reading from Left to Right*

Almost any readings you will encounter of the Ten Commandments steadfastly read them from right to left—which is my
metaphor for: adopting the ideology inscribed in the text.
Literally reading from right to left means falling in with the convention that Hebrew texts are read in that direction; as a metaphor, reading from right to left also signifies an acceptance of a
convention. It means adopting the world of the text, the world
and worldview of the author, and the original intentions of the
text.

Most of our criticism of the Hebrew Bible lives in this right to
left world. Historical criticism, form criticism and redaction criticism always read from right to left, asking as they do about origins, intentions and effects but never, in principle, critiquing
them. So too does rhetorical criticism, with its concern for the
words on the page and their articulation but with a studied
unconcern for meaning or value. There is of course nothing
wrong with reading from right to left; but it is a quantum leap
from these approaches to one that directly confronts questions of
value and validity.

[*]   An earlier version of this essay was published in *Words Remembered,
Texts Renewed: Essays in Honour of John F.A. Sawyer* (ed. Jon Davies, Graham
Harvey and Wilfred G.E. Watson; Journal for the Study of the Old Testa-
ment Supplement Series, 195; Sheffield: Sheffield Academic Press, 1995),
pp. 97-112. The essay was originally delivered as a paper to the Narrative
Research on the Hebrew Bible Group, Society of Biblical Literature, Annual
Meeting, Kansas City, November, 1991, at the Exegetical Day of the Faculty
of Theology, Uppsala, Sweden, September, 1992, and to the Society for Old
Testament Study, London, January, 1993.

For myself, I think that the only way of taking a text seriously is to ask whether I accept it, whether I buy it, whether I believe it, whether I want to call it 'true', whatever that may mean. I don't have to decide in advance that it *is* true in order to be taking it seriously; but it is only if I think that its 'truth' is an important issue, that it is worth arguing with—worth confronting, that is, from my own standpoint—that I give it any honour. I call this project of reading the text by way of critique, 'reading from left to right'—which is to say, according to the canons of reading in our time, using the standards and moral values that come into play when we pick up the newspaper, a political tract or a new novel. Without making a fuss about it, and as naturally as our eyes scan the text from left to right, we find ourselves engaged as thinking, feeling, judging persons, asking, 'Is this true? Is it the case? Can I accept it? Will I have to change if I do accept it?'

2. *The Ten Commandments as Divine Law*

The first thing I observe when I try to take this text seriously, when I ask whether I believe it, when I consider whether I can buy its ideology, is its opening words, 'And God spoke all these words, saying' (Exod. 20.10), or, in its Deuteronomy version, its closing words, 'These words the LORD spoke to all your assembly at the mountain...and he added no more' (Deut. 5.22). Taking these words seriously, and not brushing them aside as some strange Hebrew idiom, I find myself asking: Did God (if there is a God) actually speak audible words out of the sky over a mountain in the Arabian peninsula in the late second millennium BCE? That is certainly what the text seems to be saying, and I seriously want to take it seriously. Now it is not for me to say what is and is not impossible, and I readily admit that the world is no doubt a more strange and wonderful place than I have personally experienced. But it will not shock many readers of these pages if I say I do not believe that any such thing ever happened, and that I would be surprised if any scholarly reader did either. But, as I say, strange and wonderful things happen.[1]

---

1. Here, for example, is Moshe Weinfeld: 'At the dawn of Israelite history the Ten Commandments were received in their original short form as the basic constitution, so to speak, of the Community of Israel. The words

The point, indeed, may seem so obvious that some may wonder why or whether it needs to be made. I make it just because not a single commentator that I have found remarks on this datum of the text, not one confronts the claim of the text with their own personal refusal to accept its ideology, not one draws any conclusion about the status of the text once they have decided they do not believe some significant part of it.[2] Not one commentator remarks that, if God did not in fact say all these words and the text says that he did, the text is telling us lies and trying to deceive us, and that is a strange state of affairs in a text that is in the business of laying down ethical principles.

Commentators have their own ways of avoiding the issue, of

---

were chiselled or written on two stone tablets...' ('The Uniqueness of the Decalogue', in *The Ten Commandments in History and Tradition* [ed. Ben-Zion Segal; Jerusalem: The Magnes Press, 1990], pp. 1-44 [27-28]). Received from *whom?*, we are bound to ask. And chiselled by *whom?* Weinfeld does not say, but Bible readers think they know whom he means. Interestingly enough, in another version of his paper the sentence reads, 'the Decalogue was promulgated'—which sounds more human, does it not? See his 'The Decalogue: Its Significance, Uniqueness and Place in Israel's Tradition', in *Religion and Law: Biblical-Judaic and Islamic Perspectives* (ed. Edwin B. Firmage, Bernard G. Weiss and John W. Welch; Winona Lake, IN: Eisenbrauns, 1990), pp. 3-47 (32).

2.   It is not entirely surprising that the great majority of commentaries do not make even a single comment on the verse 'And God spoke all these words, saying' (Exod. 20.1). Not even the 659-page commentary of Brevard S. Childs on Exodus (*Exodus: A Commentary* [Old Testament Library; London: SCM Press], 1974) finds room for a single remark, though on p. 397 he does observe that the first-person formula 'points to direct, unmediated communication of Yahweh himself' (presumably, that is, to a literary fiction of direct communication by Yahweh). The article by E.W. Nicholson, 'The Decalogue as the Direct Address of God', *Vetus Testamentum* 27 (1977), pp. 422-33, thinks that there is a theological reason (and not just an editorial reason) for the first-person speech, but it does not consider whether the ascription of these sentences to God is *true*. Apparently all theological reasons are good ones. Others who refer to the first-person address seem to be interested only in formal analogies (e.g. Anthony Phillips, *Ancient Israel's Criminal Law: A New Approach to the Decalogue* [Oxford: Basil Blackwell, 1970], p. 4) or in its redactional history (e.g. Frank-Lothar Hossfeld, *Der Dekalog: Sein späten Fassungen, die originale Komposition und seine Vorstufen* [Orbis biblicus et orientalis, 45; Freiburg, Switzerland: Universitätsverlag, and Göttingen: Vandenhoeck & Ruprecht, 1982], pp. 164-68).

course—which is to say, of not taking their text seriously.

Method One is to tell us that someone else spoke the ten commandments, *without telling us that in so saying they are denying that God did.* J. Philip Hyatt, for example, tells us that the commandments probably 'originated in the customs and regulations of the families and clans of pre-Mosaic times, as handed down by heads of families and clans, elders, and wise men'.[3] But he makes no remark whatsoever on v. 1, which says that these are the words of God. A stunning example of this procedure is provided by a little book entitled, *The Decalogue—Words of God?*[4] Although the implied answer is of course Yes, the author invariably speaks of the Decalogue as the product of humans, locating its origin in clan wisdom, paternal instruction, and the like. Not surprisingly, Exod. 20.1 does not appear in the index.

Method Two is to change the subject, and to make the issue whether the Ten Commandments were spoken by *Moses* or not. R.H. Charles, for instance, writes: 'The two codes we are considering are ascribed both in Exodus and Deuteronomy to Moses'.[5] This is of course not true; they are ascribed to *God*.

Method Three is to tell you how foolish you are if you think that 'God spoke all these words' was ever intended to mean that God actually spoke these words. Says James Barr, in a foreword to Eduard Nielsen's book on the Ten Commandments, 'Israelite law was not, as a superficial reading of the Old Testament might suggest, dropped complete from heaven, but grew and developed through various phases of the life of the Hebrew people'.[6] So it is not that the Old Testament claims one thing and modern scholars think another. Let us have no criticism of the Hebrew Bible here. Let us rather put the blame on its readers, those superficial ones who cannot see that 'written with the finger of God' means what it has always meant to readers of any intelli-

---

3. J. Philip Hyatt, *Commentary on Exodus* (New Century Bible; London: Oliphants, 1971), p. 210.

4. Helen Schüngel-Straumann, *Der Dekalog—Gottes Gebote?* (Stuttgarter Bibelstudien, 67; Stuttgart: Katholisches Bibelwerk, 1973).

5. R.H. Charles, *The Decalogue* (Edinburgh: T. & T. Clark, 1973), p. 28.

6. Eduard Nielsen, *The Ten Commandments in New Perspective: A Traditio-Historical Approach* (Studies in Biblical Theology, 2/7; London: SCM Press, 1968), p. vii.

gence: 'developed through various phases of the life of the Hebrew people'.

Method Four is to pretend (or, talk as if) God did actually speak all these words, while at the same time making quite clear that you do not believe he did. Dale Patrick, for example, apropos of the second commandment, says, 'It is intriguing to ask why Yahweh rejected images of himself'.[7] What the commentator really believes, I am sure, is that it was some human being who *said* that Yahweh 'rejected images of himself'. Whatever Yahweh thought about the matter, we have no first-hand knowledge about it. *We have only some human's word for it.* But the commentator makes it sound as if here in the Ten Commandments we have the *ipsissima verba* of Yahweh, as if here some question in the mind of Yahweh personally is being presumed and alluded to. The commentator simply does not confront the problem of the text's claim.

Perhaps it would not matter so much if the ten commandments were a less significant part of the Old Testament. The trouble is, the very commentators who refuse to take the text seriously—by buying its ideology uncritically—generally make a lot of noise about the importance of the text. Here is James Barr again:

> The Ten Commandments constitute beyond doubt the best known and most influential single passage in the whole Old Testament.[8]

And Eduard Nielsen takes up the strain:

> Of all the passages in the Old Testament the decalogue, 'the ten commandments', is presumably the best known to western civilization.[9]

7. Dale Patrick, *Old Testament Law* (Atlanta: John Knox Press, 1985), p. 45.
8. James Barr, preface to Nielsen, *The Ten Commandments in New Perspective*, p. vii.
9. Nielsen, *The Ten Commandments in New Perspective*, p. 1. Here are some more testimonials to the significance of the Ten Commandments, which we would do well to have in the back of our minds if we plan to study them critically: (1) '...the fundamental place of the Ten Commandments in human civilization as a revelation of eternal truths' (Ephraim E. Urbach, 'Preface', in *The Ten Commandments in History and Tradition*, p. xi). (2) 'In their role as the fundamental demands made by the God of Israel on

Maybe this is true, maybe not. Maybe it seems more true if you are a Presbyterian like Barr or a Lutheran like Nielsen. Never mind. The point is that so-called critical scholars have been reading this unquestionably important text as if it contained divine words when what it really contains (and they know it) are human words, social and religious laws that their authors want to ascribe to God because they want other people to obey them. Let us not beat around the bush: reading from left to right, stepping outside the conventions and beliefs that the text wants to impose on us, which is to say, reading this text as a humanly produced text and not privileging it because we want to agree with it or want to affirm its divine origin, we have to say (do we not?) that it stands written in Exodus 20 and Deuteronomy 5 because it was in the interests of its framers to promulgate its contents.

All of us have interests. We have interests whether or not we know of them, even whether or not we are interested in them. Interests devolve from our personal, social, economic, ethnic, sexual (and so on) location. We do not have a lot of choice about what our interests are, for they are implicates of our identity. If I am rich, or if I am heterosexual, it is not in my interest to promote an egalitarian social order or to seek to outlaw heterosexual acts between consenting adults. I can of course act against my interests, whether recklessly or highmindedly; but they are my interests, and it cannot be in my interest to act against them. My interests are mine whether I like them or not; they are interests determined for me by where I fit into the web of social networks.

So when it comes to reconstructing the pattern of interests of people in societies long defunct (as I am trying to do in this essay), though we may be in the area of the contingent, we are not necessarily in the area of the speculative. Such an enquiry is,

the Community of Israel, the Ten Commandments were familiar to every Israelite loyal to his heritage. They became the crowning point of his religious and ethical tradition... [I]t was only the Ten Commandments that Israel was privileged to hear directly spoken by the Deity' (Weinfeld, 'The Uniqueness of the Decalogue', in *The Ten Commandments in History and Tradition*, p. 21). The reader is invited to decide whether Weinfeld is simply reporting the stance taken by the biblical texts, or whether he is speaking in his own voice, as a believer, and uncritically.

indeed, at the mercy of our historical knowledge or lack of it. But because it deals with social locations and social relations, and thus with typicalities, it is on rather firmer ground than we tread when we enquire after discrete historical 'facts'. And, being concerned with public and observable realities rather than private mental processes, it is on very much firmer ground than the common enquiry in biblical criticism after authors' intentions. All in all, I want to argue, the reconstruction of the interests that lie behind our biblical texts, though far from being an exact science, might well be more secure and foundational than much that has passed for biblical criticism in recent centuries.

3. In Whose Interest Are the Ten Commandments?

In whose interest?—that becomes the question for this essay. The Ten Commandments exist because it is in someone's interest for them to exist. In *whose* interest, then, are they? Since societies, like ancient Israelite society, for example, are not homogeneous, I shall be asking, In which *group's* interest are these commandments? And since groups are usually in some kind of conflict with other groups, I shall be asking, What kind of *social conflict* is alluded to, or repressed, by this text? And since it is usually the victors in any social conflict whose texts get preserved, I shall be looking narrowly at *elites and powerholders* in Israelite society for the matrix of these laws.[10]

So saying, I am already being controversial. For it is part of the accepted wisdom that the Ten Commandments do *not* serve a sectional interest, that they apply equally to everyone and promote the greater good of the community as a whole. Thus, for example, Claus Westermann takes for granted that the commandment of monolatry applies 'to everyone and for all time',[11]

---

10. Most previous studies that profess to investigate the *social* setting of the Decalogue are not interested in *class* but in social constructs like 'clan' or 'wisdom circles' (so, for example, Erhard S. Gerstenberger, *Wesen und Herkunft des 'apodiktischen Rechts'* [Wissenschaftliche Monographien zum Alten und Neuen Testament, 20; Neukirchen–Vluyn: Neukirchener Verlag, 1965]); Hossfeld, *Der Dekalog*; Christoph Levin, 'Der Dekalog am Sinai', *Vetus Testamentum* 35 (1985), pp. 165-91.

11. Claus Westermann, *Elements of Old Testament Theology* (trans.

and Walther Zimmerli that 'the law of Yahweh is addressed first and foremost to Israel as a nation'.[12] So too Brevard Childs: 'The Decalogue is not addressed to a specific segment of the population, to the priestly class, or a prophetic office within Israel, but to every man'.[13] Perhaps, indeed, the framers of the commandments did think, as innocently as Brevard Childs did when he spoke of every *man*, that they *were* addressing the whole community; we however can only gasp at the audacity of authors who manage with a word to suppress vast constituencies, whether the powerless in general or women in particular.

In the search for the interests represented by the Ten Commandments, however, it is a different question we find ourselves asking. It is not the question of the intention of the authors, not the question of whom they thought they were addressing, but rather a question about the text. It is, What does the text assume, and how does it function? With this question we deflect our attention from authors—who were real people once but are now unfortunately entirely inaccessible—and fall to discussing narrators and narratees—who, while they are nothing but mental constructs, are fortunately perpetually accessible, for they are embedded in the text, they are a function of the text.

Who *is* envisaged in the Ten Commandments, then? Who is the narratee supposed by the narrator? It is not at all difficult to profile that figure. Put together all the data we have in the commandments about who is envisaged, and what we find is: it is an individual, a male, an Israelite, employed, a house-owner, married, old enough to have working children but young enough to have living parents, living in a 'city', wealthy enough to possess an ox and an ass and slaves, important enough to be called to

Douglas W. Scott; Atlanta: John Knox Press, 1982), p. 21 (he presumably means all Israelites).

12. Walther Zimmerli, *Old Testament Theology in Outline* (trans. David E. Green; Edinburgh: T. & T. Clark, 1978), p. 138.

13. Childs, *Exodus*, pp. 399-400. Cf. also Weinfeld: 'By contrast with many laws and commands...the commands in the Decalogue obligate *everyone*. Every single individual, regardless of his condition or the circumstances in which he finds himself, is required to observe them' ('The Uniqueness of the Decalogue', in *The Ten Commandments in History and Tradition*, p. 4). Weinfeld subsequently makes clear that by everyone he means every *Jew*, but he does not make clear whether he means every *male* Jew.

give evidence in a lawsuit. It is a man who is capable of committing, and probably tempted to commit, everything forbidden here—and likely to ignore everything enjoined here, if not commanded to observe it. It is, in short, one might say, a balding Israelite urban male with a mid-life crisis and a weight problem, in danger of losing his faith.[14]

Everyone else is not so much ignored—for several other categories of persons are mentioned—as sidelined. Women, for example, are present, but they are not addressed. Apparently the work they do does not count as work, since they have nothing to rest from on the sabbath; presumably the daughters are out in the fields, Ruth-like, so they need a weekly rest like their brothers. Women's sexuality likewise passes without notice: they can be coveted by their husband's neighbour, but they themselves cannot covet their husband's neighbour—or even, for that matter, their neighbour's husband. Resident aliens are referred to; they are even required to observe the sabbath law. But they are not *addressed* as narratees. They are in the same position as cattle, obliged to obedience, but not the persons addressed. Likewise slaves, children, the unmarried, elderly parents, the disabled, beggars, the landless, the dispossessed, day-labourers and the urban poor are not the narratees.

The text screens these people out: they are not 'neighbours'. The text is busily pretending that the whole society is made up entirely of a group of 'neighbours' (Exod. 20.16-17; Deut. 5.20-

---

14. I find that my analysis of the narratee has been anticipated by Frank Crüsemann, in his *Bewahrung der Freiheit: Das Thema des Dekalogs in sozialgeschichtlicher Perspektive* (Kaiser Traktate, 78; München: Kaiser, 1983), who describes him as a middle-aged male householder, a member of the *'am ha'arets* (esp. pp. 28-35). Where I differ from Crüsemann is that while he acknowledges that there are many members of Israelite society who are excluded from consideration in the Decalogue, he too excludes them from his consideration when he esteems the Decalogue to promote an ethic of freedom. Even if it is that (and I think it is something of a *tour de force* to argue it), it is freedom only to those who share that social standing. In my view, that very fact makes the Decalogue ethically problematic. William Johnstone has helpfully summarized and commented on Crüsemann's work in 'The "Ten Commandments": Some Recent Interpretations', *Expository Times* 100 (1988–89), pp. 453-61. I am grateful to Emma Clines for drawing these references to my attention.

21), who are men of a certain income and social standing, men more or less equal to one another. It does not recognize the existence of those who are not the narratees, who are not 'neighbours'. Now we all know who it is who pretends that everyone in a society is equal, that everyone has the same chances: it is always the haves, for it is in their interest to maintain the fiction. It makes them more comfortable not to have to worry that their privilege may be the cause of other people's poverty; and, if the underprivileged can be made to believe in this equality, it lessens the chances of social friction. The poor, however, are not under the illusion that they are the brothers or neighbours or equals of the rich.

If, then, in the world of the text it is these urban middle-aged males who are the narratees, and it is (of course) Yahweh who is the narrator, the question for the real world of social relations now becomes: In whose interest is it to have a text telling these pillars of society what they should and shouldn't do, in the name of Yahweh? It will not be slaves or women or resident aliens; though they do indeed stand to benefit from some of the commandments—some of them finding it agreeable to live in a society where work is forbidden on the sabbath and others preferring the laws against theft or murder—most of the commandments leave them cold. The only group in the society that stands to benefit from observance of the commandments as a whole are those who have spent their lives in the enforcement of such commandments and who are consequently the only ones who have the authority to tell the addressees of the commandments that they must obey them, upon pain of...whatever. It is, in a word, the fathers of those addressed, that is, the old men of the society, who speak in the name of God and whose interests are represented in every one of the commandments. No word is breathed, naturally, of the inevitable tension between those who want these laws to be kept and those who do not, between those whose interests they serve and those whose interests they damage. But the moment we allow that the laws do not serve all the members of the community equally, at that moment we recognize a social conflict repressed by the text. The fathers are always *against* someone, some group, whenever they assert their own group's interests.

Now the interests of the fathers are of course principally represented by the fifth commandment, 'Honour your father and
mother' (Exod. 20.12; Deut. 5.16). On this commandment, we
might say, hang all the law and the prophets—to coin a phrase.
Not only is the physical survival of the old men dependent on
the observance of the law, but their self-esteem also will be measured by their ability to ensure that their sons maintain the family and national traditions. It is entirely in their interests to say
that God demands you 'honour' your father, for that means you
must make sure he doesn't die of hunger even though he has
stopped being a productive member of the family, and it also
means that you must uphold all the values he has lived for. For
it would be equally a dishonour to an old man to be left to rot by
his son *and* to hear that his son is kicking over the traces. Now
keeping the old folk alive may be a drain on the pocket, but it
hardly does any harm to the younger generation. Or does it?
Does it or does it not do harm to the younger generation if there
is a pressure upon them, sanctioned with the name of God, to
conform to the ideals of their elders, to be taught to regard their
time- and culture-conditioned morals as divinely authorized?

If all goes well, from the fathers' point of view, the old men
can hope that their sons will do exactly what they have done,
and be exactly the kind of people they have been. To their mind,
the commandments will have served their purpose well if no
one can be quite sure whether 'you shall not' is a command or a
prediction,[15] whether that turn of phrase commands the younger
generation how they should behave or whether it prophesies
how in fact they will behave. The Hebrew, of course, allows
either possibility. In reality, indeed, once the young have inter-
nalized the values of the old, what they are supposed to do will
be the same as what they actually do—and the imperative will
have been transmuted into a future indicative. The fate of the
younger generation is always to become the older generation,
and the addressees of the Ten Commandments are, in the nature

15. Henning Graf Reventlow is the only person I know who has suggested that any of the 'commandments' has a force other than an imperative: he argues that 'you have no other gods beside me' is an assertion of
the current state of affairs (*Gebot und Predigt im Dekalog* [Gütersloh: Gerd
Mohn, 1962], pp. 25-27).

of things, destined to become one day their speakers—to the next generation.

So we ourselves do not need for the most part to distinguish between the older generation that is speaking and the younger generation that is being addressed. The fictive narratees of the Ten Commandments that I have profiled above are very much the same as the real-life interest group whose benefit is being served by the commandments. But in the fifth commandment the exact group who author the commandments in their own interests step forward in their true colours. Honour thy father and thy mother, say the fathers—not because father and mother are on an equal footing where honour is concerned, but because a dishonour to the mother is a dishonour to the father. Honour thy father and thy mother, say the fathers, that thy life may be long in the land—which is when obedience to the command-ment comes home to roost. If we have ever wondered why this should be the first commandment with a promise, as Eph. 6.2 has it (to be exact, it is the *only* one with a promise), we know now that it is because it is the commandment with the highest chance of benefiting both its authors and its addressees. If the younger generation will honour their elderly parents and ensure that their society supports this value, it is only a matter of time before they will be on the receiving end of the honour. It is just because they undertake to keep their aged parents alive that they have a chance of their own days being long.

4. *The Sabbath Commandment*

Let us take next the sabbath commandment (Exod. 20.8-11; Deut. 5.12-15). In whose interest is *this* commandment?

At first sight it is an easy question. The people who stand to benefit from the commandment to sabbath rest are obviously those who are going to be desisting from work on the sabbath, paterfamiliases, their children, slaves and resident aliens. This is assuming of course that these people like working less than they like not working. Perhaps even in ancient Israel there were workaholics, who found the institution of the sabbath disagree-able and not in their own interest; but let us assume that in the ancient world as in the modern most workers preferred (strangely enough, say I) not to work. Is not the sabbath commandment in their interest, then?

Well, yes, it *is* in their interest. But I cannot accept that that is the *reason* for the commandment; I want to say it is only the side effect. This on two accounts. One is that that I am not disposed to believe that some of these commandments are in the interest of one group and others of other groups. At least, I will take some persuading about that, for that would mean that the Ten Commandments do not form a unity—from the interest point of view—and I think it is reasonable to suppose that they do. The second reason, though, has more weight. It is that children, slaves and resident aliens do not usually manage to have legislation effected that benefits them. Since they are never in a position of power in a society, they have no say in the rules the society makes. If they are benefited by a law, it will be coincidentally and accidentally, not through any design of theirs. No doubt it benefits the powerless to have a law forbidding murder, but it is not on account of the powerless that the law comes into being.

What, are there never any humanitarian or egalitarian impulses in a hierarchical society, which enact legislation on behalf of the needy? Are there never any demands for social justice that even the most self-interested rulers feel in sympathy with? Is it never possible for a powerful group to act selflessly against its own interests on behalf of a less privileged group?[16] My response is that such questions arise only when we are working with a restricted definition of 'interest', such as a group's economic interest or its interest in maintaining its power. Ruling elites can also have an interest in their image as benevolent or as representative of all those they rule. The natural (not the cynical) assumption is that powerful groups do nothing against their interests; if they do, they threaten their own power. And it is in the interest of the dominant (hegemonic) class to secure the assent of the greatest number of people not of their class; that makes for social stability and thus the continuance of their own power.

In whose interest is it then to have a law forbidding work on the sabbath? Perhaps it will be easier to say in whose interest it is

16. I am grateful to Martin Buss for his insistence that I address such questions.

not to have such a law. I would imagine that those on the poverty line, who need to work all day every day to make a living, will be disadvantaged by this law. And those who have animals to look after will also find this law contrary to their natural advantage. Cows have to be milked every day, sheep have to be pastured, hens have to be fed. Presumably camels can be left to get on with it every Saturday, but even the most sabbatarian farmers of my acquaintance find themselves constrained to hold a (shall we say?) flexible interpretation of this commandment.

There is a better way still of answering this question, *Against whose interest is the sabbath law?* It is to ask, What evidence is there of what people actually wanted to do or tried to do on the sabbath but were prevented by the law? Amos 8.5 has grain merchants wishing there were no sabbath; if they want to sell on the sabbath, we conclude, presumably their customers also want to buy. So the sabbath law is not in the interests of merchants or of cheatable little people[17] who need to buy their food daily and cannot afford weekly visits to supermarkets. Jer. 17.21-22 has the prophet insisting that people do not 'bear a burden' on the sabbath or 'carry a burden out of your houses'. People are unlikely to be carrying loads around Jerusalem for the fun of it, so we have to imagine what kinds of people, what kinds of loads, and for what purposes. Since they are carrying loads out of their houses and in by the gates of Jerusalem, we might well suppose that these are goods manufactured at home for sale in city markets. But the text is too unspecific for us to be sure. Neh. 13.15-16 is much more helpful. Here Nehemiah says he saw people in Judah treading wine presses on the sabbath, loading grain, wine, grapes and figs on asses and bringing them into Jerusalem. And Tyrian merchants resident in Jerusalem ran markets in fish and 'all kinds of wares' on the sabbath. So we can conclude that merchants, and perhaps home-based manufacturers, want to work on the sabbath, and are disadvantaged by the commandment. Perhaps, ironically, the only reason why they specially want to trade on the sabbath is precisely because there is a sabbath, on

17. The merchants are clearly envisaging doing business with poor people whom they can cheat, sell low quality produce to, and get into debt slavery (8.1-4).

which many other people are free enough from work to go to the market. Nevertheless, the point is that traders would not be wanting to trade on the sabbath if it were not in their interest to do so; so being forbidden to do so must be against their interest.

If these are the people *against* whose interest the sabbath law is, *in* whose interest, then, is the sabbath law? It can only be those who stand to lose nothing by it, those who can afford it, those who can make the income of six days last for seven, those whose income, that is to say, has a surplus of at least 17% to daily requirements. So they are not little people, they are not the widows or the poor. They are probably not farmers or craft-workers, and, to judge by the evidence, they are not merchants. They are certainly not priests, since they *have* to work on the sabbath, perhaps harder than on other days, if the sacrificial list of Numbers 28 (note 28.9) is anything to go by. There are not many groups left in ancient Israelite society but the urban elite, administrators, officials and the wealthiest of traders.

All the same, in what sense could it be *in their interest*, or is it that it is no more than *not against their interest*? That is a question I need to defer for the moment, until I have looked at the commandments about worship.

5. *The Commandments about Worship*

Let us ask next in whose interest are the commandments enjoining monolatry and forbidding images and preventing certain uses of the divine name (Exod. 20.3-7; Deut. 5.7-11). It is not cynical to suggest that these commandments about the deity are not simply the result of religious experience or theological thinking. Religious people do have influence on how communities think, but the moment we have *laws* about religious beliefs, enforceable upon pain of sanctions, we are out of the realm of pure ideas and into the realm of social control. The moment someone tells me I must not make an image of my god and that I will be punished if I do, at that moment I know that that person has power over me or assumes power over me. (I also know that that person has something to lose if I do not obey, so I too have a kind of power of my own; but that is not quite the point here.) Laws are a representation of a conflict of wills in a society, so I am asking here:

Whose conflicting wills are in evidence here?

Childs sets out the options in terms of a conflict between Israel and other nations. Either one can follow Eissfeldt, he says, arguing that the commandment is and always was an essential part of the Mosaic religion, or one can follow Knierim and derive the commandment from the covenant ritual at Shechem and the threat of rival Canaanite deities.[18] But the commandment, addressed as it is to Israelites, witnesses rather to a conflict *within* Israel; it is not Canaanites who are being warned off Canaanite deities, but Israelites—*other* Israelites, Israelites who are not in the position of being able to tell their neighbours whom they are permitted to worship.

What these commandments, about monolatry, against images and improper use of the divine name—and enjoining sabbath observance as well—want to do is to make Israel different from other nations. They are markers of identity, they are distinctives, they are self-definitions of Israel, they are boundaries around someone's view of what is legitimately Israel. Who then are the people who care about Israel's identity, who are anxious that without laws, with sanctions, the identity they envisage for Israel may not exist? They are not the subsistence farmer trying to jog along peacefully with Philistines in the valley of Sorek, nor the itinerant potter who has always found a Canaanite shekel to be worth as much as an Israelite one; they are not the man and the woman in the street or in the suk. They are the wealthy at the apex of power in their society, whose position becomes precarious if social change is allowed to happen, if traditional forms of national identity are undermined. They are conservatives, and they are running scared.

These are the people who want to keep insisting that they are not autochthonous Canaanites, that they have been 'brought... out of the land of Egypt' (20.2). Why do they particularly want the god whose words they invent for these commandments to define himself as the one who brought them out of the land of Egypt? Because they need to define themselves as incomers, settlers,[19] who do not have long-standing title to the land they

18. Childs, *Exodus*, p. 404.

19. Or, to use Israel Finkelstein's formulation, 'groups of sedentarizing nomads, withdrawing urban elements, northern people, groups from the

occupy but are conscious of a different, more nervous, relationship to the land than their non-Israelite neighbours have. They
want to keep alive a memory of arrival and settlement—even if
it was, in historical actuality, from over the next hill rather than
from Egypt—and they want nothing to change. Their own significance lies in the past when they were different from their
neighbours because of their origins; they need to keep difference
alive to preserve their identity and self-worth. In whose interest
are these laws about monolatry, images, the sabbath? My answer
is: these conservative old men who see themselves as inheritors
of traditional ways of life.

6. *The Social Commandments*

Whose interests are being served by the other commandments,
then?

Thou shalt not steal (Exod. 20.15; Deut. 5.19). Who needs laws
against theft except those who have property to be stolen? Who
wants to forbid coveting except those who have something worth
coveting (whatever that means[20])? Those who want to forbid
coveting, and stealing also, presumably, are not the average
Israelites in the street: they are, by their own admission, owners
of male and female slaves, of oxen and asses, of houses. They are
the grandees; they form the wealthiest stratum of the society.

Thou shalt not bear false witness against thy neighbour (Exod.
20.16; Deut. 5.20). Neighbours who have something to lose from
false witness against them are the obvious originators of this
law—because they are most benefited by it, it is in their interest.
The kind of occasion envisaged may be that pictured in 1 Kgs
21.10-13, where two 'base fellows' (בני בליעל) are 'set' (ישׁב hi.) by
the elders of the city on Jezebel's instructions to testify falsely
against Naboth. How do you 'set' false witnesses against some-

southern steppe, etc.' ('The Emergence of Israel in Canaan: Consensus,
Mainstream and Dispute', *Scandinavian Journal for the Old Testament*
[1991/2], pp. 47-59 [56]).

20. Is it simply a mental act? Perhaps so. See Bernard S. Jackson,
'Liability for Mere Intention in Early Jewish Law', in his *Essays in Jewish and
Comparative Legal History* (Studies in Judaism and Late Antiquity, 10; Lei-
den: E.J. Brill, 1975), pp. 202-34.

one, and how do you persuade 'base fellows' to waste their afternoon in a law court? Presumably money changes hands, and members of the lower orders find it worthwhile to lay false charges against a so-called 'neighbour', a member of the Volvo-driving, property-owning classes. Most references to witnesses in the Hebrew Bible are very generalized and do not evince this class differential, but when it gets down to a concrete example, isn't it interesting that *class* enters into it, that false witness is something men of property have to fear? It is noteworthy too that in Exod. 23.2 the injunction is 'not to bear witness in a suit, *turning aside after a multitude*, so as to pervert justice'. Is the law against false witness specially designed then to protect the interest of the elite against the plebs? It was never a law against lying, of course, and so it did not apply to the rank and file members of Israelite society. It was a law about a specific form of lying, lying in a law-court when property was at stake, apparently.

Thou shalt not commit adultery (Exod. 20.14; Deut. 5.18). Who is so worried about other men committing adultery with their wives as to want a divine commandment about it? It is a well-known fear of polygamous men that while they are occupying themselves with one wife, their other wives can be doing anything they like. And polygamy, we know, is largely a function of wealth. Again, it is likely to be the property-owning classes who are most anxious about property going out of the family as a result of illicit liaisons. They are the ones who stand to lose the most from adultery. No doubt every Israelite male thinks himself robbed by another who manages to sleep with his wife, but those who have landed property that goes with the offspring are the ones who want to have a law about it.

Thou shalt not kill (Exod. 20.13; Deut. 5.17). This is a difficult commandment, on any view. The verb (רצח) is most commonly used, in the legal material at any rate, of unintentional killing, manslaughter. So the commentators solemnly note, but they never remark that it is somewhat absurd to have a law forbidding unintentional acts.[21] In the only concrete example we have

---

21. So, for example, in the well-known article of J.J. Stamm, 'Sprachliche Erwägungen zum Gebot "Du sollst nicht töten"', *Theologische Zeitschrift* 1 (1945), pp. 81-90, where רצח is defined as 'illegal killing inimical to the community'.

in the Hebrew Bible of an act of רצח, we find a man cutting wood in the forest with a neighbour where the axe-head flies off the handle and strikes the neighbour dead (Deut. 19.4-5). This cannot be the sort of thing forbidden here, for no commandment, human or divine, is going to stop axeheads flying off. Perhaps the clue lies rather in the practice of blood revenge, as Reventlow has argued.[22] We would need to ask, Who is doing this killing that is forbidden in the commandment, and why are they doing it? It is not unintentional killing, for which there is no reason, and which anyone might do by accident, but the associated, subsequent killing by the avenger. רצח in fact refers both to the act of the manslayer *and* to the act of the avenger (in Num. 35.27 the גאל is said to רצח the one who has רצח'd, and in 35.30 the רצח is to be רצח'd on the evidence of witnesses). So the commandment seems to be directed against the practice of blood revenge. What precise group is practising this custom I do not know, but I can assume it is some *group* since blood revenge is, by definition, a socially condoned killing, not an act of private vengeance; and here in these commandments it is being outlawed by another social group with more power. And I assume that the ones outlawing it are the conservative fathers; for blood revenge makes for social instability, and the fathers stand for social cohesiveness and order; and they are the ones with power.

7. Conclusion

How goes the programme of reading from left to right, then? Ask any question that steps outside the framework of the text and you relativize the Ten Commandments. Somehow the standard questions, Are the Ten Commandments Mosaic?, What did they originally mean?, How were they reinterpreted in later Israelite literature?, have evaded the question of their value or 'truth'—or, enduring quality, or, continuing applicability. And the most sophisticated of historical scholars and redaction critics have gone on entertaining the most appallingly uncritical views about the ideological and ethical status of the ten commandments. Is there a chance that an analysis like the present

22. Reventlow, *Gebot und Predigt im Dekalog*, pp. 71-73.

one, that focuses on the sectional interests they support, will demythologize them—without at the same time bringing western civilization tumbling?[23]

23. It is a pleasure to record Heather McKay's stimulating contributions to the ideas of this essay.

3

Haggai's Temple,
Constructed, Deconstructed and Reconstructed[*]

1. *The Temple Constructed*

The Second Temple was not just an edifice built by Judaeans; it was also a mental artifact constructed by Haggai. It was Haggai's intention, according to the book, to get the temple constructed; but we have to ask ourselves, What kind of a temple did he have in mind? How did he himself construct the temple? What construction, we might say, did he put on the term 'temple'?

Here are eleven building materials the text of the book provides us with. Let us see whether by taking an inventory of them we can reconstruct Haggai's construction of the temple.

1. The temple is to be 'the house of Yahweh' (1.2). This apparently means a building that will be owned by Yahweh; he obviously does not need it for living in, or for being in Jerusalem himself in person; for even before the temple is rebuilt he already is 'with' the people of Judah (1.13).

2. The temple stands in need of 'rebuilding' (1.2)—which means (a) that it is to be the same building as the one that once

* An earlier version of this essay was published in *Scandinavian Journal of the Old Testament* 7 (1993), pp. 19-30, and in *Second Temple Studies* (ed. Tamara C. Eskenazi and Kent H. Richards; Journal for the Study of the Old Testament Supplement Series, 175; Sheffield: JSOT Press, 1993), pp. 51-78. The essay was originally delivered as a paper in the Persian Period Section of the International Meeting of the Society of Biblical Literature, Rome, July, 1991, to the Old Testament Seminar, University of Cambridge, March, 1992, and at the Anniversary Celebrations of the Faculty of Theology, University of Aarhus, Denmark, May, 1992. I am grateful to Sue Campbell Samuel, my teaching assistant in 1991–92 and a graduate student working on Haggai, for discussion on the book.

stood in this place (you can't rebuild a new building, only an old one), and (b) that it is at present unbuilt or derelict (as also in 1.4, where it 'lies in ruins').

3. The people, whom I will take to mean the Jews of the province,[1] say that the time has not yet come for the house to be rebuilt (1.2). This saying of theirs implies that they think there *is* a time, in the future, when the house *should* be rebuilt.[2] Now perhaps the narrator means us to believe that they will *always* be saying this, as a way of forever avoiding building the temple; but we had better not jump to that conclusion.[3] Certainly we can assume that what Haggai thinks, as against the people, is that the right time is *now*. And now *we* must ask, Why would *one* person think the time is right when almost everyone else doesn't? Must we not answer, It looks as if he knows something that the rest of the people do not know.

4. Zerubbabel and Joshua do not apparently know what the people are saying about the time for rebuilding the temple (or perhaps they are only 'thinking' it, since אמר can mean that too). For the report of what they are saying or thinking is not something Zerubbabel and Joshua know for themselves; it is informa-

---

1.   The identity of Haggai's audience has at times been a contentious issue, but scholarly opinion seems to have settled down in favour of this, the simplest, view. See e.g. David L. Petersen, *Haggai and Zecharaiah 1–8* (Old Testament Library; London: SCM Press, 1985), pp. 80-82 (with particular reference to 2.14).

2.   Some older commentators (e.g. Jerome, Rashi, Kimchi) thought that the people may have been awaiting the fulfilment of the 70 years prophecy of Jeremiah (Jer. 25.11-14). But most moderns would agree with T.T. Perowne that 'It is clear from the sharp rebuke here administered, and from the severe judgments with which their procrastination had been visited (ver. 6, 9-11), that the excuse was idle and the delay worldly and culpable' (*Haggai and Zechariah* [Cambridge Bible; Cambridge: Cambridge University Press, 1893], p. 27). This seems to me, however, to be something of a shallow moralizing interpretation that does not reckon with Haggai's notion of the eschatological 'time'.

3.   Nor had we better invent pseudo-economic and pseudo-psychological explanations such as that of John Bright: 'The people, preoccupied with the struggle for existence, had neither resources nor energy left over to continue the project' (*A History of Israel* [London: SCM Press, 3rd edn, 1981], p. 366). This does not take account of the question of the right 'time'.

tion delivered to them as a 'word of Yahweh' via Haggai the prophet (1.2).[4]

5. What is needed if the temple is to be built is timber, to be fetched from the hills (1.8). Now if we can permit ourselves a little excursion *hors du texte* in the company of the Meyers, we will find that the only trees growing on the Judaean hills are the sycamore; and their timber is unsuitable for large buildings. So the timber Haggai demands for the temple cannot be for the construction of the temple itself. It must be for the scaffolding and ladders the builders will need.[5]

6. When the temple is rebuilt, Yahweh will 'take pleasure in it' and 'be honoured' (1.8). This means that he is at the moment displeased and dishonoured by having a ruined temple.[6]

4.   Commentators do not seem to be troubled by the fact that the divine speech to Zerubbabel and Joshua consists, not of a divine oracle of judgment or promise, but only of a piece of information such as we would rely on Gallup polls to give us these days. For Petersen, the verse 'points to a demonstrable unwillingness...to participate in the reconstruction of the temple' (*Haggai and Zechariah 1–8*, p. 48); but I would have thought that if the unwillingness were 'demonstrable' there would have been no need for a divine message to Zerubbabel and Joshua to inform them.

5.   Carol L. Meyers and Eric M. Meyers give this explanation (*Haggai, Zechariah 1–8* [Anchor Bible, 25b; Garden City: NY: Doubleday, 1987], pp. 27-28), as had Koole earlier. For a lengthy list of other explanations offered, see Pieter A. Verhoef, *The Books of Haggai and Malachi* (New International Commentary on the Old Testament; Grand Rapids: Eerdmans, 1987), pp. 65-66. There are others who think that the timber may be firs, oaks, poplars, cypresses, palms or olives—and indeed *some* of these might have been used, could they be found, for the building proper; see further, Hans Walter Wolff, *Haggai: A Commentary* (trans. M. Kohl; Minneapolis: Augsburg, 1988), p. 45.

6.   The RSV tells us that the purpose of building the temple is so that 'I [Yahweh] may appear in my glory', which sounds like a 'theophany'; but וְאֶכָּבֵד can hardly mean that. Wolff also thinks that the verb is best rendered by 'I will show myself in my glory' (cf. Walter Baumgartner *et al.*, *Hebräisches und aramäisches Lexikon zum Alten Testament*, II [3rd edn; Leiden: E.J. Brill, 1974], p. 434a), which means 'the manifestation of that acceptance [as God's house] through God's presence, power, and compassion' (*Haggai*, p. 46). Peter R. Ackroyd also, in my opinion, overinterprets the word by translating, 'I will let myself be honoured', which means, he says, 'I will accept the worship which tends to my honour' (*Exile and Restoration: A Study of Hebrew Thought of the Sixth Century BC* [London: SCM Press, 1968],

7. The temple had been, before its destruction, 'glorious'. 'Who is there among you who survives who saw this house in its original glory (כָּבוֹד)?', asks Yahweh in 2.3,[7] certifying that 'glory' is something quintessential to the nature of the temple. Merely beginning the rebuilding of the temple does not make it glorious, we observe, for even a month after the work of rebuilding has been renewed,[8] it still remains without glory; for Yahweh attributes to the people the opinion that the temple must still be 'as nothing in your eyes by comparison with it [the former temple]' (2.3).[9]

8. Yet, in a 'little while' (עוֹד אַחַת מְעַט הִיא, 2.6), the temple will become full of 'glory' (כָּבוֹד). Perhaps it will by that time have been rebuilt, perhaps it will not; we do not know.[10] But what we do know is that it is not the builders of the temple who will fill it with 'glory'. It is Yahweh himself who will do that ('and I will fill this house with glory', וּמִלֵּאתִי אֶת־הַבַּיִת הַזֶּה כָּבוֹד, 2.6).

9. How the temple will be filled with glory is that Yahweh will 'shake' all the nations so that the 'riches'[11] of all nations will

---

p. 160). There is simply nothing about *worship* here.

7.   According to Meyers and Meyers, *kābôd* 'here designates splendour and perhaps also [is] a term which can be related to God's presence as bestowing glory' (*Haggai, Zechariah 1–8*, p. 50). But to see the temple 'in its glory' cannot mean 'in God's presence'.

8.   The date is 21.vii.2 compared with 24.vi.2 as the date of recommencement of building (cf. 2.1 with 1.15).

9.   The text does not mean exactly 'To you does it not seem as if it were not there?' (REB) or 'Does it not seem as though there is nothing there?' (NJB), for the issue is not whether there is anything there, but whether what is there has any glory or not.

10.   Some scholars seem to know this; Otto Eissfeldt, for example, thinks of Haggai and Zechariah 'depicting the grace of Yahweh and the coming of the age of salvation as being primarily dependent upon the building of the Temple' (*The Old Testament. An Introduction* [trans. Peter R. Ackroyd; Oxford: Basil Blackwell, 1966], p. 433). Similarly Gerhard von Rad: '[F]or these two prophets the rebuilding of the Temple is actually the necessary precondition of Jahweh's advent and of his kingdom' (*Old Testament Theology*, II [trans. D.M.G. Stalker; Edinburgh: Oliver & Boyd, 1965], p. 281). Similarly Georg Fohrer, *Introduction to the Old Testament* (trans. David Green; London: SPCK, 1970), p. 460: 'Haggai…expects, upon completion of the building, a convulsion that will shake all nature and all nations'.

11.   It does not make much difference whether we read the MT חֶמְדַּת

come into the temple (2.7).[12] *Riches* are what make the temple glorious.[13] These riches take the form of silver and gold,[14] and Yahweh lays claim to them already, even while they are still in the possession of the nations: 'mine is the silver and mine is the gold, says Yahweh of armies' (2.8)—with a certain determination if not actually aggressively.[15] Presumably '*the* silver' (הַכֶּסֶף) and

'desire of, i.e. desirable things of' (as Verhoef, *Haggai and Malachi*, p. 103) or emend to חֲמֻדֹת 'desired things of' (as Karl Elliger in *Biblia Hebraica Stuttgartensia* [Stuttgart: Deutsche Bibelstiftung, 1967], p. 1062), Meyers and Meyers, *Haggai, Zechariah 1–8*, p. 53; *et al.*).

12. I think we are right in assuming that the text speaks of an event that *will* happen, but I am nevertheless attracted by the possibility that it is all hypothetical, as Arthur Penrhyn Stanley put it: '[E]ven if the present tranquillity of the world must needs be broken up, even if some violent convulsion should once again shake all nations, yet abundant treasures would flow into the Temple' (*Lectures on the History of the Jewish Church*, III [London: John Murray, new edn, 1883], pp. 91-92).

13. So also Verhoef, *Haggai and Malachi*, p. 104: 'This is not God's glory but the abundance and preciousness of the desired things which will become available to the temple'; and Petersen, *Haggai and Zecharaiah 1–8*, p. 68: 'The possessions, rather than God, will provide *kābôd*'; and cf. Edmond Jacob, *Theology of the Old Testament* (trans. Arthur W. Heathcote and Philip J. Allcock; London: Hodder & Stoughton, 1958), p. 79: '*Kabod* designates whatever had weight—it is used of riches: Gen. 31.1...Hag. 2.7'. What we cannot say is: '[W]hat need has he of earthly splendor, when all silver and gold are his?' (Elizabeth Achtemeier, *Nahum–Malachi* [Interpretation; Atlanta: John Knox Press, 1986], p. 100).

14. What kind of interpretation is it to say: '[T]he nations' treasures consist of more than material resources, even though the text mentions only silver and gold. In Israel's history the nations contributed such cultural achievements as architectural styles, musical instruments, and melodies for singing (1 Kgs. 4–5), titles for addressing Yahweh, and consequently insights into the mysteries of faith (Ps. 29; 48:1-8; 89:5-13)' (Carroll Stuhlmueller, *Rebuilding with Hope: A Commentary on the Books of Haggai and Zechariah* [International Theological Commentary; Grand Rapids: Eerdmans, 1988], p. 30). Given interpreters like this, what does a prophet have to do to be believed if he actually means 'silver and gold'?

15. Cf. Gerhard von Rad, 'The City on the Hill', in *The Problem of the Hexateuch and Other Essays* (trans. E.W. Trueman Dicken; Edinburgh: Oliver & Boyd, 1966), pp. 232-42 (240): 'A starkly challenging sentence proclaims Yahweh's exclusive right to possess them. It is as if they have been hitherto on temporary loan, and are still held back from their true purpose as the property of Yahweh. In the eschaton, however, they will return from this

'the gold' (הַזָּהָב) mean 'silver and gold in general', 'all the silver and gold there is'.[16]

10. What this 'shaking' of the earth will amount to is unclear. The language itself suggests a *physical* cosmic upheaval, with a shaking of the heavens and the earth, of the sea and the dry land (2.6); but it is hard to see how a universal *earthquake* could bring the wealth of the nations into the temple.[17] Presumably the language of *physical* upheaval is symbolic of a *political* upheaval that will issue in Judah's dominance over all other nations. Whether the upheaval will be by military means[18] or some more pacific rearrangement we cannot tell. And how the wealth will 'come' to Jerusalem, whether as booty or as taxes,[19] is equally inexplicit.[20]

misappropriation into the exclusive control of Yahweh, their rightful owner.'

16. Similarly Petersen, *Haggai and Zechariah 1–8*, p. 69: 'Yahweh might be claiming that all silver and gold are ultimately his in order to justify taking them away from the nations'. It can hardly be a matter of the precious vessels stolen from the first temple, for they could hardly be called the 'riches of the nations' (contrast Petersen, *Haggai and Zechariah 1–8*, p. 68: 'Haggai does not expect ingots of gold but, rather, precious vessels and other metallic accoutrements for the temple cultus...[P]recious objects belonging to the temple had been lost to the nations. And their return was a necessary part of a proper restoration.'). Can it be the spoils from his victories in holy war (Verhoef, *Haggai and Malachi*, p. 105)? Perhaps (cf. Nah. 2.10 [EVV 9]; Mic. 4.13; Ps. 60.8-10 [EVV 6-8]; Josh. 6.19), but there is a marked absence of hostile intent in Haggai's depiction.

17. According to Joyce G. Baldwin (*Haggai, Zechariah, Malachi: An Introduction and Commentary* [Tyndale OT Commentaries; London: Tyndale Press, 1972], p. 48), Haggai sees 'the whole universe in such a series of convulsions that every nation will gladly part with its treasures' (why would convulsions make them do that?, I wonder), but, as Verhoef observes (p. 102), this explanation would require us to attach a literal meaning to רעש in v. 6 and a figurative meaning in v. 7.

18. Verhoef sees here the language of holy war, the wealth being spoils dedicated to the victor (*Haggai and Malachi*, p. 103).

19. Meyers and Meyers, *Haggai, Zechariah 1–8*, p. 53, envisage the nations 'send[ing] tribute through their ambassadors and emissaries'.

20. We might even consider, with Dean Stanley, whether freewill offerings from gentiles might not be in mind: 'If its own children should neglect it, the heathen whom they despised would come to the rescue' (*Lectures on the History of the Jewish Church*, III, p. 91). Cf. Achtemeier, *Nahum–Malachi*, p. 101: '[A]ll peoples will finally come with their offerings to the Lord of Hosts'.

11. There is so much silver and gold out there waiting to be shaken into the temple that, when it is all in, 'great shall be the glory of this house, the latter more than the former' (2.9).

The data are not complete and at times not entirely clear. But the resultant picture is unambiguous. Haggai constructs the temple as nothing but a *treasure-house*. It is a place where precious objects can be stored and displayed. When it is in ruins it obviously cannot serve as a storehouse and display-case. Its owner, the god Yahweh, is inevitably dishonoured by having a 'house' that is in disrepair, and worse, a house that by being in disrepair cannot display the *kābôd* that comes from owning many precious objects. It is therefore essential, for the deity's self-respect, that the house should be rebuilt. All the silver and gold in the world may belong to him by rights and in principle; but they bring him no honour unless they are gathered together in a 'house'.

There is another dimension to Haggai's construction of the temple, though. It is that there is an *urgency* about rebuilding the house. For it is only a short time, 'yet a little while', before the cosmic upheaval is going to occur that will bring the wealth of all the nations flooding into Jerusalem.[21] Preparations must be made for the arrival of all that silver and gold. The *people* do not realize that the 'time' is pressing, for they do not have Haggai's conviction about the imminent overthrow of all the kingdoms. *Haggai*, on the other hand, knows that Yahweh is about to 'shake' the heavens and the earth—perhaps he has already started[22]—so it is high time that the temple be readied to receive the treasures that will fall out of the pockets of the nations when Yahweh will imminently turn them upside down (הפך) and give them a good shaking.

Everything in the book of Haggai becomes coherent when we recognize how Haggai constructs the temple. How rebuilding

21. I can hardly agree that with the phrase 'yet a little while' Haggai 'refers not so much to the shortness of the interval as to the vastness of the powers involved' (Achtemeier, *Nahum–Malachi*, p. 102).

22. We note that the present participle in 2.21, 'I am shaking', is not preceded by 'yet a little while' (as in 2.6); does this perhaps not mean that the shaking has already begun? The commentators do not observe this difference from 2.6, and generally translate the participle as a future, even if a *futurum instans* (Verhoef, *Haggai and Malachi*, p. 143).

the temple connects with 'glory', how 'glory' connects with silver and gold, how silver and gold connect with world upheaval, and, especially, how world upheaval connects with the 'right time' for rebuilding the temple—all make sense when Haggai's temple is understood as a *treasury*.

Of course, there are many other ways of constructing the second (or, rebuilt) temple, some of which a Haggai would no doubt have consented to. It would be hard to deny, for example, that the author of the book of Haggai, whether or not that person was the historical Haggai, would have thought of the temple, or the temple to be, as a place of sacrifice. Where this essay stands, however, is on the observation that the author of the book chose not to speak of the temple in that way, ever.

It proves very difficult for modern scholars, however, to believe that an author could have such a restricted vision of the temple. We all know, and our dictionaries and encyclopaedias confirm it, that the Jewish temple had many significances, and our tendency is to recall those significances whenever we read the word 'temple', as if all of them were present in the minds of speakers and hearers of the language at every moment. James Barr has invented the *mot juste* for this habit of ours: it is 'illegitimate totality transfer' when we insist on reading all the possible meanings of a word into each of its occurrences.[23]

Here are some of the ideas that occur to commentators when they read 'temple' in Haggai.

1. It is the 'place of the presence of God'. So, for example, Verhoef (a Calvinist who nevertheless laspes into Latin in the face of the almost palpable holiness of the temple) writes:

> The second major theme of Haggai's message concerns the rebuilding of the temple... To appreciate the importance of this message, we will have to consider the theological significance of the temple. In the history of Israel the tabernacle and subsequently the temple were the places of the *praesentia Dei realis* among his people.[24]

---

23. James Barr, *The Semantics of Biblical Language* (London: Oxford University Press, 1961), p. 222 (it is 'illegitimate *identity* transfer' on pp. 218, 235 [my italics]).

24. Verhoef, *Haggai and Malachi*, p. 34.

Another way of putting it is this:

> God's presence is reestablished through the powerful symbolic
> means of his dwelling made habitable.[25]

Or,

> God's presence is made manifest in his 'glory'. In fact, God's
> 'glory', as distinct from his 'name' appears to represent an extra-
> ordinary and dramatic manifestation of God's presence and
> power.[26]

2. It is a symbol of the glory of Yahweh. So Petersen writes that
Yahweh will have

> greater prestige now that this house is finished.[27]

And Mason:

> [F]or [Haggai], the significance of the Temple is *eschatological*. It
> will be the place where God appears again in His glory.[28]

Or, more simplistically,

> [Haggai] believed that the temple must be rebuilt so the glory of
> the Lord might return and dwell with his people. Any person
> who longs for the presence of the Lord is a good man.[29]

3. It is a place of God's self-revelation. So Ackroyd:

> The divine presence...expresses itself in the Temple as the chosen
> place of divine revelation...The God who is lord of heaven and

25. Meyers and Meyers, *Haggai, Zechariah 1–8*, p. 28.

26. Meyers and Meyers, *Haggai, Zechariah 1–8*, p. 28, referring to J.G.
McConville, 'God's "Name" and God's "Glory"', *Tyndale Bulletin* 30 (1979),
pp. 149-63. Does this mean that there are unextraordinary manifestations of
this divine 'presence' in the temple? What would a 'manifestation' of a
divine presence look like? Am I alone in thinking that not a lot has been
explained when I read that God's presence is made manifest 'in' something
that is a manifestation of his presence?

27. Petersen, *Haggai and Zecharaiah 1–8*, p. 51.

28. Rex Mason, 'The Prophets of the Restoration', in *Israel's Prophetic Traditions: Essays in Honour of Peter R. Ackroyd* (ed. Richard Coggins, Anthony
Phillips and Michael Knibb; Cambridge: Cambridge University Press, 1982),
pp. 137-54 (143).

29. Ralph L.Smith, *Micah–Malachi* (Word Biblical Commentary, 32; Waco,
TX: Word Books, 1984), p. 149. The reader may care to note any female
person who would like to become a man now knows how to achieve that.

earth, who cannot be contained in a building, nevertheless condescends to reveal himself and to localize his presence in order that blessing may flow out.[30]

4. It is a place of worship, of human encounter with the divine. So Achtemeier:

> [T]he prophet concentrates almost singlemindedly on the necessity for the Judeans to restore their place of worship...When Haggai...calls for temple rebuilding, it is...an announcement that the Lord of Hosts yearns to give himself again...to enter into covenant fellowship with the Chosen People once more. Their years of abandonment under God's judgment are over. They should prepare themselves for the Lord's return...The temple will be sign and seal of their renewed hearts' devotion—the evidence that they have finally come to terms with reality.[31]

And Ackroyd:

> [T]he failure to rebuild is much more than a matter of reconstruction of a building. It is the reordering of a Temple so that it is a fit place for worship...Without a properly built temple, that is a ritually correct place for the worship of God, such worship is impossible.[32]

5. It is a sacral centre, necessary both for Israel's survival and as the focus of a universal religion. Thus von Rad:

> The Temple was, after all, the place where Jahweh spoke to Israel, where he forgave her her sins, and where he was present for her. The attitude taken towards it therefore determined the attitude for or against Jahweh...[T]he eschatological Israel was to have a sacral centre, and...this alone would guarantee her existence...It was for this time, when Jahwism would throw off its national limitations and become a universal religion—the time of the Messiah—that the temple had to be rebuilt.[33]

And Bright:

> The community desperately needed a focal point about which its faith could rally.[34]

30. Ackroyd, *Exile and Restoration*, pp. 154, 160.
31. Achtemeier, *Nahum–Malachi*, pp. 94-95, 97-98.
32. Ackroyd, *Exile and Restoration*, pp. 156-57, 160.
33. Von Rad, *Old Testament Theology*, II, pp. 281-82.
34. Bright, *History of Israel* (3rd edn), p. 368.

Similarly S.R. Driver had described Haggai's picture of the temple as

> the religious centre of the world (Is. ii. 2-4), nations coming in pilgrimage to it, delighting to honour it with their gifts, and so making it more glorious even than the temple of Solomon.[35]

6. It is the channel of salvation. Thus Wolff writes:

> Haggai does not press for the temple to be rebuilt in order that the priestly cult may function. The purpose is 'so that Yahweh may enter into it, and may appear for the salvation of the people'.[36]

7. It is also a symbol of, or, rather, a vehicle for the community itself and its identity. Thus Meyers and Meyers:

> The restoration of the sacred temple in Jerusalem is the key to the establishment of the new, largely ecclesiastical system of community autonomy under Persian rule.[37]

8. It is the economic and administrative centre of the postexilic Yahwistic community. So Petersen,[38] following the hypothesis of Joel Weinberg that the community is best understood as a 'Bürger–Tempel-Gemeinde',[39] a collectivity that provided its members with an identity and a rudimentary administration based on the 'father's house' as the primary unit of social administration.

Each of these views can be argued on its own merits, and they may well be correct accounts of ideas that were abroad in Haggai's time.[40] But whatever their validity in reference to the

---

35. S.R. Driver, *The Minor Prophets. Nahum, Habakkuk, Zephaniah, Haggai, Zechariah, Malachi* (Century Bible; Edinburgh: T.C. & E.C. Jack, 1906), p. 152.

36. Wolff, *Haggai*, p. 46. Wolff's quotation is from K.M. Beyse, 'Serubbabel und die Königserwartungen der Propheten Haggai und Zacharja', *Arbeiten zur Theologie* I/48 (1972), p. 75.

37. Meyers and Meyers, *Haggai, Zechariah 1–8*, p. xlii.

38. Petersen, *Haggai and Zechariaih 1–8*, pp. 30-31.

39. J. Weinberg, 'Das *beit 'abôt* im 6.–4. Jh. v.u. Z.', *Vetus Testamentum* 23 (1973), pp. 400-14; *idem* (J. Vejnberg), 'Probleme der sozialökonomische Struktur Judäas vom 6. Jahrhundert v.u. Z. Zu einigen wirtschaftshistorischen Untersuchungen von Heinz Kreissig', *Jahrbuch für Wirtschaftsgeschichte* (1973), pp. 237-51.

40. See for a survey of the kinds of ideas that may have been held about the temple in the Persian period, David L. Petersen, 'The Temple in Persian

historical actuality of the sixth century BCE, if we have them in our mind when we read the book of Haggai we inevitably misunderstand the book, for *it* thinks of the temple as a treasure-house, no more, no less.

2. *The Temple Deconstructed*

If I have now rightly reconstructed Haggai's construction of the temple, it remains a question whether this construction is open to *deconstruction*. Now to deconstruct a discourse, according to Jonathan Culler, is 'to show how it undermines the philosophy it asserts, or the hierarchical oppositions on which it relies'.[41] And there are in this text, to my mind, three points at which a deconstruction of such a nature imposes itself.

1. *Honour*
The book's initial set of oppositions is between the unbuilt temple and the built temple. (1) The unbuilt temple is a site of shame, lack of glory; the built temple will be a place of honour. (2) The unbuilt temple is a signal of human disregard of the divine, or disobedience (cf. 'obey', 1.12): they live in ceiled houses, while the deity's dwelling is in ruins. The built temple will be a testimony to human enthusiasm for the divine. (3) The unbuilt temple causes divine displeasure; the built temple will be an object Yahweh will take pleasure in (1.7). (4) The unbuilt temple brings economic disaster to the populace; the built temple will spell blessing upon the grain, the new wine, the oil and what the ground brings forth (cf. 1.11).

Now it comes as something of a surprise, amounting (I think) to a deconstruction, that it turns out that the rebuilding of the temple, though demanded so strongly, will *not* in fact achieve the aim of bringing 'honour' (*kābôd*) to the deity and his house. For in 2.7 we learn that it will be when the treasures of silver and gold from the other nations come into the temple that it will be filled with *kābôd*. If filling the temple with precious objects is what produces *kābôd*, then it cannot be finishing the building

Period Prophetic Texts', *Biblical Theology Bulletin* 21 (1991), pp. 88-96.

41. Jonathan Culler, *On Deconstruction: Theory and Criticism after Structuralism* (London: Routledge & Kegan Paul, 1983), p. 86.

itself that does so. And vice versa. We may call this a deconstruction because the text itself shows no hint of awareness of the
conflict between the two statements; the conflict is hidden, and
so we may say that the text *undermines* itself.

It is a further element in the deconstruction that whereas the
book initially made out that the producing of *kābôd* for the temple is entirely in the hands of the people who build or who fail to
build, 2.7 affirms that it is Yahweh's own personal filling of the
temple with treasure that will bring *kābôd*, as if the people's activity was nugatory. Perhaps, of course, we should harmonize the
text, avoiding the deconstructive possibility, and say that if the
people do not finish rebuilding the temple, there will be no
temple for Yahweh to fill with his treasures; so in that sense the
people's activity may be a *precondition* of the divine activity that
will ensure the deity's honour.[42] But the simple fact is that the
text itself does not confront the tension between the people's
contribution to the *kābôd* and the deity's, so each of the poles of
the tension tends to undermine or deconstruct the other.

2. *Uncleanness*

A more deep-seated deconstruction arises from the obligation
laid on the people to rebuild the temple, on the one hand, and
the affirmation that 'every work of their hands' is unclean (2.14),
on the other.[43]

42. Similarly Robert P. Carroll, *When Prophecy Failed: Reactions and
Responses to Failure in the Old Testament Prophetic Traditions* (London: SCM
Press, 1979), p. 161: '[U]ntil the temple was rebuilt the wealth of nations
could not flow into it. So the rebuilding of the temple had become a pre-
requisite for the expected event of salvation.'

43. I am ignoring the argument that the 'people' in question are not the
Judaeans but the Samarians (as e.g. J.W. Rothstein, *Juden und Samaritaner:
Die grundlegende Scheidung von Judentum und Heidentum* (Beiträge zur
Wissenschaft vom Alten und Neuen Testament, 3; Leipzig: Hinrichs, 1908);
D. Winton Thomas, 'Haggai', *Interpreter's Bible* (ed. George Arthur Buttrick;
New York: Abingdon, 1956), VI, pp. 1036-49 (1047); von Rad, *Old Testament
Theology*, II, p. 283; Wilhelm Rudolph, *Haggai–Sacharja 1–8–Sacharja 9–14–
Maleachi* (Kommentar zum Alten Testament, 13/4; Gütersloh: Gerd Mohn,
1976), pp. 49-50; Wolff, *Haggai*, p. 94. The most recent scholarship has gene-
rally professed itself convinced by the argument of Klaus Koch to the con-
trary ('Haggais unreines Volk', *Zeitschrift für die alttestamentliche*

To put the matter more fully: on the one hand, the people of Judah are reproached for neglecting the rebuilding of the temple, and urged to 'build the house' (1.8) and 'work' (2.4). There is indeed no way the house is going to be rebuilt apart from the labour of the Judaeans. Yet, on the other hand, Haggai seems to go out of his way to insist that everything the Judaeans do is somehow 'unclean' or 'defiled' (2.10-14). If this is so, then the temple building itself, as the work of Judaean hands, is going to be 'defiled', with evident consequences for the programme of acquiring *kābôd*. This is not an outcome the book envisages explicitly, but nevertheless, deconstructively, it sets out the impossibility of the people's achieving what it demands. The result will be that the more the Judaeans build the temple, the more they will defile it and dishonour it. And conversely, the less they build the temple, the less defiled it will be *but* the more dishonoured. So it is impossible to 'please' (1.8) this deity and impossible to honour him. It is perhaps not surprising that all the honour he expects to get will be by his own efforts ('I will fill this house with glory', 2.7).

To appreciate most fully the deconstructive possibilities in the text over this issue we have to examine more closely the dialogue of Haggai with the priests concerning the question of the transmissibility of holiness and defilement (2.10-19). There is a great deal that is uncertain about the exegesis of this pericope, and not surprisingly so, from a deconstructionist's point of view, since the text has suddenly found itself in deep and disturbing waters. Most crucial for the present purpose is the phrase 'all the work of their hands' (כָּל־מַעֲשֵׂה יְדֵיהֶם, 2.14), which seems to designate what it is that Haggai says is defiled. Now this term seems at first sight as comprehensive as it is possible to be. Nevertheless there is some evidence that it might refer only to agricultural produce.[44] For in Deut. 14.29, 16.15, 24.19, 28.12 and 30.9 we have

Wissenschaft 79 [1967], pp. 52-66; similarly H.G. May, '"This People" and "This Nation" in Haggai', *Vetus Testamentum* 18 [1968], pp. 190-97; so too, for example, Rolf Rendtorff, *The Old Testament: An Introduction* (trans. J. Bowden; London: SCM Press, 1985), p. 237.

44. It seems a mistake to restrict the 'work of their hands' to their offerings, as is done for example by Ackroyd, *Exile and Restoration*, p. 168: 'The emphasis in Haggai's own message to the people concentrates on the

the phrase 'all the work of your hand(s)'[45] in reference unmistakably to the produce of the fields; and, more importantly, within the book of Haggai itself the phrase can be shown to have this meaning. For in 2.18 we find, 'I smote you—all the work of your hands—with blight and mildew and hail'.[46] If 'agricultural produce' is all the phrase means, were we then right to think of the building of the temple when we read in 2.14 that 'all the work of their hands' was unclean?

Yes, I believe so. I would argue that it is not at all surprising that in the context of agricultural labour, such as we encounter in those passages in Deuteronomy, 'the work of your hands' should refer to field produce and not to pots, silverware or linen, or any other of the hundred and one things that could reasonably be called 'the work of the hands'. But in other contexts, 'the work of the hands' can mean quite different things. For example, in 2 Kgs 19.18 idols are called 'the work of the hands of a human'; in Jer. 32.30 the Israelites have been angering Yahweh 'by the work of their hands', presumably transgressions in general; and in Song 7.2 (EVV 7.1) jewels are 'the work of the hands of a craftsman'. Even in Deuteronomy itself the phrase quite commonly refers to human activity in general (e.g. 2.7 'Yahweh your God has blessed you in all the work of your hands' while travelling through the wilderness; 31.29 'provoking Yahweh to anger through the work of your hands', not specifically making idols, as in 4.28). Only the immediate context can give the phrase a more specific meaning than 'activity'.

The question can be answered yet another way also. Let us suppose that 'all the work of their hands' (2.14) means specifically their produce from the fields (as, admittedly, it does in 2.17). May we not go on to ask: if the people are unclean and are consequently defiling their agricultural produce, will they not

uncleanness of the people's offerings in the shrine'. On the contrary, the emphasis is on *all* the works of their hands, of which their offerings are only one example.

45. Deut. 16.15 and 24.19 have כֹּל מַעֲשֵׂה יָדֶיךָ; 28.12 and 30.9 have כָּל־מַעֲשֵׂה יָדֶךָ; and 14.29 has כָּל־מַעֲשֵׂה יָדְךָ אֲשֶׁר תַּעֲשֶׂה.

46. 'The people ("you") are defined in terms of the work of their hands...agricultural commodities' (Petersen, *Haggai and Zecharaiah 1–8*, p. 93).

equally be defiling everything they touch?[47]

Strangely enough, the text of Haggai remains very innocent over this question of defilement, not realizing its significance for the building of the temple. And so do the commentators, who only very rarely recognize how problematic is a building of a temple by workers in a state of ritual impurity.[48] Uncleanness is very contagious, so Haggai avers, and he has not needed any consultation with priests to know that; it was a commonplace for any Jew of whatever period. The idea of building a temple, by definition a holy place, using the labour of unclean builders is almost ludicrous. But Haggai represses the implicit conflict between the uncleanness of the builders and the cleanness of the building. Why? He is not stupid; he must know at some level that there is a conflict. But he cannot cope with it. Either he has to give up his dream of seeing the temple rebuilt, or he has to allow that the people are not after all in a state of ritual impurity. He cannot do either, and the result is a text that deconstructs itself.

What is truly intriguing about this deconstruction is how it comes to be inscribed in the text in the first place. Why does the whole issue of the transmissibility of holiness and uncleanness

47. How the people come to be unclean, in Haggai's view, is not a question we need to go into here. I cannot accept Petersen's elaborate argument that it is not the people but the temple that is unclean ('the impurity can only derive from the place to which the sacrifices are being brought' [*Haggai and Zechariah 1–8*, p. 84]). Cf. also Baldwin: 'The ruined skeleton of the Temple was like a dead body decaying in Jerusalem and making everything contaminated' (*Haggai, Zechariah, Malachi*, p. 33). It would be a strange way to go about demanding a ceremony of ritual purification for the temple to blame the people for letting themselves be contaminated by the temple whenever they bring offerings to it. The text implies, in my opinion, that the sacrifices are unclean before they arrive at the temple.

48. Mason, 'The Prophets of the Restoration', in *Israel's Prophetic Tradition*, pp. 137-54 (144), believes that we should see the phrase 'the work of their hands' as referring to their building activity; but he does not draw the conclusion that the temple must therefore be ritually unclean. Rather, he merely ethicizes the 'uncleanness' into an '[in]capacity for self-regeneration', observing that it is not the work of the people but the eschatological 'Coming' of God that will fill the temple with glory. He overlooks the fact that uncleanness transmits itself to temples but incapacity for self-regeneration is quite harmless to sancta.

get raised at all?[49] The elaborate question and answer process between Haggai and the priests seems designed, not to elicit authoritative answers to currently debated or unclear issues, but principally to lead up to an explanation of why the Judaean harvests have been so poor. The logic seems to be as follows (though there are no causal connectives in the text): everything the people do is unclean; their offerings at the altar are unclean; God punishes them for this infringement of cultic purity by sending blight, mildew and hail to decrease the productivity of their fields.

This is in itself a quite unexceptional line of reasoning, but its appearance at this point is startling. In the first place, it runs counter to the explanation that has hitherto been the burden of the text. From the beginning of the book, the logic has been: 'You have sown much, and harvested little...Why? Because of my house that lies in ruins' (1.6, 9). The *reason* why they do not build the temple is because they think the time has not yet come; and the *result* of not building the temple is that the deity withholds prosperity from them. The *next step* that they can take if they want to change things is to start to build the temple. Given the presuppositions, everything in this line of argument makes good (and familiar) sense. But how is this explanation to be squared with the other, that their lack of prosperity is a punishment for their *uncleanness*? Are they being punished for their *neglect* of the temple or for their *impurity*? If it is for both offences, if they are *both* negligent and unclean, why is not a word about their uncleanness breathed until three months after they have resumed work on the temple (cf. 1.15 with 2.10)?

In the second place, where is the logic in the second explanation? Where is the *reason* or *cause* why they are unclean? They have been contracting the uncleanness from somewhere, but do

---

49. It can hardly be, as Achtemeier would have it, that the temple-builders are in danger of becoming self-righteous and believing that 'association with the things of God automatically communicates moral purity... Haggai addresses this temptation with a parable and its explanation... The question is,... Having dealt with God's holy place, have they themselves become holy?' (*Nahum–Malachi*, pp. 102-103). Cf. also Ackroyd, *Exile and Restoration*, p. 169: 'There is no automatic efficacy in the temple, no guarantee that by virtue of its existence it ensures salvation'.

they know where? Since they do not, what are they to do about it as a *next step*? Assuming they do not want to remain in a state of impurity, what move can they make? Even if it is not literal impurity that we are reading about here, but some sort of moral incapacity, what are they expected to do about it? It can hardly be, can it, that the 'uncleanness' is a metaphor for their unreadiness for the work?[50] If that were so, they would surely have been 'purified' from such a uncleanness by their commencement of the work on the twenty-fourth of the sixth month, a good three months ago. And furthermore, how is the promised blessing of 2.19 connected with the uncleanness? It's all very well to be blessed, but what does that do to the impurity? Is that to be removed? And if so, how? How can the category of impurity drop out of sight, and be replaced by the category of blessing? Impurity is got rid of only by rituals of purification; impurity is impervious to 'blessing'. All the 'blessing' in the world will not turn an unclean thing into a clean, will it?

There is at bottom something gratuitous (must we not conclude?) in this excursion into matters of the holy and the clean. All that arises from it are complications that deflect the force of the original thrust of the book.

So must we conclude that the text exhibits a kind of 'bad faith', according to which the people can never be praised for doing what they are encouraged to, and can only be required to do what it is impossible for them to do? If they don't build the temple they will be punished for their negligence, and if they do build the temple they will defile it.

3. *Zerubbabel*
We have just now observed a case where the text suddenly takes off in an unexpected direction, implicitly undermining what has preceded. Now we find, in the final four verses of the book (2.20-23), an even more striking divergence from the previous course of the book, and an equally disturbing deconstructive situation.

---

50. So e.g. Perowne, *Haggai and Zechariah*, p. 24: 'Their one sin in neglecting the Temple spreads its moral pollution over "every work of their hands"'; May, ' "This People" and "This Nation" in Haggai', p. 196: 'Through their failure to honor Yahweh with proper attention to his house, they had become, as it were, unclean'.

It is fascinating that both these deconstructive texts (2.10-19; 2.20-23) are signed with the same dateline: the twenty-fourth day of the ninth month of the second year of Darius. According to this text, therefore, Haggai the prophet deconstructs the whole of his prophetic ministry on its last day![51]

The final oracle, addressed to Zerubbabel, is a quite remarkable one, designating him as nothing less than the universal and eschatological ruler. This significance of the oracle is, surprisingly, not generally recognized by commentators.[52] But the eschatological framework is quite clearly signalled by the language of cosmic upheaval we already met with at 2.6. The heavens and the earth are to undergo a 'shaking', symbolical no doubt of the political shaking that the writer envisages. More explicitly than in 2.6, where it was simply a matter of 'shaking' the nations, here we learn that Yahweh will also 'overthrow the throne of kingdoms', 'destroy the strength of the kingdoms of the nations' and 'overthrow the chariot and its riders', the horses and their riders 'going down', each by the sword of his fellow

---

51. In the older scholarship this day has sometimes been very differently esteemed, as the 'birthday of Judaism', the day when the temple was founded and the prophet definitively 'rejected willing but cultically suspect helpers, thereby inaugurating the sequestration that was to be typical of later Judaism' (Fohrer, *Introduction to the Old Testament*, p. 460).

52. Meyers and Meyers, for example, think that the day in question is 'the day in which the Yehudites will once again achieve political independence and self-rule under the Davidide Zerubbabel' (*Haggai, Zechariah 1-8*, p. 67)—which hardly seems to match the cosmic language of 2.21-22. But elsewhere they speak of Zerubbabel's appointment as an eschatological event (e.g. pp. 70, 82). And Wolff sees the announcement to Zerubbabel that Yahweh would 'overthrow (הפך) all nations' as Haggai's 'offer[ing] to the worried Zerubbabel the immediate and lasting reminder that Yahweh is the God who controls all the political conditions and affairs of the great powers' (*Haggai*, p. 102). In Zerubbabel's shoes I would not need this reminder, nor would I glean it from Haggai's words; I would be more likely to start drafting my policy as world ruler. Wolff thinks that 2.23 'designates [Zerubbabel] as the personal bearer of hope' (*Haggai*, p. 108); this is an amazingly other-worldly reading of what is transparently a political statement. Smith (*Micah–Malachi*, p. 163) also fails to grasp the immediacy of this revolution in world order when he writes: 'Zerubbabel of the line of David was only a Persian governor of a tiny community. But it would not always be that way. Yahweh was going to shake the nations.'

(2.22). This prediction signifies a new political order correspond-
ing to the picture of the dominance of Jerusalem reflected in
2.7.[53] Into that new eschatological political order there is to be
inserted Zerubbabel as its chief ruler.

The language about Zerubbabel in 2.23 is unmistakable.
Zerubbabel's appointment will take place 'on that day', which
(even if we did not recognize the phrase already as the technical
term for the eschaton) must be the eschatological time, for the
'day' when he will be appointed is plainly the time of cosmic
'shaking'. Having 'chosen' (בחר) Zerubbabel, Yahweh will 'take'
(לקח) him, as various persons have previously been 'taken' for
high office.[54] Further, Zerubbabel is termed 'my servant' (עבדי),[55]
whom Yahweh will 'set as a signet-ring' (חותם), presumably upon
his own finger as a symbol of Zerubbabel's appointment as ruler
(cf. the language used of Jehoiachin, 'Coniah, king of Judah', in
Jer. 22.23-25 as 'the signet-ring on my right hand').

So the book of Haggai ends with the announcement that

53. The text is being domesticated by Achtemeier when she writes: 'He
speaks not of the overthrow of Persia but of the subjection of all nations to
God' (*Nahum–Malachi*, p. 105)—as if Haggai dealt in ethical platitudes and
had no agenda you could call political. Ackroyd's reading is more sophisticated, but still fails to satisfy: 'The events are not necessarily to be thought
of in military terms, but rather in terms of the subordination to the divine
will of those powers which set themselves up as authorities in their own
right' (*Exile and Restoration*, p. 163). For how does he (or the prophet)
imagine such a subordination as coming about, then, if not by military
means (including no doubt supernatural military means)?

54. The term signifies 'interventions that are going to bring about a
change of place, calling, and function' (Wolff, *Haggai*, p. 105). See also
W.A.M. Beuken, *Haggai–Sacharja 1–8: Studien zur Überlieferungsgeschichte der
frühnachexilischen Prophetie* (Studia Semitica Neerlandica, 10; Assen: Van
Gorcum, 1967), p. 80.

55. According to Wolff, 'Zerubbabel is...addressed in the same way as
David...According to Haggai's line of thinking, this relationship will have
been related to Zerubbabel's efforts for the building of the temple' (*Haggai*,
p. 105). I doubt this, for why would Joshua, equally responsible for the temple building, not be in view here also? And in any case, was David responsible for the first temple? I doubt, in other words, that the promise to
Zerubbabel is connected with temple building at all. And that 'Zerubbabel,
as Yahweh's seal, would then be the guarantor of the temple's completion'
(Wolff, *Haggai*, p. 106).

Zerubbabel is to be appointed world ruler.[56] No matter how brief the oracle, the claim it makes is astounding. When we recollect how the envisaged eschatological ruler is portrayed elsewhere in the prophetic literature (e.g. Isa. 9.6-7; 11.1-3; 16.5; 55.4; Jer. 23.5; 30.9; Ezek. 34.23-24; 37.24-25; Mic. 5.1-4 [EVV 4.14–5.3]; Zech. 3.8; 6.12-13), we are drawn up sharp by the realization that here for the first time in Old Testament prophetic books a prophet actually knows the name of this hoped-for figure, and moreover that it turns out to be the name of a contemporary of the prophet,[57] a man who is at this moment walking about the streets of Jerusalem. The historical Zerubbabel was, so far as we know, only a governor (פחה) of the Persian province of Yehud and a member of the Judaean royal house, nothing more startling, so the astonishing boldness of the identification can hardly be exaggerated. He must be the first real person in history to have been identified with the eschatological son of David.[58]

Now where a deconstruction begins to open up is over the question, So what is the important thing for this prophetic text? What is the *point* of the book of Haggai?

56. Wolff is remarkably reticent in only allowing that 'it is not entirely improbable that...Zerubbabel will in the future be declared the new David. But it must be stressed that this promise is couched in extremely muted terms.' His argument is that important messianic terms like משׁח and מלך are missing and there is nothing said of the struggle, victory and peace of the messianic age (*Haggai*, p. 106). I myself find what Haggai says much more persuasive than what he doesn't say. In contrast to Wolff, von Rad, *Old Testament Theology*, II, p. 284, says: 'He clearly and unequivocally designated as the coming anointed one David's descendant Zerubbabel'; cf. Rendtorff, *The Old Testament: An Introduction*, p. 236: 'a clear messianic expectation'; J. Alberto Soggin, *Introduction to the Old Testament* (trans. J. Bowden; London: SCM Press, 1976), p. 325: 'The messianic kingdom was about to be inaugurated, its sovereign was to be the last scion of the house of David, Zerubbabel'.

57. According to the chronology of the book of Zechariah, Zechariah will be saying something very similar in two months' time (cf. 1.7) about 'the Branch'; but although the identity of the Branch is an open secret, Zechariah does not go so far as Haggai in giving his name as Zerubbabel.

58. Von Rad says that 'It is common to point out that Haggai here differs radically from the pre-exilic prophets by naming a living member of the house of David as the coming anointed one' (*Old Testament Theology*, II, p. 284); but I have not found any other traces of this 'common' observation.

Until we have read to within four verses of the end of this book we are in little uncertainty about its overall point. No one doubts that it concerns the rebuilding of the temple, the consequences of ignoring it and an encouragement to begin it.[59] But, suddenly, in the last four verses we encounter an entirely new theme, the appointment and naming of the world ruler. And the former issue of temple building suddenly becomes invisible—just as, for its part, the universal significance of Zerubbabel had been in all that preceded.

Any book, of course, may have more than one topic, more than one aim. A book does not deconstruct itself merely by taking up a new topic, even in its last four verses. Where the deconstructive aspect lies, I think, is in the fact that the two topics, each of such moment, and each not self-evidently subordinate to the other, are nevertheless not brought into relation with one another, so that the reader experiences an aporia over what should be designated the overall theme of the work.[60] It is not that the two purposes flatly contradict one another, as if, for example, part one had said that Joshua was to become the world ruler and part two had said Zerubbabel. It is that in the first and major part of the book the one thing worthy of attention is the glory of

59. So too Wolff, *Haggai*, p. 22: 'Haggai is impelled by a single question: how can the devastated temple in Jerusalem be rebuilt?' Wolff relates the address to Zerubbabel to this theme by the assumption that Zerubbabel is 'appointed authorized guarantor of the temple's completion' (*ibid.*); but of course there is nothing in the Zerubbabel oracle about the temple. A focus on the temple has not however been universally recognized; cf. e.g. Perowne, *Haggai and Zechariah*, p. 22: '[I]t was the stern call, "Repent ye", with which he was principally charged'. Here the pragmatic demands of the text have been moralized, as so often happens.

60. Attempts to relate the two parts of the book are extraordinarily unsuccessful; thus Petersen, *Haggai and Zecharaiah 1–8*, p. 105: 'Through [Haggai's] efforts...the temple was well on the way to reconstruction. Now it was time to focus on other issues, including the civil polity of Israel.' Is that what 2.20-23 is about, 'the civil polity of Israel'? And is a phrase like 'now it was time to focus on other issues' not an elaborate way of saying that we cannot see the connection between the first issue and the second? See also Stuhlmueller, *Haggai and Zechariah*, p. 16: 'Haggai's focus was exceptionally clear. All of his energies were directed toward two goals: the rebuilding of the temple and the restoration of the Davidic rule.' But he does not even hint at what the relation of the two goals might be.

Yahweh evidenced by the influx of treasures to the temple and in the second part of the work the one object of attention is the glory of Zerubbabel as world ruler designate. Zerubbabel is not, it is true, in *competition* with Yahweh for glory, for it is Yahweh who is appointing Zerubbabel to his glorious office. But it is hard to see how the two themes are related.

It is not that Zerubbabel himself is going to bring about the achievement of the glory of Yahweh which the first part desiderates; for it is not Zerubbabel as distinct from Joshua who leads the work of rebuilding (1.1, 12, 14; 2.2, 4); and in any case it is not the rebuilding that is going to acquire glory but the filling of the temple with wealth by Yahweh himself (2.7). Nor does the completion of the temple bring about in any way the success of Zerubbabel, for his appointment is not linked to the completion of the temple (in fact, the *completion* of the temple hardly seems to be the issue; it is the *working on* the temple that seems to matter).

As a result, every attempt we make to state the aim or theme of the book seems doomed. In this major respect too the book deconstructs itself, professing to be about one thing and then, without telling us that it has changed its mind, turning out to be about something different (without ceasing to be about the first thing at the same time).

3. *The Temple Reconstructed*

I always worry about what to do with a text after it has been deconstructed. In this essay I want to propose a *reconstructive* process. I will focus first upon reconstructing the realities surrounding the text's composition, and secondly upon reconstructing the eventualities surrounding the text's reception.

a. *The Composition of the Text*
Why was this text written? I will not try to answer that question by speculating about the author's intention or the psychology of the prophet, of course, and especially not by double-guessing Persian political strategy or extrapolating from archaeological artifacts. Taking a leaf out of Frederic Jameson's book,[61] I will

---

61. *The Political Unconscious: Narrative as a Socially Symbolic Act* (London: Methuen, 1981).

assume that this text, like others, is written in order to suppress or repress (using the Freudian metaphor) a social conflict. Texts are written on paper, and paper is used for pasting over cracks, especially cracks in the social fabric. The question, Why was this text written?, can then be answered by reconstituting the social reality it implies. Now this is not quite the same as reconstructing the actual social reality in Jerusalem in 520 BCE, to which of course we have no access, since all we have are texts, texts that purport to give us access to those times, indeed, but that are, being texts, constitutionally incapable of doing so. No matter; we cannot access the actual first *readers* of Haggai's book either, but we *can* reconstitute its implied readers. We cannot ever grasp the social reality of Haggai's time, but we *can* profile the social reality implied in the book.

If texts are written to suppress conflicts, and we want to bring those conflicts to the surface, deconstruction seems to me a good way of doing it. In a deconstruction, a chasm in the text opens up; and we have the choice of timidly averting our gaze from the giddy depths or of boldly peering down into them to what lies hidden (or partly hidden) at the unconscious level.

1. The first deconstruction I identified concerned the issue of honour. It appeared that the people are dishonouring the deity by not rebuilding the temple, and yet for all their rebuilding they will not achieve the honour the deity requires. There is a conflict here between the people and what they can do, on the one hand, and the leadership (the prophet and his accomplices, the high priest and the governor) and what they want on the other. There is, in other words, a social conflict lurking beneath the text and coming to expression in its deconstructability.

In this case, of course, the conflict is not entirely latent. For the text itself portrays the very same conflict, though it doesn't tell us the whole truth about it. It represents the conflict as being between the enthusiasts for rebuilding the temple and the 'people'. On the one side are Haggai the 'prophet', Zerubbabel the governor and Joshua the high priest. These leaders will have their support groups, presumably of prophets, administrators and priests. On the other side are the 'people', everyone else. They are farmers and householders. The conflict comes about when the people with power think that the people without power should stop farming and putting ceilings in their houses and should spend their days in unpaid labour on building the temple. The people without power do not think this is a good idea.

In whose interest is this rebuilding? Not the people's. Even if they are not economists, they can see that temple building is not contributing to the gross national product, and even if they are not atheists they can see that the worship of the deity is not being impeded in any way by the incompleteness of the temple. Sacrifices are being offered, prayers are being said, priests and levites are being fed by tithes. The temple is a prestige project promoted by the elite, and its construction serves *their* sense of fitness, their vanity. The people at large are understandably not so enthusiastic, for they have little to gain and plenty to lose by the project.

So there is a social conflict beneath the text, implied by the text. The text by no means obscures it completely, but it does try to suppress it. And the way it does so is to tell the story of how the conflict was overcome, i.e. resolved. We recall that Jameson regards texts as attempts to suppress *unresolved* social conflicts. If a conflict has been resolved, it won't generate a text; if everything in the garden is lovely, there is nothing to write home about. Now the way this text tries to suppress the conflict that generated it is to claim that the people were won over to the opinion of the leadership, and so set about rebuilding the temple, thereby removing the tension. What the text suppresses (almost) is that the conflict was *not* resolved, for not all the people *did* co-operate in the building of the temple. Only a *remnant* worked on the temple—which implies that the majority did not. We can tell that this is the case, for while 'the people' as a whole are claimed to say that the 'time is not yet come' (1.2), and it is the people as a whole who are unclean and defiling the temple (2.14), it is only the 'remnant of the people' who obey the prophet's demand, have their spirit stirred and are addressed as its builders (1.12, 14; 2.2).[62] A remnant is a good thing to be; it is

---

62. Another way of suppressing the conflict is to translate שאר as 'the rest' of the people (as REB at 1.12, 14; 2.2); everyone knows, on the contrary, that '[i]n Hg and Zc "the remnant of the people" means the faithful grouped around Jerusalem' (so NJB footnote)—or rather, the supporters of

the nearest the proletariat can get to being an elite. If you are a remnant, you are still there; you are still in the reckoning. If you don't belong to the remnant, you have been written off. Now the text of course says not a word about the non-remnant, those who did *not* obey the prophetic word; it tries to write them out of existence. But the word 'remnant' gives the game away; for any semiotic square with 'remnant' at one corner is bound to have 'non-remnant' at another. In short: after Haggai had finished all his prophesying, the conflict between those who wanted the temple built and those who did not remained—so a text was called into being. *That* is the implication of the text.[63]

2. The second deconstruction, concerning the issue of uncleanness, points up more sharply the same implied social conflict, between the leadership and the populace. Where it differs from the first is that it expresses not just the fact of the conflict but the feelings of the elite about the conflict. The prophet, and therewith his class, cannot cope with the fact that they despise the people they are dependent on, and they express their anxiety about the tension by creating a deconstructable text. That is to say, they recognize that without the labour of the 'people' there will be no temple building; indeed, without the free and voluntary labour of the lower orders the prestige project of the elite will not be accomplished. Haggai (the character in the book of Haggai) expresses his distaste for the 'people' by pronouncing them 'unclean', and he attempts to gain a secure vantage point for himself over against the people by setting up an artificial dialogue with the priests as his power base. But his categorization of the people as 'unclean' backfires on him when it leads him to declare 'all the work of their hands' unclean. Implicitly that must include the temple building, but he and the class he represents cannot allow that; the text is generated by the unresolved conflict.

the leaders in Jerusalem. It is, incidentally, not a problem for the distinction between 'the people' and 'the remnant of the people' that in 1.12 'the people' fear before Yahweh and in 1.13 Yahweh says to 'the people', 'I am with you'; for the 'people' in question in the verses have just now been defined by 'the remnant of the people'at the beginning of 1.12.

63. Whether it was the historical reality is more than we can say, of course.

3. The third deconstruction, concerning Zerubbabel, evinces a different social or political conflict implied by the text, namely over the status of the governor. At its most simple, the point is that Haggai doesn't need to pronounce this oracle about Zerubbabel if everyone already agrees with it, and he doesn't need to write it down if everyone has accepted his prophecy about Zerubbabel at the time when he delivered it. The very existence of the Zerubbabel oracle in the text is prima facie evidence of resistance to it in the historical reality the text implies. Commentators indeed often recognize that the oracle addresses a situation of conflict, but, since they tend to think in psychological, personalistic and theological categories, they don't see that it is a *political* conflict. They think it is a conflict within Zerubbabel's own psyche, that he needs 'encouragement'. Maybe anyone in Zerubbabel's position *does* need encouragement, but more than that he needs a public announcement of support from his various power bases. Haggai provides that here on behalf of the prophetic cadre.[64]

There is bound to be conflict in a society when one group begins promoting one of its number as a world dictator and promising a shaking of all fixed points of reference. Shopkeepers and farmers are not going to welcome a cosmic upheaval; they need weather they can rely on and steady trade. A shaking of the heavens and the earth that will result in one ruler being substituted for another is more attractive to potential rulers and their hangers-on than to folk who have to earn a living by the 'work of their hands', to coin a phrase. And even if the wealth of all the nations is going to come pouring into Jerusalem, no one expects it to end up in the pocket of Joe Citizen; turning the local shrine into Fort Knox is not everyone's idea of eschatological bliss. Everyone under their own vine and fig tree...now that's a different matter. Haggai's elite do not know this; they think everyone should be impressed by the idea of Zerubbabel's being the signet ring on the deity's finger. The text actually represents this elite as so out of touch with reality as needing to be informed by a divine oracle what their people are thinking: the time is not yet

---

64. Cf. the notation of Ezra 5.2 that, at the rebuilding of the temple by Zerubbabel and Jeshua, 'with them were the prophets of God, helping them'. How? We may presume that the prophets did not carry stones.

come, say the people, says the Lord, by the hand of Haggai. Do rulers so ignorant deserve to be rulers?, we ask ourselves. The gulf between the governors and the governed is intolerably wide; even the surface of the text witnesses to that fact, and the deconstruction confirms it.

b. *The Reception of the Text*
Haggai's book was plainly not a 'popular' work; it is not the product of the 'people'. Rather, it portrays, from the point of view of the leadership, a conflict between them and that section of the people that does not belong to the 'remnant'. But equally plainly, it found its way into the biblical canon, and was accepted by the 'people'. How did they cope with its inconcinnities? Why did they not notice its self-deconstructability? Why did no one see through its papering over of the social conflicts it so revealingly attests?

Being professedly the words of a prophet has a lot to do with it. Being a *book* attributed to a prophet was even more important. It is writing that creates truth, for the truth about the past is what is remembered about the past. Writing a book of prophecy is therefore what makes a prophet a true prophet—even if that prophet tells palpable falsehoods like 'yet a little while and I will shake the heavens'.

That is to say, if you regard the words of Haggai as essentially the words of the deity written down 'by the hand of' Haggai', which means to say, if you believe 1.1, all tensions in the text have to be explained away, for everyone knows that the deity does not contradict himself. In fact, you don't need to explain away tensions, for if you believe that these are the words of the deity you will not be expecting to find tensions, and you will not believe the evidence of your eyes when you encounter one. It will also not occur to you to side with anyone in the text except Haggai, for he is the prophet of the god; the people therefore *are* unclean, and the temple most certainly *should* be built, the moment Haggai says it should. In short, through most of the history of the reception of the book, its deconstructability and its suppression of social conflict has simply been ignored because of the authentication of the prophet by the religious community.

What has happened, however, in the days since the interpretation of the Bible was wrested from the control of ecclesiastical authorities? Sad to say, not a lot. The prophet's book remains canonical scripture, and most interpreters feel some constraint to offer readings in accord with the parameters of doctrinal purity.

Two quotations from latterday readers of the book of Haggai should be enough to testify to the reception the book enjoys these days. In response to the depiction of the wealth of the nations flowing into Jerusalem, in which many a reader might well see a touch of the grandiose and of wishful thinking, Hans Walter Wolff writes:

> What is being expressed here is not greed on Israel's part, or some kind of Jewish egoism; it is the sovereign claim of Yahweh, who turns to his impoverished people in their necessity.[65]

Compare with this the words of Wolff's Heidelberg predecessor, Gerhard von Rad:

> There is no question here of greed for gain, but a proclamation by Yahweh which the prophet sets down with uncompromising boldness, and any exegesis which casts doubt upon this mighty purposefulness of Yahweh in the present world-order stands self-condemned in its own supposed spirituality.[66]

The text, that is to say, cannot possibly represent any kind of unlovely motivation on the part of the prophet or his supporters. In fact, say Wolff and von Rad, what we find here are not really words of the prophet himself, but 'the sovereign claim of Yahweh', 'a proclamation by Yahweh' that is consequently as unassailable as the moral character of Yahweh himself. These are not the words of some postexilic Jew, poverty-stricken and marginalized in some far-flung outpost of empire, giving voice to a fantasy about world dominion and economic supremacy for his kinsmen; no, these are the very words of the 'mighty purposefulness' of the universal god, 'turning to his impoverished people in their necessity'. Let no reader of these esteemed Old Testament scholars reflect for a moment on the social divisiveness of Haggai's book, or remark that it is a funny way of turning to your empoverished people to promise them all the silver and gold lining the pockets of the Gentiles and then do nothing about it. Such exegeses stand self-condemned, von Rad

---

65. Wolff, *Haggai*, p. 82.
66. Von Rad, 'The City on the Hill', pp. 232-42 (240-41).

assures us, so we know in advance where we stand with the guild of biblical scholars if we try to write an essay like the present one. The text owed its origin to its suppression of a social conflict in ancient Israel; and it owes its continuing existence (does it not?) to its facility to suppress conflict among its readers. And in the same way, and in the same 'prophetic' succession, the works of Wolff and von Rad also owe *their* continued existence to *their* power to suppress divergent readings, outlawing in advance 'any exegesis that casts doubt'.

This is the depth of the corruption in our academic discipline that surrounds us, even in this year of grace 1995, for all the splendours of the Enlightenment and the glories of scientific biblical criticism. It would be ironic if Haggai's book should come to serve for the unmasking of the abomination of religious authority standing where it should not and for the breaking loose of conflicts within the scholarly community that have been too long hushed up in the name of collegiality and tolerance.

4

Metacommentating Amos[*]

Metacommentary, what is that? Let me try this formulation: When we write commentary, we read what commentators say. When we write metacommentary, we notice what commentators do.

This plain and symmetrical account of metacommentary seems to collapse, however, the moment it has been formulated. For what do commentators *do* apart from what they *say*? Apart from playing squash or lying late in bed, which we do not want to know about, what do commentators do other than what they say?

Well, the main thing they do but don't say is not say what they don't say. Not many say, Of course, I am failing to ask this question of the text, or, I am hiding from you, dear reader, my own opinion on the matter, or, I come to this text with a prejudice about what it ought to mean. These are really very interesting matters, for they are being concealed. What is written on the page is only what the author has chosen to reveal; but to every text there is a subtext, which the author has suppressed, repressed, forgotten, ignored, kept from us—and not even told us that it has been kept from us. We innocent members of the public, who go on laying out good money on commentaries,

* An earlier version of this essay was published in *Of Prophets' Visions and the Wisdom of Sages: Essays in Honour of R. Norman Whybray on his Seventieth Birthday* (ed. Heather A. McKay and David J.A. Clines; Journal for the Study of the Old Testament Supplement Series, 162; Sheffield: JSOT Press, 1993), pp. 142-60. The essay was originally delivered as a paper at Loyola College, Baltimore, September, 1991, in the Israelite Prophetic Literature Section, Society of Biblical Literature Annual Meeting, San Francisco, November, 1992, and at the Ehrhardt Seminar, University of Manchester, May, 1993.

need protection against these commentators who are failing to tell us what it is they are failing to tell us. So it becomes an urgent public duty to create a neighbourhood watch committee of metacommentators who will investigate for us how we are being shortchanged.

You can search high and low for metacommentary on Amos and Amos commentators, for it is a rare scholar who will step outside the ideology of the text and notice how severely traditional commentary has been constrained by the outlook of the text. But I did find one, whose feminist perspective gave her a vantage point, outside the text, from which the Amos landscape suddenly took on new and surprising contours. Judith Sanderson, in *The Women's Bible Commentary*, noticed, as everyone else has, how the oracles of Amos vigorously condemn the wealthy women of Samaria for oppressing the poor, but also, as no one else has, that they they do not champion the women among those poor. And when Amos condemns the wealthy women of Samaria, because Sanderson is a feminist reader she does not automatically adopt the prophet's standpoint, but suspects that his condemnation is yet another scapegoating of women, who are being blamed now not only for sexual sins (as usual) but for social and economic injustices in society as well.[1] 'A survey of modern commentaries on Amos 4.1 reveals the alacrity with which women are blamed for societies' evils, [and] their relative powerlessness is disregarded', she writes, metacommentatingly.[2] She is quite right; but her feminist critique is only a paradigm for several types of criticism that can be made.[3]

---

1.   These women, we must recall, are 'the pampered darlings of society in Israel's royalist culture...ruling the society of Israel from behind the scenes with sweet petulant nagging for wealth to support their indolent dalliance' (James L. Mays, *Amos: A Commentary* [Old Testament Library; London: SCM Press, 1969], p. 72).

2.   Judith Sanderson, 'Amos', in *The Women's Bible Commentary* (ed. Carol A. Newsom and Sharon H. Ringe; London: SPCK, 1992), pp. 205-209 (205-206).

3.   I am speaking here only of more or less contemporary commentators. Some older commentators, especially when writing from an avowedly Christian perspective, did not feel the same degree of inhibition towards evaluation of their text. Here, for example, is Richard S. Cripps: '[T]he Prophet's conception of God is not perfect. One of the mistakes which the

Metacommentating Amos myself, I propose noticing some of the things commentators do. First, they adopt the view of the text regarding the social and economic situation in ancient Israel. Secondly, they adopt the ideology of the text regarding the existence of God and the authenticity of the prophetic vocation. Thirdly, they conceal from their readers that this is what they are doing.

1. *Commentators and the Social Critique of Amos*

I take here the woe against the rich in Amos 6.4-7:

> Alas for those who lie on beds of ivory,
>   and lounge on their couches,
> and eat lambs from the flock,
>   and calves from the stall;
> who sing idle songs to the sound of the harp,
>   and like David improvise on instruments of music;
> who drink wine from bowls,
>   and anoint themselves with the finest oils,
>   but are not grieved over the ruin of Joseph!
> Therefore they shall now be the first to go into exile,
>   and the revelry of the loungers shall pass away (NRSV).

Let me engage first in a little *Sachkritik* as a backdrop to reading some commentators. There is undoubtedly a great deal of anger in this passage against the rich in Samaria, and its spirit of denunciation against idleness and luxury strikes a chord with democratically minded and hard-working readers. But a reader who has not yet opened a commentary pauses, at least long enough to ask, What exactly is the crime of these Samarians for which they are being threatened with exile? Is there some sin in having expensive ivory inlays on your bedframe? (Amos, we

---

Christian Church has made, resulting in damage impossible to calculate, has been to standardise as eternal and ultimate truth that which was but a stage—however lofty—in the slow process of its revelation and discovery... If any picture of God found within the O.T. had been perfect, then one of the reasons for the appearing of Jesus would have become unnecessary' (*A Critical and Exegetical Commentary on the Book of Amos* [London: SPCK, 1929], p. 25). However unacceptable today the theory of 'progressive revelation' may be, at least it enabled its adherents to adopt a critical stance toward their texts.

presume, is not worried about the fate of elephants.) No doubt meat of any kind was something of a delicacy in ancient Israel, and these people are eating the meat of choice animals prepared for the table; but is that wrong?[4] (Again we can suppose that Amos is not vegetarian and that the text has no fault to find with the farming methods.)[5] And as for singing idle songs, who among the readers of Amos can cast a stone? Has karaoke suddenly become a sin, as well as a social disease?[6] Drinking wine out of bowls instead of cups does admittedly sound greedy, and

4.   Oh yes, say Andersen and Freedman (F.I. Andersen and D.N. Freedman, *Amos: A New Translation with Introduction and Commentary* [Anchor Bible, 24A; New York: Doubleday, 1989], p. 562). 'The details of the menu supplied by v 4b indicate the unconscionable extravagance of the feast... The sumptuous provision of beef and lamb, and young and tender animals as well, points to eating on a scale far beyond the means of the ordinary worker or farmer.' But are we to read a 'menu' in the reference to 'lambs from the flock' and 'calves from the stall'? Can we even say that Amos means that both are eaten at the same feast? In any case, would it be 'unconscionable extravagance' to have two kinds of meat served at the one banquet? How many unconscionably extravagant restaurants have Andersen and Freedman eaten in, I wonder, and shall we say that if Andersen orders lamb and Freedman veal that their 'excessive behavior' is 'its own condemnation' (cf. p. 563)? And, incidentally, exactly how many items are on this 'menu' anyway? Either it is 'beef and lamb' or it is 'young and tender animals', but it is not 'young and tender animals *as well*'. And is there something reprehensible in eating lamb rather than mutton, Wienerschnitzel rather than Hungarian goulash? Or is it perhaps that the reference to 'young and tender' animals—whom we all feel sensitive about—is nothing more than a rhetorical ploy to make the unsuspicious reader take sides uncritically with the prophet against his opponents?

5.   The cryptic remark of Hammershaimb, however, gives pause for thought (Erling Hammershaimb, *The Book of Amos: A Commentary* [trans. John Sturdy; Oxford: Basil Blackwell, 1970], p. 100). 'It hurts the feelings of the shepherd of Tekoa that good animals are used for feasts of this sort', he says, and the reader wonders whether Amos perhaps thinks the rich should serve diseased animals for dinner, or whether he is against them having opulent feasts but would find no fault with, shall we say, humble feasts—or whether, perhaps, the 'shepherd of Tekoa' entertains tender vegetarian feelings toward his charges.

6.   The commentators think that the phrase 'like David' is an inauthentic addition to the text; but they *would* say that, wouldn't they, because otherwise it would be altogether too hard to say what was wrong with it.

anointing yourself with the finest (and presumably most expensive) oil rather than bargain basement value-for-money oil is certainly self-indulgent. But how serious is self-indulgence? Is it a crime? Is it a sin that deserves a sentence of deportation? Does being wealthy and conspicuously consuming renewable natural resources (wine, oil, mutton and elephant tusks) put you in line for exile, by any reasonable standards? What are the rich supposed to have been doing? If expensive oil is on sale in the market and you have the money in your pocket to buy it, where is the sin?

Ah well, say the commentators, it's more serious than that. The prophetic criticism is that these people have been indulging themselves *and at the same time* not feeling any pain at the ruin of their people (6.7). So, says the metacommentator, if they *had* been worried about the fate of the nation, it would have been all right for them to be self-indulgent? Well, no, not quite. Actually, they are being hit on both counts. Anyway, says the metacommentator, how does the prophet know that they do not feel pain about their nation? He is presumably not invited to their parties—surely he wouldn't have the nerve to complain about the extravagance if he were—so how does he know what they feel and don't feel? Ah well, it's obvious that if they felt any pain they wouldn't be having parties. Is it? If Rome really is burning, what else is there left to do except fiddle?

Would it perhaps be just as true to say, Amos hates the rich because he is not one of them? If he were richer, he would be using more expensive aftershave himself. It's easy to condemn other people's lifestyle and to blame the ills of society on them. But the truth about political and economic disaster and well-being is probably far too complex to be explained by the behaviour of individuals. The fate of nations is determined much more by structural matters, the operation of markets, demographic changes, disease, war and chance. To be sure, the personal behaviour of other people is not a negligible factor in everyday life; we would all like our fellow citizens to behave better, and we know we would feel less envy and less fear if they were all more like us. But if you are a little country being targeted for annexation by a big one, as Israel was by Assyria, the high-mindedness and moral sensitivity of the average citizen are not going to make a lot of difference.

In short, it would be uncritical of us to accept Amos's analysis of his society, to simply buy the ideology of the text. Somehow we need to distance ourselves from the prophetic voice, and recognize that the prophet's is only one voice in his community. The prophet, and the text, have a corner to fight, a position to uphold, and we for our part need to identify that position, and to relativize it, not so as to discard it but only so as to give it its proper due. But, hardly surprisingly, most of the books about Amos simply take Amos's point of view for granted. Amos is right, his opponents are wrong; Amos is fair; Amos is accurate; Amos is immensely perceptive; Amos is inspired.[7]

In order to practise metacommentary, we need to do some close reading of commentaries. Here is my first exhibit:

7.   Here is a striking example of commentators' incapacity to distinguish between the text and themselves. Andersen and Freedman (*Amos*, pp. 88-97) have a section on 'The God of Israel in the Book of Amos'. It opens by saying, 'Our purpose is to present Amos' picture of the deity, not ours, and to keep it within the thought world of the ancient Near East and the Bible rather than to translate it into contemporary theological or philosophical language' (p. 88). That sounds scholarly and objective enough. But the section concludes by saying: 'What it finally comes down to is the nature of the God of the Bible, the person with whom the prophet must deal (and vice versa) and the person around whom everything turns. When all of the superlatives have been exhausted and when all of the authority or majesty have been accorded and the recognition given to the one incomparable deity who stands uniquely alone and against everything that is perishable, vulnerable, corruptible, and the rest, he nevertheless remains a person. That is the fundamental and ultimate category in the Bible, as without it nothing else matters...Once it is agreed that this God—creator and sustainer of heaven and earth, sole and unique—is the God of the Bible and Israel and Amos and the rest of us, then we may draw closer and ask him who he is, what he is like, and how things run in this world' (p. 97). By this point, plainly, we readers are not reading any more about Amos and the ancient world, for Amos had no Bible and thus no God of the Bible. Nor are we reading about Amos's God when we read that God is 'against everything that is perishable, vulnerable, corruptible'—for are those terms not true of humanity, and is Amos's God 'against' humanity in general? And when, at the end, we start to read about what is 'agreed' and are told that 'we' may 'draw closer and ask him who he is' (how?), we can feel sure that the authors' trumpeted scholarly interests in the ancient world have been submerged by their own ideological beliefs.

> In eighth-century Israel the rich got richer and the poor got poorer... Amos sketches the well-being enjoyed by the upper classes in the capital cities, the splendid society that was built upon the misery of the weak and poor... Expensive furniture, indolent ease, succulent food, the sound of music, and extravagant indulgence—so the affluent in Samaria live. Every item represents a luxurious sophistication that had been possible in earlier times only for royalty, and remained a world apart from the life in the villages. The hollowness of it all only becomes apparent in 6c where this heedless hedonism is thrown into relief against the 'ruin of Joseph' from which it is completely insulated.[8]

Such a rich text repays close reading.

In eighth-century Israel the rich got richer and the poor got poorer.[9]
If it is true that the rich got richer, can we be sure that the poor got poorer? The gap between rich and poor can widen even while everyone's standard of living is improving. What about those who were neither rich nor poor (? the majority). And in any case, how can we possibly know whether the poverty portrayed in Amos was widespread; how can we know whether the rich were in some way responsible for the poverty of the poor or whether there was some structural cause, which was really no one individual's fault, for the poverty of a minority?

Amos sketches the well-being enjoyed by the upper classes in the capital cities, the splendid society that was built upon the misery of the weak and poor.[10]
'Splendid' is ironic, is it not? It is not an objective scholarly description, is it? It is actually representing Amos's (ironic) point of view in the guise of a scholarly description, is it not? And does the author literally mean, 'built upon the misery of the weak'? It is no doubt true enough that in a competitive and entrepreneurial society the weakest go to the wall if there are no programmes for social care; but we cannot simply assume that a prosperous society owes its prosperity to the deprivation of its poor.[11] You

8. Mays, *Amos*, pp. 114, 116.
9. Mays, *Amos*, p. 114.
10. Mays, *Amos*, p. 114.
11. Mays actually says that 'The economic base of such luxury is violence...against the poor' (p. 117). What economic theory, we suddenly

couldn't say that about modern Switzerland, for example. Should not biblical commentators have to do a course in economics before they deliver themselves of opinions about Israelite society that they proffer in their own voice? Certainly, they shouldn't be allowed to parrot the prophets and pretend they are doing scholarly analysis.

Expensive furniture, indolent ease, succulent food, the sound of music, and extravagant indulgence—so the affluent in Samaria live. Every item represents a luxurious sophistication that had been possible in earlier times only for royalty, and remained a world apart from the life in the villages. The hollowness of it all only becomes apparent in 6c where this heedless hedonism is thrown into relief against the 'ruin of Joseph' from which it is completely insulated.[12]

What authority has the commentator to take this high moral tone? Would he care to compare his own living standards in, let's say, Richmond, Virginia, with those of the affluent in Samaria of the eighth century BCE? Why does he seem to sneer at the spread of wealth and sophistication from the court to a wider section of the populace? Why does he not approve, as a loyal American, of the democratization of privilege that his text attests? Why does he suggest that if the villages cannot have cable TV no one else should? And what right has he to talk of 'heedless hedonism' when he himself, if he is anything like most of us academics, has probably never contributed to the gross national product, having devoted himself to the selfish pursuit of non-practical knowledge, and being parasitic, like most scholars, upon the wealth-creating sectors of the community for his own bread and butter?

And here is my second exhibit:

> The prophet brutally smashes the attraction of these banquets of the chosen few in society which go on long into the night, by a mournful *hoy* ['woe']. He disturbs the fastidious and dubious atmosphere of these ceremonies where the other man's fate is completely disregarded... There are some who profit at the

wonder, does Mays subscribe to? Can it be perhaps that he is a Marxist? Or is this not a serious economic and political remark, but only preacher's rhetoric?

12. Mays, *Amos*, p. 116.

expense of the community; they enjoy life while the rest weep in misery. Amos does not desire a prosperity founded on oppression. That is why this fastidious set will be deported and this refined but rotten society will vanish away.[13]

From whose point of view does Amos 'brutally smash the attraction' of these banquets? Not that of the readers, presumably, since they will not be very attracted to a party where everyone has long since gone home. It will be that of the partygoers themselves; Amos thinks the national situation too serious for people to be enjoying themselves. And so, apparently, does the commentator. Without thinking, without questioning, he assumes that if Amos says it, it must be right. And what is more, it must be effective. So if Amos stands outside the window and shouts *hoy*, 'woe' (remember, he hasn't been invited to the party), everyone inside finds the party entirely spoiled, its attraction smashed and its fastidious atmosphere fatally disturbed. Really?

Amos doesn't desire a prosperity founded on oppression, says the commentator, no doubt quite correctly. But he omits to mention that neither do the wealthy of Samaria, in all probability. No one except the most depraved and cynical people walk around boasting about founding their prosperity on oppression. So the difference between Amos and those he opposes is not that he is evidently in the right and they are evidently in the wrong; it is a difference in conviction about what is and is not fair dealing. Perhaps Amos is in the right, but perhaps he is not. All I am saying is that to jump to the conclusion that he is in the right is not a scholarly procedure; it is simply the reflex of an uncritical religious belief that assumes that what a prophet in the Bible says must be the truth. And yet that very Bible gives us plenty of evidence about the existence of false prophets in ancient Israel, and about the capacity for error even of those who are genuine.

2. *Commentators and the Religious Ideology of Amos*

Amos, or the book of Amos, is full of religious ideology (or theology, as we tend to call it when we are not being critical but

13. R. Martin-Achard, *A Commentary on the Book of Amos*, in R. Martin-Achard and S. Paul Re'emi, *God's People in Crisis* (International Theological Commentary; Edinburgh: Handsel Press, 1984), pp. 48, 49.

giving our implicit assent to it). The question the metacommentator asks is whether the commentators on Amos recognize ideology when they see it. Here are some ideological statements you find in the book and in the commentaries.

a. *The Prophetic Sense of Vocation*
The book of Amos is founded on the belief that Amos the prophet had actually been spoken to by God. This is what he claims when he says, 'Thus says Yahweh'. It is an amazing claim, and a shocking one. Most of our acquaintances, we ought to recall, think that people who claim to hear voices from the sky should be locked up. Commentators are hardy souls, however, not easily alarmed, and generous of spirit. How else to explain the fact that almost every textbook on Amos accepts Amos's claim, the book's ideology?

Here is the commentary of that learned German, Hans Walter Wolff. Under the heading 'The Man Amos' he tells us, with due scholarly caution:

> When Amos was born and when he died, we do not know. How old he was at the time of his appearance around 760 BC remains hidden from us... Amos was not a native of the northern kingdom, but a Judean come from Tekoa... As a sheep breeder (and as such to be distinguished clearly from a lowly shepherd) he was probably not exactly poor.[14]

'Probably not exactly'; it is the very quintessence of scholarly reserve. But then, in the very next paragraph, scholarship is thrown to the winds and pious statements of belief in the intangible and unknowable are paraded as if they belonged to the same world of discourse:

> It was the hand of Yahweh which uprooted him temporarily from his familiar realm and made him break the silence of the wise in evil times (5.13). Whenever he reveals the basis for his prophetic appearance, he points exclusively to Yahweh's irresistible insistence... To those who attribute his appearance to his own brazen self-will, he directs the question whether then terror at the sudden roar of a lion could be self-willed; it is Yahweh's address that has

14. Hans Walter Wolff, *Joel and Amos: A Commentary on the Books of the Prophets Joel and Amos* (Hermeneia; Philadelphia: Fortress Press, 1977), p. 90.

> irresistibly impelled him to make proclamation (3.8)... [B]ecause
> he has been constrained by Yahweh to proclaim his judgment,
> Amos also exposes Israel's guilt as reason for this judgment.[15]

So there is a God, and his name is Yahweh, and Yahweh did
indeed speak to Amos, just as Amos claims, and I am telling you
this with all my authority as a German professor.[16] There were
those, no doubt, in Amos's own time who 'attributed his appearance to his own brazen self-will'—though the text, if I read it
rightly, tells us only of those who demanded that Amos go home
and stop prophesying at Bethel; whether they implied that it was
not God who brought Amos to Bethel but Amos's own self-will
is rather harder to determine. Anyway, says Wolff, Amos has the
better of that exchange because he can whip out the lines, 'The
lion has roared; who will not fear? The Lord GOD has spoken;
who can but prophesy?' (3.8). Somehow that proves that Amos is
in the right, that he has been sent by God, that there is a God,
and all the rest of it. And any modern readers, by the same
token, who attribute Amos's appearance at Bethel to his own
brazen self-will—or even say, more modestly, that they suppose
Amos just thought it was a good idea to go to Bethel and say
what he believed—they too stand condemned by the prophet
himself. Amos's rhetorical question is unanswerable. No matter
that it is only a claim. No matter that you can't prove the validity
of one claim by making another. Amos *has* been impelled by
God, he *has* been constrained by Yahweh; this is historical fact.
No, we do not know when he was born, and no, we cannot be
sure whether he was rich or poor, but yes, we do know he was
sent by God and that he was in the right and Amaziah was in the
wrong.

---

15. Wolff, *Joel and Amos*, p. 91.

16. American professors are no different, of course. Says Mays, opening
his section on 'The Message' of Amos: 'Amos was Yahweh's messenger to
Israel' (*Amos*, p. 6)—which six words, being interpreted, mean, Yes, there is
a Yahweh, and yes, Amos is his authentic prophet and Amaziah is a fraud; I
know, and I am telling you. It has all the critical finesse and scholarly sobri-
ety of the muezzin's call to prayer: There is no god but God and Muhammad is the prophet of God. There is of course nothing wrong about the
muezzin's claim, especially if you are a believer (I don't disbelieve it myself,
actually); it's just that it's not critical scholarship.

b. *Inner-Religious Conflict*

There's another thing, the matter of Amaziah. I don't mind admitting that my own antipodean sympathies and prejudices every time are with the rough-hewn prophet from down under by comparison with the smooth authoritarian toady, the priest Amaziah. But I can't help thinking, But this Amaziah wasn't an atheist, he wasn't a pagan, he wasn't an irreligious man. He worshipped the same God as Amos, and he and Amos believed in almost all the same things. From my perspective, from the perspective of an Assyrian, from the perspective of almost anyone who is not caught up in the political and religious situation of the eighth century BCE, the conflict between them was no more than a minor sectarian dispute. And since we only have Amos's side of it—and that, moreover, is couched in the colourful rhetoric of poetry—how can we ever decide where right and wrong lay? and what, for that matter, would right and wrong in matters of this kind actually be?

c. *Knowledge versus Belief*

Let me try a rather more subtle example, this time from the Danish scholar Erling Hammershaimb. The reader is invited to detect the point at which the scholarship stops and the religious assumptions begin:

> Amos not only knows the land of Israel...; he is also familiar with his people's history and the accounts of Yahweh's acts of kindness to the people. For him Yahweh is the creator God, who has led the people out of Egypt and preserved them during the forty years of wandering in the wilderness, and then defeated the Amorites in the land of Canaan, so that Israel could dwell there (2.9ff.; Amos 9.7). He knows too that Yahweh has continuously cared for the spiritual well-being of the people, and sent prophets to speak to the people and remind them of his commandments (Amos 2.11). Amos does not therefore regard himself as proclaiming something completely new...[17]

Amos is familiar with his people's history—that is an uncontroversial inference from the text of the book itself (provided, of course, that we leave aside the trifling matter of whether the author of the book is actually the prophet Amos). He knows the

17. Hammershaimb, *Amos*, p. 12.

'accounts' of the national god's deeds; no problem there. 'For him' Yahweh is this and that—which is the scholarly way of representing the views of others without at the same time committing oneself to them. But when we read, 'He knows too that Yahweh has continuously cared for...his people', we are bound to ask, 'Knows, does he?' How can he *know* something that is not a fact? He knows the *tradition* that Yahweh has cared for his people, but Hammershaimb cannot say that Amos 'knows' it unless Hammershaimb believes it. He cannot mean that Amos knows it but Amos might be wrong; we don't say someone 'knows' it is four o'clock if we ourselves believe it is six. Hammershaimb, though he hasn't done anything very wicked, has let his guard slip nevertheless. He persuaded us at the beginning of the paragraph that he was speaking purely as an 'objective' scholar, dispassionately describing the views of Amos, but by the third sentence he let us see that in fact he was not a disinterested observer of Amos at all, but an adherent and promoter of Amos's theological ideas. Any reader who thinks that such an analysis of the scholar's religious commitment is hypercritical might like to consider how the sentences would sound if we substituted Zeus for Yahweh, and, shall we say, Aeschylus for Amos. For Aeschylus, Zeus is the creator. Fine, we say. He knows too that Zeus has continuously sustained the Greek people. Has he indeed?, we cannot help asking.

d. *The Contrast between 'True' and 'False' Prophets*
Take another example, the matter of the terms in which the contrast between Amos and the 'professional prophets' is cast. In insisting he is not a prophet nor a prophet's son, Amos, says Hammershaimb, 'means that he is not a prophet by profession, does not belong to a band of prophets, and has not uttered his prophecies for financial gain like the professional prophets'.[18] Does this mean that *Amos* claims that the 'professional prophets' utter their prophecies for financial gain, or that *Hammershaimb* believes that the 'professional prophets' did so? Given that sentence alone, it is hard to tell. Certainly, when we read that 'Amaziah himself forbids Amos to prophesy in the Northern Kingdom, and orders him out, as being a professional prophet

18. Hammershaimb, *Amos*, p. 11.

who had appeared there for the sake of gain',[19] we have no doubt that the point of view being reported is that of Amaziah and not of the modern critic. But when we read, a few pages on, that Amos 'wishes to protest at being included in the same class as the professional prophets, whose preaching was not dictated by Yahweh, but by the wish to earn money',[20] the relative clause beginning 'whose preaching' can only be taken as the words of the scholar.[21] It is the scholar who advances the view that the prophets Amos dissociates himself from are false prophets ('not dictated by Yahweh'), and not even sincerely mistaken, but corrupt, and motivated only by the desire for money. Amos himself (the character Amos in the text, I mean) never says that other prophets are false prophets, and never hints that the preaching of prophets and the sons of prophets is dictated by the wish to earn money. He only says that he is not a 'professional' prophet.[22]

19. Hammershaimb, *Amos*, p. 113.
20. Hammershaimb, *Amos*, p. 117.
21. It is the comma after 'professional prophets' that proves it: if there had been no comma, the 'whose preaching' clause could be understood as defining the professional prophets, and in that case could be representing the perspective of Amos; but the comma turns the clause into a descriptive clause, which can only represent the perspective of Hammerschaimb. The distinction is the same as that between 'that', which introduces a defining clause, and 'which', which introduces a descriptive clause. If it is protested that the comma may have been introduced by the translator, I offer my apologies to Hammerschaimb, and fasten the blame on the translator. And if is protested that I am making a lot of fuss about a comma, I will reply that, in this case, on that comma hangs the difference between giving the impression that one is uncritically adopting the opinions of Amos or being a critical scholar. Real critical scholars will go to any lengths to prevent a comma cheating them of their reputation.
22. He may even be saying that he *was* not a professional prophet, but he *is* now. If Yahweh has *taken* him from following the flock, he is not being a shepherd any longer, is he? And if he is not earning a living from shepherding, is he perhaps earning it from prophesying?
    But where does the idea of 'professional prophet' come from, anyway? Does *nabi* mean that? Was Ezekiel, who was a professional priest, also a professional prophet? And in any case, is Amaziah implying that Amos is prophesying for the sake of income, and is he urging Amos to earn his living from prophesying elsewhere, or does 'eat bread' mean what it means everywhere else, 'eat', not 'earn'? In sum, has the whole idea of 'gain' perhaps been entirely imported into the text?

As far as we know, he may have nothing against professional prophets; the sum and substance of his reply to Amaziah might well be simply his affirmation of the genuineness of his own calling. And we too might do well to think twice before assuming that 'professional' prophets are in the business of prophesying just for the money; Hammershaimb was a professional biblical scholar, but we wouldn't dream of saying that he was motivated by the wish to earn money.

e. *Punishment*

It is an essential element in the text's ideology that sin should be punished. The book opens with a powerful indictment of the nations that surround Israel for their crimes, and a repeated threat of punishment. As each nation comes into focus, the prophetic message is: 'For three transgressions of X and for four, I will not turn away the punishment thereof' (e.g. 1.3).[23] Any 'departure' from God is visited with punishment, as in the catalogue of disasters in ch. 4 (famine and plague and war) that failed to make Israel 'return' to the Lord. And the repeated 'therefore' is a further sign of the prophetic ideology; the familiar pattern is: an account of a sin, followed by the 'therefore' that introduces the punishment. The denunciation of the rich that we have already looked at, 'Woe to those who lie on beds of ivory', likewise comes to a conclusion with such a 'therefore': 'Therefore they shall be the first of those to go into exile' (6.7). And to the sin of Amaziah in forbidding Amos to prophesy, there is the same 'therefore' of punishment: 'Therefore thus says the LORD, Your wife shall be a prostitute in the city...' (7.17)— which Amos, interestingly enough, thinks of as a punishment of *him*.

What do the commentators make of this ideology? They never discuss it; they only repeat it. They *agree* with Amos that both Israel and the surrounding nations *deserve to be punished*, and that such punishment should be *capital*. Here, for example, is John Bright:

---

23. Actually, the Hebrew text does not have a word for 'punishment', but it is obvious—from the ideology of the book as a whole, really—that it can only be punishment that is inevitable after a crime.

> Amos's message was a devastating attack on the social evils of the day, particularly on the heartlessness and dishonesty with which the rich had ground down the poor..., but also on the immorality and the careless pursuit of luxury which had sapped the national character...—all of which he viewed as sins that Yahweh would surely punish.[24]

The metacommentator is bound to ask whether modern scholars are aware of what they are doing. They are adopting the view, and presenting it as their own, that the best way, or perhaps the only way, of dealing with heartlessness, dishonesty, immorality and luxury (to adopt Bright's terms) is to wipe the offenders out of existence. The metacommentator observes (but is not surprised) how, when it is the deity who is punishing, high-minded commentators who would not harm a fly themselves suddenly join the hanging and flogging brigade and think no punishment too severe.

Nor do the commentators seem to notice the conflict between the apparent justice of punishing those who deserve it and the obvious injustice of punishing those who do not. Mays, for example, can write that the 'prophecy of Amos can be heard as Yahweh's response to their [the poor's] cry, for the weak and poor are the special objects of Yahweh's compassion and concern';[25] but at the same time he can say that 'the consistent burden of his [Amos's] oracles is to announce the disaster that will fulfil Yahweh's decree of an end for his people'.[26] He doesn't seem to notice that Yahweh can't be very compassionate to the poor if he intends them to be carried into exile because of the wrongdoing of their leaders, or that the prophet's demand for justice does not seem to apply to the deity.[27]

---

24. John Bright, *A History of Israel* (London: SCM Press, 3rd edn, 1981), p. 262.

25. Mays, *Amos*, p. 10.

26. Mays, *Amos*, p. 9.

27. Here is a typical commentatorial utterance on the subject: 'The conception of Yahweh which Amos entertains is that of a god of justice... [Amos] makes the idea the very centre of his conception of God... Righteousness being a vital element in Yahweh's character, he not only will demand it in those who profess to be his followers, but will also enforce the demand...It is a demand for justice, which, in its simplest and most natural form, includes honesty, integrity, purity, and humanity... It demands the

These commentators surely know that they have many options open to them when they themselves are wronged by someone else, and that inflicting injury on others is either a raw instinctive impulse or else a cruel cold-blooded decision that they come to at the end of their tether, feel guilty about, but try to justify nevertheless on some rational grounds. But once they start commentating on Amos they accede to Amos's simple moral defeatism. Not one of them has the courage—or the intellectual capacity—to extract himself (they are all males) from the ideology of the text and to pronounce a moral judgment upon the prophecy. To be sure, the future *was* very much as the prophecy says—whether it predicted it or wrote it up in hindsight. Things *were* awful, for rich and poor alike. But it is even more awful to ascribe the destruction of a state and the forceable deportation of its citizens to an avenging God. If that is how a believer finds himself or herself impelled to conclude, that it is a terrible thing to fall into the hands of the living God, the metacommentator can respect that. But to affirm it casually, to pretend that it is unproblematic—*that* is not scholarly, it is not even human.

Must the metacommentator be so waspish?, readers are likely to be asking themselves. Does everything have to become so *personal*, and is it truly scholarly to question the motives and interests of our colleagues, as I have been doing throughout this paper?

The answer is, Yes. It must be, once we admit that we are not all engaged in some objective quest for determinate meanings, and that our ideologies, our locations, our interests and our personalities determine our scholarship—and separate us from one

---

utmost consideration of the poor and weak,—*moral* justice' (William Rainey Harper, *A Critical and Exegetical Commentary on Amos and Hosea* [International Critical Commentary; Edinburgh: T. & T. Clark, 1905], pp. cxvii-cxviii, cxx). It simply does not occur to this commentator to ask whether in Amos's conception this moral standard applies to Yahweh, and whether the threats of famine, fire, exile and the like can be accommodated with 'the utmost consideration of the poor and weak'. At least Harper does not try to argue that the punishments are 'a token and proof of divine concern and commitment' (Andersen and Freedman, *Amos*, p. 383), a disingenuous claim if ever there was one.

another. Strip away the bonhomie that passes for scholarly interchange in the corridors of the international congresses, and we find that there is a lot we don't like, don't approve of, and will not stand for, in our colleagues, a lot that has yet to be brought into the light, taken the measure of, and fought over. Managing personal conflict within the academy may well be the new skill, harder still than Assyriology or deconstruction, that scholars will need to acquire in this decade.[28]

28. Examples of the 'new brutality', as we might term it, in biblical scholarship, may be found in the recent pages of the *Journal of Biblical Literature*; witness the paper of Ben F. Meyer against E.P. Sanders ('A Caricature of Joachim Jeremias and his Scholarly Work', *Journal of Biblical Literature*110 [1991], pp. 451-62), and that of Meir Sternberg against Danna Fewell and David Gunn ('Biblical Poetics and Sexual Poetics: From Reading to Counter-Reading', *Journal of Biblical Literature* 111 [1992], pp. 463-88). I neither welcome it nor deplore it; the tensions that come to the surface in such acerbic reviews are already in existence, and no good can come of suppressing them.

5

Why is There a Song of Songs
and What Does It Do to You If You Read It?*

There exists in the Hebrew Bible a text we know as the Song of Songs. My project here is to consider how this text happened to be created as a text in the first place and what the effect of its existence is. I choose the Song of Songs because these sounded quite difficult questions to address to this particular book.

The first of these questions, Why is there a Song of Songs?, may sound like an historical one, about writers, and the second, What Does It Do to You?, like an interpretational one, about readers. But I am not sure how distinct those categories are, for readers are always historically conditioned and how readers respond to texts is therefore essentially an historical matter; and, on the other hand, apparently historical questions about the origins of texts are only ever readers' concerns anyway, to which there are no objective answers 'out there' but only responses more or less satisfactory to the hermeneutical programmes or 'interests' of readers. So in principle I am disposed to collapse the familiar distinction between origins and interpretation, between writers and readers. But in practice I do want to enquire about two things: the causes of the text and the effects of the text; and so I have given my questions the form, Why is there a Song of Songs?, and, What does it do to you if you read it?

1. Why is There a Song of Songs?

I could think of two meanings for 'Why is there a Song of Songs?', depending on whether I focused on the text as a text—

 *   An earlier version of this essay was published in *Jian Dao: A Journal of Bible and Theology* 1 (1994), pp. 3-27. The essay was originally delivered as a paper in the Wisdom Literature Section, Society of Biblical Literature International Meeting, Münster, July, 1993.

on the conceivable demand for it at the time of its composition and on the circumstances of its production—, or whether I focused on its producer—the personal desires, needs and demands that generated the work. I did not of course imagine that I would be able to reconstruct historical actuality, like the name of the author or the date of the text's composition, and I felt it would be merely speculative to try to describe the actual social matrix of the text or the psychology of its actual author. What would be less problematic, I thought, was to try to identify the *implied* author and the *implied* social setting of the text—to draw inferences from the text, that is, about the circumstances of its origin. My purpose was, then, not to attempt a move from the text to the historical actuality that generated the text, but rather to sketch the kind of historical matrix the text implies; and not to try moving from the text back to the actual author and his or her psyche, but rather to construct the kind of psyche implied by the text he or she authored.[1]

Whether these sketches of the implied social setting of the text and the implied author are like or unlike historical actuality I have no way of knowing—but then neither does anyone else, so I am not greatly troubled. The *advantage* of my scheme is that it is open to debate; that is, my conversation partners can riposte that such and such is not a reasonable inference from the text, or that I have left out of account certain other aspects of the text. The *disadvantage* of my scheme is that it rather assumes that the text is somehow typical, that it is such and such a kind of text, of a kind that typically comes from such and such a situation—when all the time, in historic actuality, it might have been a maverick text by an eccentric author. But I do believe that most texts are typical, and that therefore this text is likely to be a typical text.[2]

1.   These are different aims from those of the traditional historical literary criticism. The Old Criticism (as we might call it) interested itself in *real authors* (their names and identities, when exactly they lived, what they had read, who influenced them, and so on) but recognized only *ideal readers* (like scholars, or like subtle, observant and unforgetting readers); the New Criticism that I profess (no relation to the Anglo-American New Criticism of the mid-century), on the other hand, is interested more in *implied authors*, while searching out the opinions of *real readers*, ancient and modern.

2.   My programme may be thought to have some affinities with that of

a. *The Implied Circumstances of the Text's Production*
Why is there a Song of Songs? The first response concerns the circumstances of the text's production, the social matrix, the material causes, the economic and political realities that the text itself might point to.

1. *The textuality of the text.* For the question that is now on the agenda, Why is there (at all) a Song of Songs?, we need to begin with the idea of the Song of Songs as a *text*. The curious thing is that, in the scholarly literature, the textuality of the Song of Songs is quite transparent, invisible. No one seems to take any account of the fact that it is a *text*, and to ask what brings a text of this kind into being or what it signifies that there was a text of this character in ancient Israel.

Roland Murphy, for example, one of the more subtle of Canticles commentators, does not notice that his text is a *text*. 'Does the work represent', he asks,

> folk poetry (*Volksdichtung*) or is it a sophisticated, elitist artistic composition (*Kunstdichtung*)? Those who favor associating the work with popular culture posit its origins in concrete social settings, such as ancient Israelite celebrations of betrothal and marriage. Those who view the Song as a refined literary creation attribute its composition and transmission to the educated elite of ancient Israel. Again, such arguments are unconvincing. It is evident that love poetry in particular is at home in all strata of society, and at all times. There is, in any event, no compelling way of discriminating between what was 'popular' and what was deemed courtly or 'cultivated' in ancient Israel. It is noteworthy that the question of cultural provenance reflects the division of

Lucien Goldmann, for whom literary texts attempt to be the coherent expression of the world view of a social group. According to him 'the work constitutes a collective achievement through the individual consciousness of its creator, an achievement which will afterwards reveal to the group what it was moving toward without knowing it' ('Genetic Structuralism in the Sociology of Literature', in *Sociology of Literature and Drama: Selected Readings* [ed. Elizabeth and Tom Burns; Harmondsworth: Penguin, 1973]). On Goldmann, see David Forgacs, 'Marxist Literary Theories', in *Modern Literary Theory: A Comparative Introduction* (ed. Ann Jefferson and David Robey; London: Batsford Academic and Educational, 1982), pp. 134-69 (151-55); Terry Eagleton, *Marxism and Literary Criticism* (London: Methuen, 1976), pp. 32-34.

scholarly opinion regarding 'folk wisdom' and 'school wisdom'. Here, too, a doubtful distinction is sometimes drawn between the cultural lore generated and nurtured within the Israelite family or the general populace and the higher 'wisdom' supposedly cultivated in courtly circles.[3]

What he does not take into account is that the Song is not just poetry, but written poetry,[4] and it is not just a composition, artistic or otherwise, popular or learned—it is a *written text*. No doubt love poetry is 'at home' (or out of the home) in all strata of society, but texts are not, especially in an only partially literate

3.   Roland E. Murphy, *The Song of Songs: A Commentary on the Book of Canticles or The Song of Songs* (Hermeneia; Minneapolis: Fortress Press, 1990), p. 5. Even when he asks, '[H]ow are we to understand the literary compilation and promulgation of the Song itself?' (p. 99), he simply takes refuge in Audet's ascription of 'this secondary level of work' (!) to postexilic sages; but this is strange, because the wisdom teaching of the 'sages' usually adopts a heavily moralizing tone on sexual matters—which is certainly not the case in the Song of Songs, the editors having added nothing more, apparently, than 'their own generalizing, self-consciously didactic signature in 8:6b-7': love is as strong as death. What postexilic sages thought they were doing in 'promulgating' this book of erotic poems is not explained. It is not very convincing to say that it was they who promoted the book because it was 'compatible with their intellectual curiosity about natural phenomena' (is that what sex had been reduced to in the postexilic age?) and with their 'pragmatic recognition of what contributed to ideal connubial bliss and marital fidelity' (p. 99; the idea of the Song of Songs being *pragmatic* is certainly an original one). Brevard S. Childs also wants to say that the poem is essentially wisdom literature, 'wisdom's reflection on the joyful and mysterious nature of love between a man and a woman within the institution of marriage' (*Introduction to the Old Testament as Scripture* [London: SCM Press, 1979], pp. 574-75). This is the 'canonical context', he says. But what are the wise doing 'reflecting' on marital love, and why, especially, do they compose a book of love poems by way of 'reflection' (is the Song of Songs really so cerebral, we ask)? Like many others, Childs has no vision of the work as a text prior to its incorporation in a canon.

4.   The same is true of Michael V. Fox, *The Song of Songs and the Ancient Egyptian Love Songs* (Madison, WI: University of Wisconsin Press, 1985), pp. 244-50, who, no doubt rightly enough, describes the kinds of poems written in the Song of Songs and in the Egyptian collections of love songs as 'entertainment', but completely overlooks the fact that what we have in these books are not songs but texts, and that entirely different questions have to be asked about texts than about songs.

community. If not many people could actually *read* the Song of
Songs, why was it *written*?

Do we not need to consider what a *text* is?

1. A text is not a performance. Whatever else the Song of Songs
is, it is not a song. Songs can be melodious, loud, communal, and
so on, but the Song of Songs cannot be any of those things, for it
is not a song. It may be the imitation of a song. It may be the
record of a song, or the preparation for a song, but it is not a
song itself. It is no more than the words of a song, and it is the
words written down. There is no music and there is no speech.
The only thing you can do with it is read it. No doubt, *as* you
read it you can perform it, but then you are making the text into
something other than a text.

2. A written text purporting to be a 'song' represents the priva-
tization of song. A song implies, for its realization, a singer and a
hearer—at least one, but often many. A text implies, for its realization, only a reader. It actually requires a single, lone reader,
for only one person can usually read a text at a time (of course, if
one person reads a text aloud to other hearers, then it becomes a
sort of performance).

3. A text is a production, a product, made in order to be
copied, to be circulated. It is, moreoever, a commodity, created
to be sold in the market place, consumed by customers. That is
what texts are, if they are not private texts like letters and contracts, but literary texts. Furthermore, an author of a text has had
the intention of a readership for the work, and has had the conception of a public that would desire the work, enough to put
their hand in their pocket for it. And the author has envisaged a
public that would want ownership of the work, either in order to
read it again whenever they wanted, or to possess in some way
what they saw as the essence of the work even if they never
opened or unrolled it. All these things are of the nature of literary
works, ancient and modern. No doubt there are from time to
time works that come into the public's hands by some freakish
route, as when private diaries enter the public domain after their
author's death and against his or her wishes; but there is no reason in this case to suspect any unusual origins of the text.

2. *The social matrix of the text*. The Song of Songs being a text, we
need to ask, if we are interested in its origins, What kind of

author?, and What kind of public? To both I answer, Male, and Israelite. I can argue that the implied author is male, and I think the balance of historical probability about the actual author is overwhelmingly in the same direction.[5] And I think I can argue that the book's public is male, too. There is no evidence for female literacy in ancient Israel,[6] so in all probability we can suppose a male readership. That is to say, the Songs of Songs is a text written by an Israelite male to meet the desires and needs of other Israelite males. I think that is fairly obvious, but it needs to be said. None of the commentaries says it, which is a pity, because I think recognizing that probability may be an important factor in how we read the book.

Now for this text, the next question is, What is its social context? Where does it fit into the life of ancient Israel? The book offers one clue that has never been taken up, so far as I know. It calls itself the 'Song of Songs', which everyone acknowledges must mean 'the best song', 'the supreme song', 'the songiest of songs'. But I ask, Says who?, Who's judging? Under what circumstances, that is, would a claim be made for any text that it is the best of its kind? The Book of Isaiah does not claim that it is the best prophecy, and Chronicles does not represent itself as superior to Kings. No matter whether the title to the Song of Songs is 'original' or not (whatever that might mean), the title, unlike that of all the other biblical books, is a competitive one. It

5. So I take issue with Athalya Brenner, Fokkelien van Dijk-Hemmes and others who would argue that female authorship of the Song is probable or at least a distinct possibility; see A. Brenner, 'On Feminist Criticism of the Song of Songs', in *A Feminist Companion to the Song of Songs* (ed. A. Brenner; Sheffield: Sheffield Academic Press, 1993), pp. 28-37 (32); *eadem*, 'Women Poets and Authors', *ibid.*, pp. 86-97 (87-91, 97); Jonnecke Bekkenkamp and Fokkelien van Dijk, 'The Canon of the Old Testament and Women's Cultural Traditions', *ibid.*, pp. 67-85; and cf. also S.D. Goitein, 'The Song of Songs: A Female Composition', *ibid.*, pp. 58-66.

6. At least, none that Alan R. Millard can mention in his article on 'Literacy (Israel)', *Anchor Bible Dictionary* (ed. David Noel Freedman; New York: Doubleday, 1992), IV, pp. 337-40—with the possible exception of the reference in 1 Kgs 21.8-9 to Jezebel writing letters in Ahab's name. But, as Millard himself says, though references to kings and officials writing could mean they themselves wrote, 'equally, secretaries ("scribes") may have acted on their behalf' (p. 338a).

implies a competition (by males of course, who else?) to find the best song, the top of the pops, the ancient equivalent of the Eurovision Song Contest.

That is the *implied* social context; but it is of course impossible to say whether that was the *actual* social context. Perhaps there were in fact song contests at the Israelite court, or in the palaces of wealthy nobles of the postexilic age, as there were at the ducal courts of Languedoc by the troubadours of the twelfth and thirteenth centuries of our era.[7] But perhaps the musical competition that is implied is entirely fictive, being modelled on military contests like that of the warriors of Abner and Joab in 2 Sam. 2.14, for example. No matter, the social context implied is that of the male competitive world, in which song can be pitted against song, love song against love song, indeed. The text constitutes, therefore, not a transcript of happy Mediterranean hours al fresco, nor the recollection in tranquillity of bucolic emotions, nor yet a record of village festivities at a tipsy peasant wedding—but *a contrivance representing itself as a prizewinner*. The Song of Songs does not exist for the sake of love (well, not just), but for the sake of winning. That is what it says about itself; and if it is kidding, then it is deceptive as well.

The material cause of the Song of Songs is, then, the need of a male public for erotic literature (the title Song of Songs implies that there are other texts of the same kind).[8] The economic context is the existence of a market, with a choice for the consumer, and a publishing industry with copying facilities, a promotion

7. The female troubadours (see Meg Bogin, *The Women Troubadours* [London: Paddington Press, 1976]), whose very existence was long unacknowledged, could admittedly serve as a possible analogy for a female poet of the Song of Songs. We do hear of (professional, no doubt) female singers in 2 Sam. 19.36 (EVV 35) (Barzillai's), Eccl. 2.8, 2 Chron. 35.25, Ezra 2.65 = Neh. 7.67, and perhaps also in Amos 8.3 (of the temple).

8. Interestingly, the oldest evidence we have for the actual use of the Song of Songs reflects such a setting: 'Rabbi Aqiba says, "Whoever sings the Song of Songs with a tremulous voice in a banquet hall and (so) treats it as a sort of ditty has no share in the world to come"' (*Tosefta to Sanhedrin* 12.10; cf. *Babylonian Talmud, Sanhedrin* 101a). We presume that, despite his severity, there remained men who put the evening's entertainment ahead of the world to come. The 'tremulous voice', by the way, couldn't be of a male impersonating a female, could it?

department that bills the text The Song of Songs, and sales out-
lets. And the social context is one that approves the existence
and distribution of erotic literature that verges on soft pornography. It is much the same male public as Ezekiel depicts when
Yahweh tells him his audience will listen to him as to an enter-
tainer, not as to a prophet whose words must be obeyed: 'My
people will come to you as to a public gathering (כִּמְבוֹא־עָם) and sit
before you. They will listen to your words but not do them.
For they have a taste for erotica (עֲגָבִים)...As far as they're concerned you're just a (singer of) erotic songs, who sings nicely and
plays well. So they'll hear your words—but *do* them they will
not!' (Ezek. 33.31-32).[9]

3. *The political matrix of the text.* What of the *political* context? All
texts, according to Fredric Jameson,[10] owe their existence to a
desire to repress social conflict, to make life easier for both
oppressors and the oppressed, to allow the oppressors to deny
their role and to enable the oppressed to forget their suffering.
They carry out that programme by papering over cracks in the
social fabric, minimizing the conflict, writing it out of existence.[11]
Now we do not have to analyse social conflict in terms of *class*
conflict, which is what Jameson is most interested in. Gender
relations are no less a site of social tension, and manifest a
struggle for power no less than class relations do. The Song of
Songs implies the author's desire to repress the conflict of interests between the sexes by representing the female and male
lovers as more or less equal, and their desire, capacities and sat-
isfactions as more or less identical. The social reality in ancient
Israel, as in most societies known to us, is quite different: it is the
reality of men having power over women, of women as a class
having no power to speak of outside the domestic setting, and of
a system in which women are regarded and treated as effectively
the property of men. A text therefore that presents the relations

9.   Translation by Fox, *The Song of Songs and the Ancient Egyptian Love
Songs*, p. 248.
10.   Fredric Jameson, *The Political Unconscious: Narrative as a Socially Symbolic Act* (London: Methuen, 1981).
11.   For an application of this outlook to a biblical text, see Chapter 3
above, 'Haggai's Temple, Constructed, Deconstructed and Reconstructed'.

between the sexes in the language of 'I am my beloved's, and my beloved is mine'—which is to say, of a mutual possession—can only be an attempt, politically speaking, to drive underground the pervasive social reality with pillow talk, to develop, in Jamesonian terminology, a strategy of containment for the social tension, to achieve coherence and closure by shutting out the truth about history.[12] The patriarchal social system not only created the Song of Songs; it needed it.

Why then is there a Song of Songs? Because there was an economic, a social, and a political need for it. This is not the whole story, but it is a story that has to be told, especially when the prevailing story, in all the handbooks, is that it represents the cultured sensitivities of its author or the 'real' relations between the sexes in ancient Israel, and that it is nothing but an innocent recording of real life love poetry.

But there is another way of answering the 'Why is there...?' question. It is to enquire after the psychological profile of the author as it is implied by his text.

b. *The Implied Psychological Profile of the Author*
The text was called forth by a complex of social needs that it addressed. But it would not have come into existence if there had not been an author who was able and willing to produce the work. Its production must have satisfied some personal psychological need of his. Or rather, I should say, the implication of his text is that it did. That is the implication of texts in general, that they come into being at the free decision of their authors, who feel some internal compulsion to compose them, and derive some personal satisfaction, some lowering of interior tension, from completing them. That may not always be the actual case, of course. Some authors, no doubt, write at gunpoint, others are driven by financial necessity or greed to write works they have no personal involvement in, others are automata; but the implication we may reasonably draw from the existence of any text is that some author intended it, and satisfied psychological needs of his or her own in writing it. What need on the author's part

12. Cf. William C. Dowling, *Jameson, Althusser, Marx: An Introduction to the Political Unconscious* (Ithaca: Cornell University Press, 1984), p. 77.

did the Song of Songs satisfy, then? Or, rather, since we are studying not historical actuality but implied reality, What need does it imply that it satsified?

My route into this question is to regard the text as a dream, its author's dream.[13] Texts are of course products of the *conscious* mind, and most authors are unconscious of the psychological needs and drives that their works arise from, preferring to speak of their writings in terms of their conscious intentions and of their works' overt content. So if we desire to penetrate to the unconscious layer of the writing, it will, no doubt, have to be without the author's knowledge or consent.

The author of the Song of Songs has dreamed a dream in which the lovers are perfectly and equally desirous of one another.[14] To be sure, their love encounters some difficulties and hindrances from sources outside themselves: the watchmen beat the woman as she wanders though the city seeking her beloved (5.7), and social constraints forbid her from expressing her love to him in public and taking him to her home (8.1-2). But the lovers have no doubt of one another—even if he is sometimes difficult to find (3.1-3), and disappears from the door after he has knocked on it in the middle of the night (5.2-6). There is no pain in their love, except for the inexplicable absences; there is no cruelty, no rejection, no faithlessness, no agonizing 'He loves me, he loves me not'.

What is more, the dream is a man's dream about a woman's love: it is hers that is the speaking voice throughout the poem.

---

13. Marvin H. Pope, in his commentary (*The Song of Songs* [Anchor Bible, 7C; Garden City, NY: Doubleday, 1977], pp. 133-34), refers to the endeavour of the pyschiatrist Max N. Pusin to understand the book in Freudian terms, identifying the woman's first dream (1.2–3.4) as a 'happy, wish-fulfilling dream', and the second (5.2-16) as 'an anxiety dream, a depressive night-mare...in which there is frustration and punishment of forbidden desires'. Pope professes himself 'not convinced' (p. 134), as does Harold Fisch (*Poetry with a Purpose: Biblical Poetics and Interpretation* [Bloomington: Indiana University Press, 1990], pp. 98-99); but the point seems obvious to me.

14. If anything, the woman is even more desirous than the man. In Francis Landy's eyes, she is certainly 'the more active partner, nagging, restless, decisive. The man on the other hand is predominantly passive and complacent' (*Paradoxes of Paradise: Identity and Difference in the Song of Songs* [Bible and Literature Series, 7; Sheffield: Almond Press, 1983], p. 69).

This is *her* poem, even though it was a man who wrote it. The
opening words (1.2) are hers, 'Let him kiss me', and the closing
words also (8.14), 'Run, dearest'. Her voice frames the whole
Song: a woman encompasses a man. When he is present, he is
present only through her imagination, through her conjuration.
She is daydreaming about him, so when he speaks it is because
she is calling him up, recalling him. The opening words tell us
what kind of a dream this is, for they speak the language of
conjuration: 'Let him kiss me with the kisses of his mouth!' It is
'him', 'his', for *he* is not present. When lovers are together, or
even when they are writing poems to one another, they speak
the language of 'thou'. Here, they are not together. In his
absence, she dreams him into presence, she conjures him up

Her language is the language of conjuring, is it not? 'Let him
kiss me', she says, 'with the kisses of his mouth.' With what else
than kisses would he be kissing her, and with what kisses but
the kisses of his mouth?[15] This is the conjuring, bewitching language of 'eeny, meeny, miny, mo', but in the erotic mode. The
superfluity of the words is of the essence of her desire, the excess
springs from the wishing for his presence. Since he is *not* there,
he can be brought there only by language, which is to say, by
conjuring, by verbally dreaming him up. Sometimes it is explicit
in the text of the Song that she is dreaming; but even when it is
not, the text is representing itself as a dream, a fantasy. For what
else can it be? It is not a speech addressed to another person who
is present, but neither it is a letter or a message sent to someone
who is absent. It is not a narrative of what has been the case,
though it contains such narratives, and it is not a description of
the lover, though it contains such description. It is not a psalm,
or law, or prophecy. What else can it be?

So the Song is the dream of a dream. The male author is
dreaming a love poem, and the love poem takes the form of a
woman's dream, of a woman dreaming her male lover's words.
It is a fetching ventriloquy, this voice that is doubly thrown.[16]

15. With the kisses of his nose, thinks Fox (*The Song of Songs and the
Ancient Egyptian Love Songs*, p. 97), taking a lead from some allusions in
Egyptian love songs; but I don't believe him.

16. I think of the collection of poems by Carol Ann Duffy, *Thrown Voices*
(London: Turret Books, 1986), where she writes, in turn, in the voice of a

Can it be perhaps that this is the reason why it is the Song of Songs? Can it have earned its supremacy on account of the male author's giving such an excellent imitation of the woman's voice?—by male standards, that is. May he be like the Japanese Kabouki actors who play female parts, and are surrounded by admiring male fans, who see in them—not real women, but—women as imagined by men.[17] Here too, the author as dreamer plays the part of a woman. And here the woman in the man's dream dreams of a man, and speaks in his voice.

What sort of a dream is this Song of Songs? Self-evidently, it is a wish-fulfilment dream. The male author dreams a text about a woman who is forward in love, who initiates the love-making,[18] who boasts about her lover to other women, who professes herself sick with love (2.5; 5.8),[19] who does nothing all day but daydream and fantasize about him (even when she is down in the nut orchard to see if the pomegranates are in bloom, 6.11-12), volunteers to lose her honour by coming to visit him at siesta time when he is out in the fields with his flocks (1.7), and all night imagines him at her bedroom door (5.2). She is bold in love, wishing she could kiss him in the street,[20] turning tradition upside down by devising a *wasf* about *his* charms and the parts of *his* body,[21] imagining speeches for him in which he invites her

spinster, a transvestite vicar, a psychopathic rapist, a cat, an adulterous wife—and a ventriloquist's dummy.

17. This is only one of the several places in this paper where Heather McKay gave me a welcome idea or bibliographic reference.

18. So Phyllis Trible, 'Depatriarchalizing in Biblical Interpretation', *Journal of the American Academy of Religion* 41 (1973), pp. 30-48 (42).

19. Lovesickness is a male complaint in Egypt, apparently; see the texts in Fox's *The Song of Songs and the Ancient Egyptian Love Songs*, pp. 13, 38 (21F [C]), 55; though the woman's heart stands still in Pap. Harris, B 12 (p. 210), it leaps out of its place in Chester Beatty I, A, 34 (p. 53), and she collapses from love (*ibid.*).

20. Like the 'loud' woman of Prov. 7.13.

21. I am assuming, perhaps wrongly, and certainly contrary to the textbooks, that the *wasf* is a male literary form, used by a man to compliment his woman lover. The woman in the Song is so forward in love that she turns the form back on him. This is perhaps why some have found '[t]he poetic imagination at work in 5.10-16...less sensuous and imaginative than in the *wasfs* of chs. 4 and 7', a failing that is hardly to be put to the account of 'the difference in erotic imagination between poet and poetess' (Richard

to 'come away' into the countryside, to secret clefts of the rocks (2.14), and inviting him to 'come to his garden' (4.16) and to go out to the fields and lie with her among the henna bushes (7.12 [11 REB])—as brazen in her own way as the seductive woman of Proverbs 7. She talks explicitly, teasingly and allusively about her sexual experience; and she lets him speak intimately of her body without reticence on his part or coyness on hers.

She is a strange one, this woman in the Song of Songs.[22] She is, literally, a strange woman, an *'ishshah zarah*—and that is because she does not exist. She is not a real woman, she is a figment of the poet's imagination. What's more, she is his wish-fulfilment dream. He dreams her up precisely because she does not exist. What we have we do not wish for.[23] He is a certain kind of man, who wants a certain kind of woman, a type that is not generally available in his culture. He fantasizes such a woman, he writes his dream, he finds an audience of like-minded men, his poem becomes a best-seller.

Perhaps there really were women like this in ancient Israel. But the text implies that the author of the text does not have one. Otherwise what would he be doing writing a text? The truth is, we know nothing about the love life of the actual author. But the text, read psychologically, implies (probably, that is—though perhaps wrongly, in fact) that its author transforms his unfulfilled desire into a text, that that is *why* there is a Song of Songs.

N. Soulen, 'The *waṣf* of the Song of Songs and Hermeneutic', in *A Feminist Companion to the Song of Songs*, pp. 214-24 (216 n. 1) (originally in *Journal of Biblical Literature* 86 [1967], pp. 183-90). But see Marcia Falk's comments, in 'The *waṣf*', in *A Feminist Companion to the Song of Songs*, pp. 225-33 (232).

22. 'This domination by the woman may seem strange in a Near Eastern setting', allows Landy (*Paradoxes of Paradise*, p. 69).

23. Francis Landy (personal communication) thinks all this is too reductive, that the fantasy is not compensation (as in classical Freudianism) but fulfils a desire for its own sake, the desire of the imagination as well of as reality. It's a good point, but I think I am disposed to 'reduce' imagination to compensation nevertheless. I stick by Freud's dictum, '[A] happy person never phantasies, only an unsatisfied one' ('Creative Writers and Day-Dreaming', in *The Standard Edition of the Complete Psychological Works of Sigmund Freud*, IX [trans. and ed. James Strachey, in collaboration with Anna Freud; London: Hogarth Press and the Institute of Psycho-Analysis, 1959], pp. 143-53 [146]).

2. *What Does It Do to You If You Read It?*

The question of the effect of our texts has rarely been raised in our scholarly tradition. This is perhaps the worst consequence of the historical-critical method (which was all very necessary in its own day and remains valid, please don't misunderstand me), since in its quest for origins it screened out the present, and, with that, the ethics of interpretation—including the ethics of keeping alive these texts by study and commentary and writing. The practitioners of the historical-critical method, like the inventors of the atomic bomb, were ethically irresponsible. Their commitment was to the 'truth', whatever that might be and wherever it might lead. And that is unquestionably a whole sight better than a commitment to falsity.[24] But it systematically ignored the question of effects on readers, and it is about time we regarded such study as part of our scholarly discipline and task.

There are two ways of coming at this question. One is to examine the ways the text has been received and interpreted by readers of the past. The other is to study the effects on readers of our own time.

a. *The reception of the text by former readers*
Now the first sounds like 'the history of interpretation', which, if not a fashionable form of biblical study, has at least been made respectable in recent years by its promotion by scholars such as Brevard Childs,[25] and, in relation to the Song of Songs, by Marvin Pope and Roland Murphy especially.[26] I have in mind,

24. As Qoheleth would say, 'Wisdom excels folly as light excels darkness' (Eccl. 2.13)—but it is nevertheless *hebel*.

25. Systematically throughout his *Introduction to the Old Testament as Scripture*, and specifically on the Song of Songs (p. 579). Cf. also J.W. Rogerson, C. Rowland and B. Lindars, SSF, *The Study and Use of the Bible* (The History of Christian Theology, 2; Basingstoke: Marshall, Morgan & Scott, 1988); and John F.A. Sawyer, 'Interpretation, History of', in *A Dictionary of Biblical Interpretation* (ed. R.J. Coggins and J.L. Houlden; London: SCM Press, 1990), pp. 316-20.

26. Note also Ann W. Astell, *The Song of Songs in the Middle Ages* (Ithaca: Cornell University Press, 1990); Anne-Marie Pelletier, *Lectures du cantique des cantiques: De l'énigme du sens aux figures du lecteur* (Analecta Biblica, 121; Rome: Editrice Pontificio Istituto Biblico, 1989); and, from an earlier period,

however, a rather more critical understanding of ancient interpreters, one that does not principally seek to *understand* them
and their interpretations within their own historical context, but
to critique them and judge them by a standard of reference other
than their own—that is, by my own, by our own.[27] I am rather
insistent on a programme of judging interpretations by standards
other than their own; for if we do not judge them by our own
standards of reference, we cannot be ethical. If we judge the
references in our texts to slavery or to the oppression of women
by the standards that operated in the ancient world, we might
well find ourselves approving those practices, or at least being
less antithetical to them. We do not owe any such debt to the
past, however, and it is a more truly human activity to make

H.H. Rowley, 'The Interpretation of the Song of Songs', in his *The Servant of
the Lord and Other Essays* (London: SCM Press, 2nd edn, 1965), pp. 195-245.
Note also James Doelman, 'Song of Songs', in *A Dictionary of Biblical Tradition in English Literature* (ed. David Lyle Jeffrey; Grand Rapids: Eerdmans,
1992), pp. 727-30.

27. So I cannot approve of the programme of Roland Murphy, for
example, who thinks that whether or not the hermeneutical principles evidenced in traditional Jewish and Christian interpretation 'are true or false
from a modern perspective is not the primary issue. If such judgments are
to be made, they should be preceded by an effort to understand the why
and the how of our exegetical forebears' (*The Song of Songs*, pp. 11-12). Who
is to say, I respond, what the 'primary issue' should be? It is just a convention that it is not the business of scholarship to make decisions, or that
views on the validity of ideas are 'secondary' to a primary task of
'understanding'. Of course I am not in favour of ignorance or of trying *not*
to understand; but it is curious how often the 'preceding' task of understanding precludes the 'subsequent' task of 'judgment'. Murphy's own scin-
tillating and penetrating analysis of the history of interpretation, for
example, limps to the lame conclusion that 'shifting views in the history of
the interpretation of the Song...tell the story of new generations becoming
aware of the hermeneutical limitations of their predecessors. Hence it
would be foolish to suppose that our methodology has resolved, once and
for all, the issues of the Song's meaning that baffled our precritical
forebears' (p. 41). That is his total critique. Nothing in the history of interpretation, apparently, is silly, far-fetched, excessive, wrong-headed,
myopic, strained, implausible, impossible—or wrong. To understand all is,
apparently, to forgive all. But what has happened to critical evaluation?

serious and well-informed judgments than merely to acquire knowledge or 'understanding'.

It's not just a practical question of our sponsors and our public getting the judgments and evaluations they need, though it is that, at least. It's an ethical one—an ethical question for the professionals in biblical studies themselves.[28] The question is whether it is moral to restrict one's scholarly concern to mere understanding when the subject matter is offensive or questionable to oneself. No one thinks an objective seminar on the feasibility of making lampshades out of human skin is an ethical possibility. So long as evaluation is not prejudice, is there anything that should not be evaluated? And if you ask, Evaluated according to what norm?, there is no special difficulty; for there are no absolutes, no universal standards, and so there is nothing wrong with using your own standards. Not only is there nothing wrong, nothing else would be right; for 'ethical' can only mean 'ethical according to me and people who think like me', and if I don't make judgments according to my own standards, according to whose standards shall I be making them, and in what sense could those judgments be *mine*?

What it boils down to is this: To be truly academic, and worthy of its place in the academy, biblical studies has to be truly critical, critical not just about lower-order questions like the authorship of the biblical books or the historicity of the biblical narratives, but critical about the Bible's contents, its theology, its ideology. And that is what biblical studies has notoriously not been critical about at all.[29] To be critical, you have to take up a

28. On this question I found very stimulating the article by Stephen Fowl, 'The Ethics of Interpretation; or, What's Left over after the Elimination of Meaning', in *The Bible in Three Dimensions: Essays in Celebration of the Fortieth Anniversary of the Department of Biblical Studies, University of Sheffield* (ed. David J.A. Clines, Stephen E. Fowl and Stanley E. Porter; Journal for the Study of the Old Testament Supplement Series, 87; Sheffield: JSOT Press, 1990), pp. 379-98. In my view he takes the discussion well beyond the point reached by Elisabeth Schüssler Fiorenza in her important 1987 Society of Biblical Literature presidential address, 'The Ethics of Interpretation: Decentering Biblical Scholarship', published in *Journal of Biblical Literature* 107 (1988), pp. 101-15.

29. Nor literary critics who write about the Bible, for the most part. These days, they don't write like J.H. Gardiner, assistant professor of

standard of reference outside the material you are critiquing;[30] but, traditionally, biblical scholars have been believers, ecclesiastics or, at the least, fellow-travellers and sympathizers with the ideology of the Bible. When the academy begins to view the Bible as a cultural artifact, and is not seduced or pressured by religious commitments, the hallmark of its criticism will be that it steps outside the ideology of the text.[31]

What has reading the Song done to its ancient readers?, I ask, then. The main thing is that it has persuaded them that it is not about the one thing that it is self-evidently about: human sexual love. I say self-evident when I mean evident to me, of course, because I find it hard to imagine anyone denying it. But I have to confess that most readers of former times whom I know about, in fact, have read the Song as celebrating the love of God, or of Christ, for the church, or for Israel, or for the individual believer, or for Mary. They cannot have failed to recognize that the Song gives a very strong impression of being about something altogether different, and at times they allude to a literal meaning that, collectively, they have not wished altogether to deny. But in their reading of the Song of Songs they have been able to evade almost entirely the sexual significance of the text. They have been able to read it, and to commend it, as a holy and religious work. I see, for example, in the Bibliography to Pope's commentary, a work by one P. Simson, *The Song of Solomon, called the Song of Songs. Fitter to be sung with any of the common tunes of the Psalms. Very necessary to be taught children at school* (In the Gorbals

English at Harvard in 1906, and author of *The Bible as English Literature* (London: T. Fisher Unwin, 1906): 'It is obvious...that no literary criticism of the Bible could hope for success which was not reverent in tone. A critic who should approach it superciliously or arrogantly would miss all that has given the book its power as literature and its lasting and universal appeal' (p. vii). But they're all mightily respectful, Harold Bloom, Frank Kermode, Gabriel Josopovici, Robert Alter, and all.

30. My colleague Philip Davies gave me this crucial idea.

31. I learned this important phrase, and what it stands for, from my colleague J. Cheryl Exum, who has developed her feminist criticism of the Hebrew Bible under its aegis (see, for example, her *Fragmented Women: Feminist (Sub)versions of Biblical Narratives* [Journal for the Study of the Old Testament Supplement Series, 163; Sheffield: JSOT Press, 1993]).

[Glasgow], 1701).[32] Did those Scots school pupils never imagine, we wonder, that there might perhaps be another earthly, earthier, sense to the text beside the authorized interpretation? There was no shortage of commentaries, for example in the seventeenth century, with titles such as the following: John Cotton's *A Brief Exposition of the whole Book of Canticles, or, Song of Solomon, Lively describing the Estate of the Church in all the Ages thereof, both Jewish and Christian, in this day: And Modestly pointing at the Gloriousnesse of the restored Estate of the Church of the Jewes, and the happy accesse of the Gentiles, in the approaching daies of Reformation, when the Wall of Partition shall bee taken away;*[33] William Guild's *Loves entercovrs between the Lamb & His bride, Christ and His church. Or, A clear explication and application of the Song of Solomon;*[34] and Richard Sibbes's *Bowels opened: or, A discovery of the near and dear love, union and communion betwixt Christ and the church, and consequently bewixt Him and every believing-soul. Delivered in divers sermons on the fourth, fifth, and sixth chapters of the Canticles.*[35]

My purpose here is not to unravel the causes for such egregious misreadings, strong misreadings indeed,[36] though they certainly need unravelling, being not at all obvious. For the transmission of the Song within the context of the scriptural canon might not necessarily have constrained readers into an allegorical reading, any more than they were constrained into a mystical reading of tales and commands about warfare against Canaanites; and the fact that the Song was read largely by avowedly celibate clerics prior to the Reformation[37] does not

32. Cf. W.J. Cowper, 'A Gorbals Imprint of 1701, with Notes on Patrick Simson's "Spiritual Songs"', *Records of the Glasgow Bibliographical Society* 6 (1920), pp. 1-13.

33. London, 1642.

34. London, 1658.

35. London, 1648.

36. To use Harold Bloom's phrase, in *A Map of Misreading* (Oxford: Oxford University Press, 1975).

37. Murphy recognizes the importance of this social context of the Song's readers: 'When one realizes...that most of the Christian exegesis on the Song until the Reformation was produced by clerics and monks, it becomes understandable that a mystical interpretation thrived' (*The Song of Songs*, p. 12).

explain everything; it does not account for the allegorical reading prevalent in Jewish interpretation of all periods or in Protestant interpretation until the nineteenth century,[38] or for the tendencies to allegory even in uncloistered critics of our own day.[39]

It is more to my point to observe the effect of the book upon its male readers and students (as far as I can discover, only one woman wrote on the Song of Songs prior to Cheryl Exum in 1973[40]). Not having researched the erotic literature, I am in no

---

38. A naturalistic reading goes back to Erasmus, Grotius and Bossuet in the seventeenth century, and to Lowth and Herder in the eighteenth.

39. See for example Fisch, *Poetry with a Purpose*, ch. 6 'Song of Song: The Allegorical Imperative', for whom the text is so overdetermined that it demands allegorical interpretation. 'If the ancients had not already taken this path, modern literary critics would certainly have felt obliged to do so', he writes (p. 95). 'Critics will be driven by the text itself to construct allegorical schemes of greater or lesser validity that will account for the hold that its strange and compelling language has upon us, to account also for the ineffable longing that this love song of a shepherd and a shepherdess calls forth. When so much metaphorical energy is expended on a shepherd and a shepherdess, they themselves become metaphorical' (p. 96). (Might they have stayed more real if they had been more aristocratic?, we wonder.) See also the view of Hans-Josef Heinevetter that the erotic in the Song of Songs is itself a metaphor for a different way of being in the world: 'Damit wird aber die Erotik selber zur Metapher: zur Metapher für eine andere Lebensweise, ein anderes gesellschaftliches Miteinander, für die Abkehr vom Leben gegen die Natur' (*'Komm nun, mein Liebster, Dein Garten ruft Dich!' Das Hohelied als programmatische Komposition* [Athenäum Monographien, 69; Frankfurt: Athenäum, 1988], p. 226).

40. I refer to the work of the French quietist and mystic, Jeanne Marie Bouvier de la Mothe Guyon (1648–1717), *Le cantique des cantiques* (1688), translated as *The Song of Songs of Solomon. With Explanations and Reflections Having Reference to the Interior Life* (tr. James W. Metcalf; New York: Dennett, 1865). For a less than generous notice of Mme Guyon, see F.L. Cross (ed.), *The Oxford Dictionary of the Christian Church* (London: Oxford University Press, 1957), pp. 598-99. Johanna Lürssen wrote a mongraph on *Eine mittelniederdeutsche Paraphrase des Hohenliedes* (Germanistische Abhandlungen, 49; Breslau, 1917), and Pope mentions in the Bibliography to his *Song of Songs* a work by one Ann Francis, *A Poetical Translation of the Song of Solomon* (London, 1781), which I have not been able to trace. These two works are, however, not strictly studies of the Song itself. The work of J. Cheryl Exum referred to above is 'A Literary and Structural Analysis of the Song of Songs', *Zeitschrift für die alttestamentliche Wissenschaft* 85 (1973), pp. 47-79.

position to say whether the book has influenced authors in that genre; but what I do know is that the history of its interpretation is one of a massive repression of sexuality,[41] of denial of the book's ostensible subject matter, a testimony especially to male fear of female sexuality. Sexuality has been thought by such readers to be an unsuitable, unworthy, undignified subject for a work of this rank, for a work in this canonical scriptural context. And that is not merely a harmless misunderstanding or a curious hermeneutical aberration. It is witness to a refusal by its male readers over the centuries to come to terms with their own sexuality, to acknowledge its power and to recognize its acceptability. Their own sexual behaviour, and especially their feelings about sex and themselves as sexual beings, has evidently been distorted by the existence of the Song of Songs. The interpretational tradition of this book has authorized its male readers to repress its subject matter.[42] And what has it done to women, I ask, if their men's scriptures have so consistently been read as teaching that in every legitimate and desirable expression of sexuality there is a transcendental signified (God, the church, and so on), which, whatever it is, is not *women*?

I find myself asking, Is the book to any degree responsible for the way it has been read? Can a book, indeed, be innocent of its reception? What is it about this book that has allowed, even legitimated, a reading so against its own grain? I don't rightly know how to answer this question; but I have the suspicion that a work that came into the world as an erotic, perhaps pornographic,

Note also, from 1973, Phyllis Trible's article, 'Depatriarchalizing in Biblical Interpretation', *Journal of the American Academy of Religion* 41 (1973), pp. 30-48, in part concerned with the Song of Songs (pp. 42-48).

41. But it can only have been a repression, for the drive that led commentators to pore over the book cannot have been suppressed by their allegorical interpretations.

42. I have seen such a view expressed only in one other place—a place I did not expect to find it—by G. Lloyd Carr, in his *The Song of Solomon: An Introduction and Commentary* (Tyndale Old Testament Commentaries; Leicester: Inter-Varsity Press, 1984), pp. 50-51: 'The traditional allegorical and typical approaches assume that the Song is intended to teach something of the relationship between God and his people...Implicitly or explicitly, this approach denigrates the very physical beings we are by virtue of our creation.'

literature for the male taste proves ultimately to be irredeemable in polite society. It was of no use—I mean, on its own subject, sex—to the preachers and moralists of the patriarchal age (I mean, of all ages up to and including our own) because they could not handle its sexual candour and its challenge to patriarchal norms of female submission. In a feminist age too, it will not do, for it cannot shake off all traces of the needs it was created to serve, and, however refreshing it may be when compared to other productions of a male-oriented society,[43] it is indefeasibly male—as we shall shortly further see.

b. *The effects of the text on contemporary readers*

To prepare this part of the chapter, I should have liked to carry out a survey of contemporary readers of the Song of Songs, and to have elicited their reactions to the text and their views both of what the text encourages and what it ignores. In the absence of any quantifiable data or documentary evidence, I shall have to ask my readers to take my word for the effects of the text on this reader, and to consider whether their own experience offers any parallels. Except insofar as I deceive myself, the effects of the text on me are real effects; and while my experience might not be very interesting or very typical, it *is* my experience, and I believe it is possible to analyse some significant elements in it. Above all, I hope that such an analysis will help to legitimate the putting of reader effects on the agenda for critical study of our texts.

1. The book's whole-hearted concentration on love, and the experience of the two lovers, keeps other issues entirely off the agenda. It is hard for a reader of this book, I mean a serious and committed reader, a well-wishing and appreciative reader, to worry at the same time about global warming or the fate of whales, about even more important things like social injustice or

---

43. We might compare, for example, the three focal points in biblical views of female sexuality that T. Drorah Setel has analysed: procreation, ritual purity, and possession ('Prophets and Pornography: Female Sexual Imagery in Hosea', in *Feminist Interpretations of the Bible* [ed. Letty M. Russell; Philadelphia: Fortress Press, 1985], pp. 86-95 [88]; reprinted in *A Feminist Companion to the Song of Songs*, p. 146). None of these elements figures in the Song of Songs.

even the politics of gender relations. Everything in its time and place, for goodness sake, one might respond—but the reality is that the book is so seductive that it is hard to keep its concerns constrained to their own time and place. It is hard to believe that the book is not saying, 'That is all ye know on earth and all ye need to know', that it is not affirming that there is no truth but beauty,[44] no way of being in the world that matters apart from the erotic, no focus for existence but the personal Other. But, as Phyllis Trible puts it so well, its silences portend its limits. 'If we cannot return to the primeval garden...we cannot live solely in the garden of eroticism.'[45] However happy we are for the lovers, we cannot help observing that their world is a very narrow one, and we worry about what will happen to their love when they leave the garden, as they needs must, for the world of economic and social necessity.

2. The Song of Songs represents a return to Eden, an 'inversion of the Genesis narrative', as Francis Landy puts it; it is 'not merely a commentary on the garden of Eden, but a reenactment, almost a hallucination of it'.[46] That makes it a very charming text, charming in the magical sense. It is not surprising that commentators are seduced by its vision of primal bliss, and never have a bad word to say about it. But the fact is that any text that proffers the possibility of a return to Eden is a Utopian text in the literal sense, a text about an Erewhon, a Nowhere. For the Garden of Eden does not exist, it never has; and even if it did, it was not paradise, and it was never the case that everything in the garden was lovely. In my opinion, no paradise worth the name has a snake in it, especially a theologian of a snake, nor the possibility of losing one's immortality, nor a woman whose only purpose is

44. I refer of course to John Keats's *Ode on a Grecian Urn*: 'Beauty is Truth, Truth Beauty'.

45. Trible, 'Depatriarchalizing in Biblical Interpretation', p. 47.

46. Landy, *Paradoxes of Paradise*, p. 183 (reprinted in *A Feminist Companion to the Song of Songs*, p. 129). Cf. also Phyllis Trible, *God and the Rhetoric of Sexuality* (Philadelphia: Fortress Press, 1978), ch. 5 'Love's Lyrics Redeemed' (pp. 144-65). But note also Athalya Brenner's insistence that '[b]eyond the structural framework...the attitudes and messages of the two texts are fundamentally different' (*The Song of Songs* [Old Testament Guides; Sheffield: JSOT Press, 1989], p. 83).

to be a 'helper' to the man. I have no desire to return to the naivety and ignorance of childhood, to be at the mercy of an all-seeing father, or to be responsible for someone else's garden, which I did not even plant myself. And as for running around naked in a tropical jungle (we should refer to it as the Jungle of Eden, shouldn't we?), I think 'sunburn' and I think 'shoes'.

Deep down, and in its essence, the Song of Songs is fantasy, escapist literature, and its dream stuff signals that. Fantasy is no wickedness, but it does create an ambivalence about the text in the mind of this reader, an ambivalence that, interestingly enough, none of the textbooks encourages one to contemplate. Reality can be awful, and escaping from it into an imaginary world can at times be the only sensible thing to do. The downside of fantasy is that it can deflect attention from what needs to be done in the real world, and so for Marx, for example, it was counter-revolutionary, like utopianism in general. And there can be little doubt how well utopian literature can serve the purposes of social control.[47] The upside of fantasy, of course, is that it envisages an alternative reality, which can subvert or at least critique the real world of quotidian experience. It can even be argued that no change is possible without a prior fantasy, that fantasy is the precondition for social transformation.[48]

As it happens, we do not have any evidence of the Song of Songs being used in the transformation of power relations between the sexes in ancient Israel. If Tamara Eskenazi is right in arguing that the status of women suffered no decline after the exile,[49] as has commonly been claimed, we still can hardly give much credit for their status to the Song of Songs' depiction of a sexually autonomous woman. One might have thought that the

47. Cf. James M. Kennedy's analysis of how Genesis 2–3 will have functioned as a legitimation of power in ancient Israel ('Peasants in Revolt: Political Allegory in Genesis 2–3', *Journal for the Study of the Old Testament* 27 [1990], pp. 3-14).

48. See Rosemary Jackson, *Fantasy: The Literature of Subversion* (London: Methuen, 1980), and George Aichele and Tina Pippin (eds.), *Fantasy and the Bible, Semeia* 60 (1992), and in particular their 'Introduction: Why the Fantastic?' (pp. 1-6 [2-3]).

49. Tamara C. Eskenazi, 'Out from the Shadows: Biblical Women in the Postexilic Era', *Journal for the Study of the Old Testament* 54 (1992), pp. 25-43.

Song of Songs would have served as ancient Israel's *Joy of Sex*, and, like it, have functioned not so much as an instructional manual but as an opinion-forming and permission-granting tract. That does not seem to have been the case, and one can only suppose that patriarchy found the egalitarianism of the Song (such as it is) too hot to handle, and suppressed its subversiveness by recourse to an authorized and normative allegorical interpretation, that is, to its de-eroticization.[50]

And it is by now no doubt too late for the Song to have any major impact on social change, since there are in existence already many other, more home-grown, models for the relations between the sexes. Only perhaps in communities that are both essentially patriarchal and committed to the authority of the Bible may the Song still have a liberating effect and be able to suggest a vision of an alternative style of being.

3. The final point on which I wish to report on the Song's effect on this reader is the matter of the representation of the woman in the book.

I start again here from the assumption that we are dealing with a male text, and I am interested in how that text constructs the woman. Even feminist critics sometimes ignore the fact that what we have in this book is not a woman, not the voice of a woman, not a woman's poem, not a portrayal of female experience from a woman's perspective, but always and only what a man imagines for a woman, his construction of femininity. But the situation is worse than that; it is not just that the text presents a male, patriarchally constituted view of a woman, or offers a male point of view on sexuality; it is, as Susan Durber puts it, that 'the very symbolic order of which [the text is] a part is subject to the "Law of the Father" [in the Lacanian sense] in which the "I" is always male...[The text is] part of the (patriarchal)

---

50. As Fisch puts it, '[H]owever far back we go, we cannot discern any traces of an earlier "literal" interpretation of the Song such as we can with Homer. Gerson D. Cohen has indeed argued very plausibly that "allegorizing activity took place not long after the Song itself was compiled"' (*Poetry with a Purpose*, p. 97; the reference is to Cohen's article, 'The Song of Songs and the Jewish Religious Mentality', in *The Samuel Friedland Lectures 1960–1966* [New York: The Jewish Theological Seminary, 1966], p. 16).

symbolic order which constructs our subjectivity, whether we are biologically male or female.'[51]

Typically, the symbolic order in which we all operate constructs the woman as the other, as the object to the male subject, and as the object of the male look; 'woman' connotes 'to be looked at'. John Berger writes that a woman is someone who has been taught that she is to be watched:

> [M]en act and *women appear*. Men look at women. Women watch themselves being looked at. This determines not only most relations between men and women but also the relation of women to themselves.[52]

So the reader of the Song of Songs is assumed to be a male, an anonymous bystander who shares the author's perspective on the watched woman—as on David's rooftop: 'Is this not Bathsheba?' (2 Sam. 11.3). The woman, for her part, is offered the subject position as the focus of male gaze, and not unwillingly (for she knows no alternative) she adopts that subject and subjected position, misrecognizing herself.[53]

In the Song, the woman is everywhere constructed as the

51. Susan Durber, 'The Female Reader of the Parables of the Lost', in *Women in the Biblical Tradition* (ed. George J. Brooke; Studies in Women and Religion, 31; Lewiston: Edwin Mellen Press, 1992), pp. 187-207 (194). The following paragraph owes much to her excellent article. It cannot possibly be true, given these observations, that 'Canticles affirms mutuality of the sexes. There is no male dominance, no female subordination, and no stereotyping of either sex' (Trible, 'Depatriarchalizing in Biblical Interpretation', p. 45).

52. John Berger, *Ways of Seeing* (London: BBC, 1972), p. 47. On the matter of the male gaze in biblical literature, see J. Cheryl Exum, *Fragmented Women: Feminist (Sub)versions of Biblical Narrative* (Journal for the Study of the Old Testament Supplement Series, 163; Sheffield: JSOT Press, 1993), pp. 170-201; Mieke Bal, 'The Elders and Susanna', *Biblical Interpretation* 1 (1993), pp. 1-19.

53. The language here derives from Louis Althusser's view of the human subject as constructed within the discourses and practices of culture, which are developed on the basis of ideology (*Lenin and Philosophy and Other Essays* [London: New Left Books, 1977]). Jacques Lacan speaks of the subject as misrecognizing itself as the producer of meaning, when the truth is rather that the subject is itself the product of discourse (*Ecrits: A Selection* [trans. Alan Sheridan; London: Tavistock, 1977]).

object of male gaze. In the opening lines she is made, by the male author, to describe herself as 'black, but beautiful' (1.6), 'black' because she has been forced to work in the vineyards under the sun, but 'black' also because she has been forced by the male gaze—and by patriarchal binary thinking—to construct 'white' as beautiful and any other shade as its complete opposite. 'Do not stare at me', she says to the Jerusalem women, for she feels their scorn at having offended (though she had no say in the matter) against the norms for female beauty, complied with by women,[54] but instituted by men, no doubt as a symbol of female alterity (the brothers in the vineyard must be equally sunburnt, but there is no shame in that for them). To her male spectators, the readers of the poem, of course, she cannot say, 'Do not stare at me'; for she has been brought into existence precisely to be stared at, and the veil she would willingly cover herself with is disallowed by the poet's gaze. She has been the victim of male violence and anger (1.6), and she bears the marks of it on her face; and now the poet invites his readers to share his sight of the woman's humiliation. That is the very stuff of pornography.[55]

The man and the woman in the poem are by no means equal in this matter of the gaze. It is typical of the poem, though admittedly not universal in it, that he describes her in physical terms whereas she speaks of him in symbolic and metaphorical language. He compares her to a mare of Pharaoh's chariots (1.9), no doubt for her beauty and ornaments,[56] and his instinct is to decorate her further, with ornaments of gold studded with silver (1.11). She is the subject of his objectifying *waṣf*s (4.1-7; 6.3-7; 7.1-7), fragmented into her bodily parts, each in turn the object of his gaze. She may be all fair, with no flaw in her (4.7), but she hardly moves; his vision fixes her, like a photographic image.

She, on the other hand, images her lover with metaphors, as a sachet of myrrh lying between her breasts (1.13), as an apple tree among the trees of the wood, as a gazelle leaping over the

54. As usual, the patriarchal norms set women against women.
55. See Setel, 'Prophets and Pornography', p. 145. It is perhaps not a very severe humiliation she has undergone, and she has not come to feel that she is no longer beautiful; but it is nevertheless very powerful symbolically.
56. So Murphy, *The Song of Songs*, p. 134.

mountains (2.8-9, 17; 8.14), as Solomon carried in his palanquin (3.6-11), as a prince in a chariot (6.12). She does address a *waṣf* to him (5.10-16), but there is something odd about it, and its signifi-cance remains a little elusive.[57]

He is all action, in her eyes, kissing and drawing her (1.2, 4), lying with her (1.12-14), taking her into the wine-garden (2.4), holding her in his arms (2.6), bounding over the mountains (2.8-9), peering in at the windows (2.9), bidding her rise up and come away (2.10-14), grazing his flock among the lilies (2.16), and so on and so on. She in his eyes is more of a statue; she comes to life only when she speaks in her own voice, telling then of her nightly search for him (3.1-2; 5.6), her encounters with the watchmen (3.3; 5.7), her conjuring up of the north wind (4.16), her desperate addresses to the Jerusalem women (5.8), her pledges of love in the vineyards (7.11-13).

So the male author is not incapable of constructing a vital woman, but he does not choose to do so, on the whole. The woman he creates remains caught in her domestic setting, inter-minably waiting for her lover to arrive, seeking him but finding him not, calling and gaining no answer (3.1; 5.6). He has the transport (3.6-10), and he has the freedom. She longs for him (1.2; 2.6), but he is mostly disturbed by her (4.9; 7.5). Above all, he in-sists on constructing her; the keynote is 4.1: 'Behold, you are beautiful, my love; behold, you are beautiful'. That repeated 'behold' (הִנָּךְ) says it all: she is to behold herself, herself as seen by him. She is to have no vision of herself; he will impose that upon her. And he will be content with nothing less than her

---

57. See Soulen, 'The *waṣfs* of the Song of Songs and Hermeneutic'; Athalya Brenner, '"Come Back, Come Back the Shulammite" (Song of Songs 7.1-10): A Parody of the *waṣf* Genre', in *A Feminist Companion to the Song of Songs*, pp. 234-57; J. William Whedbee, 'Paradox and Parody in the Song of Solomon: Towards a Comic Reading of the Most Sublime Song', in *A Feminist Companion to the Song of Songs*, pp. 266-78 ('the male who appears as bigger-than-life, standing somewhat awkwardly as a gargantuan, immo-bile, distant figure' [274]). Landy most perceptively observes, '[O]n his face, the expressive articulate part of his body, we find animate images of the woman; whereas the rest of his body, though appropriately formidable, is coldly metallic and disjointed. By a curious paradox that which is alive in him and relates to her is feminine' (*Paradoxes of Paradise*, p. 80; cited by Whedbee, 'Paradox and Parody', p. 274).

acceptance of the subject position he is offering. She is to see herself as he sees her; otherwise she has no identity.

This is a dangerous text, not a gross one. A more blatantly sexist text would do less damage than one that beguiles. On the other hand, once you see its programme, perhaps you sharpen up your reflexes. 'What does it do to you?' depends a lot on how you have already constructed *yourself*.[58]

58. Francis Landy wrote some detailed comments on this chapter for me, which I have gratefully used.

6

Why Is There a Book of Job,
and What Does It Do to You If You Read It?*

The programme of this chapter is the same as that of the previous chapter on the Song of Songs. Why is there a book of Job? means, What are the necessary conditions of its existence?, How did it come to be created as a text in the first place? What does it do to you if you read it? means, What effects does it have?, What difference does it make that this text exists?

The first question, Why is there a book of Job?, may sound like one of the old conventional questions, like What problem is the book addressing?, What is its intellectual matrix?, What were the influences upon it?, What theological needs did it serve? They are not my questions here, for what I have in mind, rather, are the *material* causes as distinct from the *mental* causes.

The second question, What does it do to you if you read it?, may sound like one of the newer conventional questions, like, What is the history of its interpretation? How have the differing social and historical contexts in which it has been read influenced the interpretation of the book? They too are not my questions here, for what I have in mind, rather, is *critique* rather than *description* of the history of interpretation, *evaluation* rather than mere *understanding*.

*   An earlier version of this essay was published in *The Book of Job* (ed. W.A.M. Beuken; Bibliotheca Ephemeridum Theologicarum Lovaniensium, 104; Leuven: Leuven University Press / Peeters, 1994), pp. 1-20, and, in abbreviated form, as 'Deconstructing the Book of Job', *Bible Review* 11/2 (April, 1995), pp. 30-35, 43-44. It is reprinted by permission of Leuven University Press and Peeters. The essay was originally delivered as a paper at the Journées Bibliques / Colloquium Biblicum, Katholieke Universiteit te Leuven, August, 1993, and to the Narrative Research on the Hebrew Bible Group, Society of Biblical Literature Annual Meeting, Washington, DC, November, 1993.

1. *Why Is There a Book of Job?*

a. *The Implied Circumstances of the Text's Production*

Why is there a book of Job? The first set of questions concern the circumstances of the text's production, the social matrix, the material causes, the economic and political realities that the text itself might point to. These are not the questions that scholars writing on Job tend to ask about this text; if they ask about origins, they usually speak of mental causes, of ideas the author wanted to promote or to dispute. Here, though, I want to focus on material causes for the existence of the text.

1. *The Text*. We need to begin with the idea of Job as a *text*. The curious thing is that, in the scholarly literature, the textuality of Job is quite transparent, invisible. No one seems to take much account of the fact that it is a *text*, and to ask what brings a text of this kind into being or what it signifies that there was a text of this character in ancient Israel. For most scholars, the book of Job is a transcript of the author's mind, a window on the ancient Israelite thought-world, a discussion of a theological problem— anything other than a writing, a product, a *text*.

A text is a production, a product, made in order to be copied and to be circulated. All texts are, if they are not private texts. It is, moreover, a commodity, created to be sold in the market place, consumed by customers. That is what texts are, if they are not private texts like letters and contracts, but literary texts. Furthermore, the author of a text such as Job had the intention of a readership for the work, and had the conception of a public that would desire the work—desire it enough to put their hand in their pocket for it. And the author envisaged a public that would want ownership of the work, either in order to read it again whenever they wanted, or to possess in some way what they saw as the essence of the work even if they never opened or unrolled it. All these things are of the nature of literary works, ancient and modern. No doubt there are from time to time works that come into the public's hands by some freakish route, as when private diaries come into the public domain after their authors' death and against their wishes; but there is no reason in the case of the book of Job to suspect any unusual origins of the text.

2. *The Public.* If then a text implies a public, for the book of Job we need to ask, What public? Thereafter we can ask, And what kind of author, socially speaking, does such a public imply?

What public does the book of Job imply? Obviously, it implies a Hebrew-speaking (or rather, Hebrew-reading) public, which is to say, no doubt, an Israelite one, even though the central character of the book is not an Israelite. And it implies a male audience, since all its principal characters are male, and women and women's interests are ignored or repressed.

It implies a highly literate public, with a rich vocabulary, a taste for imagery and a stomach for elaborate and extended rhetoric. It implies a readership that is not literal-minded, one that delights in irony, exaggeration, misdirection and whimsy.

It implies an intellectual public, for the issues it ventilates are conceptual ones, the points of difference among the various characters in the book being sometimes quite fine—and the argument rarely being stated in concrete and direct language. It implies a public that is intellectually curious, that is open to being teased and is willing to be left unsatisfied by its conclusion. It does not imply a readership that wants clear, quick answers.

It implies a leisured public. Not only does it take several hours to read the book—if you are a very fluent reader, that is—but its public must be of a type that has a lot of time and patience to take an interest in theoretical and conceptual matters generally, as well as the time to process the arguments of this particular book by means of reflection, re-reading, and discussion with other readers.

Further, the book implies a public of individuals who are free to read the book or desist from it, consumers who have the choice to pick it up or lay it down. For it does not belong to any institutional structure as a necessary and constitutive text—in the way a lawbook or a collection of psalms might, for example. And the book does not imply the existence of a ready-made market, unlike the Song of Songs, for example, whose name implies the existence of other texts of the same type. The book of

Job had to win its readers one by one. It is hard to imagine a Job fan-club, eager consumers of every new book on the market about its loquacious hero, or a Job 'school', transmitting the Job tradition to generations of reverential pupils picking up their copies from the college bookstore year by year.

No, the book implies a very small readership, even among those who are literate in its society. It does not imply any ritual or socially occasioned use, but presents itself as an intellectual art-work for a leisured class.

Without that readership, however, the book could hardly exist, *as a book*. Perhaps the author could have written it purely for self-expression. But without a readership, without a circulation, it is unlikely that the book could have survived, or, if surviving, would have been included in a collection of Hebrew books. So the readership is constitutive of the book as a text, as a text that survives into the modern world.

3. *The Author.* If such is the public that the book implies, what kind of author, then, from the point of view of class and social structure, does the book imply? What is its matrix, socially speaking?

a. *The class matrix.* Let us suppose that in the society in which the book was produced there were two classes, rich and poor. No doubt societies are generally more complex than that, but most societies have at least those classes in them. We hardly need to *suppose* the existence of such classes as the matrix of the book of Job, of course, because the book itself testifies to the existence of rich and poor in the world of the story—and it is unlikely that the author would have envisaged such a social structure for his fiction if he had not been familiar with it in real life.

Very well, then. If there are rich and poor in the social world of the text's production, from which class does the book arise? Job is a rich man, in fact the 'greatest of the sons of the east' (1.3), so prima facie this is a rich man's story—not only a story *about* a rich man but also *by* a rich man.

Or is that conclusion too premature? Does not the story tell us that Job is not only rich but also becomes poor? Perhaps then it is a poor man's story. And, in any case, why should not the poor also tell stories about the rich? I reply, in the first place, that the Job of the book is *not* a poor man—not even a poor man who once was rich—but a rich man, through and through, a rich man who loses his wealth, indeed, but who regains it and becomes richer than ever. And secondly, the experience the poor have of the rich is, overwhelmingly, of oppressors—of landlords, money lenders, despots. They do not know, on the whole, of *pious* rich men. If Job is rich *and* pious, the implication is that the story is a rich man's story, told from the perspective of the wealthy. Of course, we can allow, it is always within the bounds of possibility that in this case an exceptional storyteller from the poorer class told a story about a rich man with the piety and integrity of Job. That may indeed be true (I don't believe it myself), but, true or not, that is not the natural implication of the narrative.

Once we recognize that the narrative implies the perspective of the rich, other features of the book fall into place.

1. The first is the lack of realism in the book about poverty. Job has lost all his property, and his income: his 7000 sheep, his 3000 camels, his 500 yoke of oxen and his 500 she-asses. All that he owns is 'touched' or struck by disaster (1.11). Yet he is still able to support his wife, his four friends who have come to visit him for a week at least (2.13)—*and* the four servants who have survived the disasters (1.15, 16, 17, 19). He still has guests in his house (who ignore him), maidservants (who are treating him as a stranger), and his own personal valet (19.15-16). He is, in short, maintaining a considerable household—on nothing, on no income and no resources. And he is never hungry. He is distressed by his skin complaints, and he cannot sleep (7.4; 30.1), but he never complains that he has no food. So he is not really a very poor man. Or at least, the author does not know how to depict him as a poor man. The truly poor are not worried about their status, as Job is; they are worried about where their next meal is coming from.

2. When truly poor people *are* described in the book, they are either despised or glamourized. In ch. 30 Job depicts men who from 'hard hunger' (30.3 RSV) have to gnaw the dry ground, picking mallow and the leaves of bushes, living in gullies and caves, warming themselves by burning the roots of the broom

(30.3-7). But there is no sympathy on Job's part or the author's for these desperately poor people; rather, they are a senseless, disreputable brood who have been 'whipped out of the land' (30.8). True, they are said to 'make sport of' Job (30.1)—which is not very nice, but everyone else is rejecting Job too (or at least, that is how it seems to Job)—men in general who have gaped at him and struck him on the cheek (16.10), friends who scorn him (16.20), mockers who surround him (17.2), and all his family who ignore him (19.13). But it is his truly poor despisers who come in for the severest criticism, and are themselves despised for their poverty and not just for their attitude to Job. The implication must be that the book does not originate among them, or represent their interests. From the way they are portrayed we can infer that it is the interests of those at the opposite end of the social spectrum that are represented by this book.

Where the truly poor are depicted elsewhere in the book, however, in ch. 24, it may seem at first sight that their poverty is sympathetically portrayed. Here 'the poor of the earth', who have been dispossessed of their property by the wicked, have to go out into the wasteland like asses to scavenge food for their young (24.5). They are so poor they go about naked, they have no covering in the cold, and they are wet with the rain of the mountains (24.10, 7-8). They have no share in the food they are producing: 'though hungry, they carry the sheaves...they tread the wine presses, but suffer thirst' (24.10-11 NRSV). This is not an unsympathetic depiction, but it shows the hand of the rhetorician rather than of the fellow-sufferer. For the author can imagine poverty only as the deprivation of wealth: the poor people he describes in ch. 24 are widows and orphans whose flocks, donkey and ox have been seized by the wicked (24.2-3). In other words, they have suffered the fate of a Job, though on a smaller scale. Theirs is not the systemic poverty of the long-term poor, who never owned cattle and who were never rich enough to feel the absence of a donkey a loss. The poor of ch. 24 glean in other people's fields and vineyards (24.6), and work as day-labourers, carrying sheaves in the field, pressing olives and treading grapes (24.10-11). They are not starving, and they are not—not literally—'scavenging in the wasteland food for their young' (24.5). The picture of the poor in ch. 24 is not a depiction of real poverty; it is a glamourization of poverty; it has an eye for the photographic opportunities in it, but it does not know the world of the poor from the inside.

3. The third feature of the book that makes sense when its social context among the rich is recognized is the way in which wealth is regarded as unproblematic. In the world of the book, there is no question to be raised about one man having such wealth that he can own 'very many' slaves or servants (1.3), no question about a social and economic system, that is, in which the existence of many men functions to support the status and wealth of one man, a system that produces a narrative in which humans are listed as property of the rich man, like, and after, sheep and camels and oxen and she-asses.

Nor is it regarded as problematic by the book that Job's 'friends' do not live in his own community. There is room, apparently, for only one Job in the land of Uz; he cannot have friends of his own standing in his country, for he is the greatest of the sons of the east, and the only friends he can afford to have (given his dignity) are sheikhs like himself, from foreign lands. Job's intimates, indeed, are members of his household (19.19), but his equals, those who are alone are called his friends (or rather, his 'neighbours', רעים) do not come from his community. This is a sad, and socially conditioned, state of affairs, but the author of the text sees nothing problematic about it, for he him-self—so the inference may be drawn—has experienced, and has come to regard as natural and commonsensical, the fact that wealth creates a barrier and that distinct social classes are an inevitable feature of society.

b. *The gender matrix.* What of the gender matrix of the book? Not surprisingly, it must be characterized as patriarchal—but that is too general a term, and the nature of its patriarchy needs to be further analysed. 'Patriarchy' is often used today to designate a social system in which men have unproblematic power over women—and we can undoubtedly infer that the book repre-sents the interests of patriarchy in that sense. For example, whatever Job's wife means by her speech, to curse God and die (2.9), it is evident that she plays her role in the story only as a foil to Job, his patience being contrasted with her impatience, his piety with her blasphemy, his wisdom with her speech 'like one of the foolish women' (2.10). There are no wise women in the book of Job, we notice, only foolish ones. We cannot help wondering whether, when Job says his wife is speaking like one of 'the foolish women', he actually means 'women in general'—as if to say, dismissively, 'There you go, talking like a woman'. For who else, as a group, would the 'foolish women' be? In his language, they *are* a group, for she is speaking 'like one of' them. Yet in reality, in real societies, foolish women are not a group or class. How many foolish women has Job been listening to, anyway, to know how they talk? In fact, he knows very little about foolish women—a patriarch like him will hardly be mixing with such persons. He is simply presuming, from his position of patriarchal power, that women have nothing important to say. Perhaps there is a class aspect here as well, and 'foolish women' means, in particular, 'lowerclass women'; perhaps also it is the pious snob, who has pitched his tent on the moral high ground, who speaks here, equating 'lowerclass' with 'godless'. But more likely, as I was suggesting, it is simply the male speaking, the patriarch, who lumps all women together as foolish chatterers, expects better of a patriarch's wife, and is disappointed but not surprised when she shows herself typical of her sex.

Job's wife, in any case, suffers, as women do, at the hands of the patriarchy of the book. In the first place, the suffering she experiences is ignored, though her husband's is everywhere trumpeted. The fact is, she has lost as many children as Job has, and she, every bit as much as Job, has lost her status and standard of living. But she has, in addition, to endure a suffering that Job does not: she has to go on living with a spouse whom everyone in the society now regards as a heinous sinner. Secondly, her very existence is ultimately repressed by the narrative; for though we hear in the epilogue that Job again has seven sons and three daughters (42.3), not a word is said of her, the woman who by now has spent fifteen whole years of her life being pregnant with Job's children. The children that are born are Job's, not hers; she has been effaced.

Patriarchy, in the sense of male control of women, also expresses itself in the way Job's second set of three daughters is treated. At first it may seem that they are more highly esteemed than women generally are in their culture, for they alone of Job's children are named and they, uniquely in the Hebrew Bible when there are surviving sons, share their father's inheritance (42.14-15). But the syntax of the narrative is very revealing. 'In all the land there were no women so fair as Job's daughters; and their father gave them inheritance among their brothers' (42.15), says the narrator. But we mistake him if we think that these are just two unrelated facts about Job's daughters: that they were beautiful, *and* that they gained an inheritance from him. No, that 'and' (the *waw* consecutive) functions just like the 'and' of 1.2: there, Job was blameless, *and, and so* there were born to him seven sons and three daughters and he had 7000 sheep...Here, Job's daughters are the fairest in the land, *and, and so* he gave them inheritance. But the male orientation is even more marked than that. Typically, in a male world, women exist to be looked at by men; 'fair' is the judgment of the male gaze, whether it is Job's, the narrator's, or the author's. No doubt the brothers are more or less as good-looking as their sisters, being the children of the same father and mother; but they are not called 'fair'. No, they inherit because they are sons; the daughters inherit because the man is charmed by them. And what names he gives them: names of cosmetics! Men must act but women have only to *be*.

Patriarchy, however, does not only concern the relations between men and women. It also comes to expression in the way older and more powerful men treat younger and less powerful men. Job's nostalgic speech in ch. 29, for example, is a classic text for a repressive and thoughtless patriarchy. In his 'autumn days' (29.4), as he recollects them, Job would prepare his seat in the square at the city gate, the young men would see him and withdraw, and even those esteemed in the society would refrain from speech and lay their hand on their mouth; the voice even of the nobles would be hushed and their tongue would cleave to the roof of their mouth (42.7-10). Job portrays himself here as the dominant male, and he behaves like any dominant male among primates: others must make gestures of submission to him. This dominance is what gives him identity and pleasure, and in the time of his loss of it he can only wish that it was restored: 'Oh, that I were as in the months of old' (42.2).

Consider a further expression of this patriarchal dominance:

> Men listened to me, and waited,
> and kept silence for my counsel.
> After I spoke they did not speak again,
> and my word dropped upon them (29.21-22).

That is to say, once Job arrives at the gate all conversation stops, and, once he has spoken, the matter is decided. He has total control over his interlocutors as his words 'drop' (נטף) upon them (29.22); he prevents discussion, and insists on having his own way. Whether or not this is what actually happened in his salad days (what would 'actually' mean, I wonder), this is what he remembers, and this is what he desires.

Now this very unpleasant mode of dominance is not remarked on by male commentators (they are all male), no doubt because that is the role they secretly or subconsciously aspire to. Which man among you, my readers, I might ask, given the choice between giving your authoritative view on a matter and thereupon having the whole issue finalized, and submitting to hours of free-floating discussion by less experienced and lower-ranking members of a committee, would instinctively opt for the latter?

The conflict between groups that such patriarchal dominance arouses is well displayed in the intervention by the young Elihu. He has been compelled to hold his peace until the four patriarchs have finished all they want to say, and he is, not surprisingly, 'angry'; the verb occurs four times (32.2, 2, 3, 5). Not surprisingly, too, the anger is intellectualized by the author as an anger that arises 'because of' the arguments of Job and the friends—but that 'because of' merely signals a displacement of the source of the anger. For one does not become *angry* because someone else holds a different view from oneself on esoteric points of theology; it is in cases where one's own identity is in some way threatened by that view or its expression that intellectual disagreement connects with the emotions.

Because of the patriarchal rules of order and protocol (which are, of course, far from innocent and natural, and which exist in order to preserve the power structure), Elihu feels obliged to construct an elaborate and apologetic justification for his entry into the conversation. The conflict between old and young, between patriarchal dominance and the submission of the less powerful male, is evident throughout. The text tries to repress the conflict that patriarchy engenders by having Elihu submit, ostentatiously, to the patriarchal norms and so 'resolve' the conflict; but the text is transparent to the social anger between the generations. It is an interesting possibility that the omission of Elihu from the narrative framework of the book is not an accident of literary history but a classic Freudian slip on the part of a patriarchal author, who identified with Job and the three friends, and with God—elderly gentlemen, all of them—, rather than with the young Elihu.

c. *The political matrix*. What of the *political* context? This text, the book of Job, which is so directly and overtly concerned with wealth and poverty, telling as it does the story of a rich man who becomes empoverished, is at the same time exercising a repression of the conflict between the social classes that are determined by wealth and its absence. In so doing, it deploys various strategies.

1. It portrays the concentration of wealth in the hands of one man as unproblematic.

2. It tells a story of movement from riches to poverty, and from poverty to riches; it tells of a man who in his lifetime is both rich and poor, and then is rich again—as if the boundaries between the classes can be casually crossed. But we know that such is not a possibility for the vast majority of humans.

3. It deflects attention from the political to the ideational, and elevates theology above economics. It transmutes the issues of wealth, power and class into issues of human innocence and the divine governance of the universe. Even if we think theology is more important than economics, we can hardly deny that it's a different subject—and changing the subject is a classic way of repressing conflict.

All texts, according to Fredric Jameson,[1] owe their existence to a desire to repress social conflict, to make life easier for both oppressors and the oppressed, to allow the oppressors to deny their responsibility and to enable the oppressed to forget their

1. Fredric Jameson, *The Political Unconscious: Narrative as a Socially Symbolic Act* (London: Methuen, 1981).

suffering. They carry out that programme by papering over cracks in the social fabric, minimizing the conflict, writing it out of existence. A book about a rich man, about the richest of men, indeed, who loses his wealth, must have something to do with class—which is to say, with class conflict. The book's existence, and its narrative, implies a situation of conflict, of tension and variant interests if not of open conflict, in which the rich feel the need to explain themselves and re-invent themselves, under the figure of Job. The fact that no one, even today, reads this book as a document of class struggle is evidence of how successfully it has repressed the conflict it presupposes.

Why is there a book of Job? Because there was a social, gender and political need for it. This is not the whole story, but it is a story that has to be told, especially when the prevailing story is that all it represents are the cultured theological sensitivities of its author. But there is another way of answering the 'Why is there...?' question. It is to enquire after the psychological profile of the author as it is implied by his text.

b. *The Implied Psychological Profile of the Author*
The text was called forth by a complex of social needs that it addressed. But it would not have come into existence if there had not been an author who was able and willing to produce the work. Its production must have satisfied some personal psychological need of his. Or rather, I should say, the implication of his text is that it did. That is the implication of texts in general, that they come into being at the free decision of their authors, who feel some internal compulsion to compose them, and derive some personal satisfaction, some lowering of interior tension, from completing them. That may not always be the actual case, of course. Some authors, no doubt, write at gunpoint, others are driven by financial necessity or greed to write works they have no personal involvement in, others are automata; but the implication we may reasonably draw from the existence of any text is that some author intended it, and met psychological needs of his or her own in writing it. What need on the author's part did the book of Job satisfy, then, or, rather, what need does it imply that it satisfied?

a. *The text as a dream.* My route in to this question is to regard the
text as a dream, its author's dream. The author, I argue, has conceived or imagined his story, consciously or subconsciously,
from much the same stuff and in much the same way as he
nightly created his dreams. The author was no doubt largely
unaware of the psychological needs and drives that his work
arose from, and would have spoken of his work—if he were
asked—in terms of his conscious intentions and of the work's
overt content. Most of us authors would do the same. So if we
desire to penetrate to the unconscious layer of the writing, it will,
no doubt, have to be without the author's knowledge or consent.

What kind of dream is the book of Job? Obviously, it is a
death-wish, a dream in which the unconscious explores the
possibility of ceasing to be—of ceasing to be altogether, or
ceasing to be what one is at present. In fantasy too, that is, in a
semi-conscious mode, we find ourselves imagining 'what if'
scenarios in which our worst fears become reality. In entertainment too we have the phenomenon of the horror movie, or the
video nasty—or the Greek tragedy—as an outworking of the
death-wish on the author's part, and, complicitly, on the view-
ers' or audience's part as well.

If the author of Job is a well-to-do man, he is obliged to, and
needs to, for his own psychic security, play out—in dream or
fantasy or imaginative literature—his fear that his wealth may
not last, and to imagine himself as something other than a
member of the wealthy ruling class. He needs to affirm his
identity, and his role within his class, by contrasting his present
identity with other potential identities he could be obliged to
adopt. He creates the character Job as an image of himself; or
rather, he dreams himself as Job.

The book of Job exists, that is, because its author needed it to
exist: that is the implication of a book that consists of such a narrative. He needed to externalize his fear, to see its shape, to try it
on for size; and, at another level, he was driven willy-nilly to
fantasize about the loss of what was precious to him. This is not
a poor man's dream, incidentally, for poor people do not fear
becoming poor. It is the dream, and so the text, of a man who
has something to lose.

In this fantasy, however, the dreamer does not only give

shape to the death-wish; he also wills the overcoming of the death-wish, and writes of the restoration of what he has both feared and wished to lose. He wants, and yet he does not want, to lose his status and his wealth, and so his dream has a dream-like happy ending, which brings to the dreamer more than he had to begin with, which assuages the fear in the death-wish by the gratification of a dream of wish-fulfilment.

b. *The dream as a text.* There is a further aspect of dream interpretation that is relevant here, and it concerns the transformation of the dream material into text, the realization in textual form of the psychic realities that gave rise to the text. It is the principle that all the characters in a dream represent the dreamer, or aspects of the dreamer. As I have said, the author dreams himself as Job, and is the hero of his own dream. But he is also Eliphaz, Bildad, and Zophar, Elihu, God—and the narrator too, no doubt.

This is to say more than that there is something of the author in all of these characters, more even than that the author recognizes himself in his characters—consciously or subconsciously. What is implied by the existence of this gallery of characters through whom the author dreams himself is that the author experiences a conflict over the issues he raises in the book. He has created a fiction of a dialogue about innocent suffering in which different speakers adopt different points of view because he himself, whatever his conscious mind thinks, feels uncertainty about the answer. The book is structurally, then, an expression of the author's psychic conflict—especially the conflict between a sense of fitness in the concept of retribution and the experience of suffering that he inscribes in the character of Job.

On the overt level, of course, the book allows this inner conflict to appear: for the book as a whole is a sustained debate, which is never fully resolved—it is never entirely clear what the 'message' of the book is, how the divine speaker answers Job and the friends—if at all—and what the final restoration of Job does to the case presented by the character Job throughout the book.

Not far below the surface, also, the book exhibits inner conflict; for it involves itself in a deconstruction, affirming throughout its course that piety does *not* lead to prosperity and then at its end telling how Job the supremely pious becomes the supremely wealthy.[2] This deconstructability of the book is, I would say, a literary manifestation of the author's own psychic uncertainty.

Deeper still, there is a psychic conflict that the book witnesses to—a conflict we can legitimately *infer*. Consciously, the author may have believed he had resolved the problem, or resolved it as much as it can be resolved. But reading his text as a dream, we can infer that the plurality of its characters represents a certain psychic fragmentation on the author's part. Through the literary process, through naming, distinguishing, externalizing and distancing, he hopes to achieve psychic equilibrium—but only at the cost of alienating parts of himself. So it is not surprising that his project falters literarily, given that it is the manifestation of his psychic disorder.

Why then is there a book of Job? The material causes implied by the book's existence are these: a reading public, a social conflict and an author's psychic needs. For this book to come into being, there had to be a reading public that desired the work, and wanted to consume it as a commodity. The social tension between riches and poverty had to exist—that is, the distinction between rich and poor—for the narrative of a rich Job who loses his wealth to be invented. And there needed to be an author who attempted to relieve, to some extent, his own psychic anxieties by the composition of the work.

2. *What Does It Do to You If You Read It?*

As in the previous chapter, on the Song of Songs, I shall be trying to answer this question in two ways. One is to examine how the text has been received and interpreted by readers of the past. The other is to study the effects on readers of our own time.

2.   See my chapter, 'Deconstructing the Book of Job', in *What Does Eve Do to Help? And Other Readerly Questions to the Old Testament* (Journal for the Study of the Old Testament Supplement Series, 94; Sheffield: JSOT Press, 1990), pp. 106-23 (also published in *The Bible as Rhetoric: Studies in Biblical Persuasion and Credibility* [ed. Martin Warner; Warwick Studies in Philosophy and Literature; London: Routledge, 1990], pp. 65-80).

a. *The Effects of the Text on Former Readers*
I think that we can identify four strands in the history of interpretation of the book of Job. In the first, Job has been seen as the
ideal patient man, piously and fatalistically accepting his suffering as the will of God. This view prevailed in both Jewish and
Christian interpretation up to the Renaissance. There then
appeared the reading that saw Job as the champion of reason
against dogma, of empirical observation against tradition. In the
modern period, another image of Job has been developed, that
sees him as the victim of a cruel and absurd world, and that
finds even in the divine speeches a defence of a cosmic
irrationality. The character Job, in other words, has been constructed according to the ideals of each age. The fourth strand in
interpretation, which has persisted up until the present, is the
conception of the book as 'wisdom'. In traditional interpretation
that meant that the speeches as well as the narrative were didactic or moral literature, and moral truth could be supported
equally by the speeches of the friends and by Job's (if anything,
the friends' speeches were more serviceable for sound morality
than the angry and intemperate speeches of Job). In modern critical interpretation, the categorization of the book as 'wisdom'
continues by means of the construct of the 'wisdom movement'
or 'wisdom school' in Israel. Questionable though the idea is
that there was such a movement or group within ancient
Israelite society, it is currently the prevailing paradigm for
reading the book.

Now the effects of those styles for interpretation have been
either a misreading of the book (I mean, a reading that I cannot
accept or even sympathize with or tolerate), or an unnatural and
dogmatically conditioned limitation on the interpretational
possibilities for it.

In the case of the most ancient, and (to judge by its longevity)
most persuasive, interpretation—of Job as the ideal patient sufferer—the reading is so palpably untrue to the book as a whole
(as I and people who think like me would say) that I feel constrained to offer a reason for its existence. There is of course
some colour for the picture of Job's patience in the narrative of
the first two chapters—but then there is always *some* ground for
misreadings. We could perhaps suggest that readers have rarely

got beyond the first two chapters and therefore have thought that the character of Job was adequately presented in these chapters. Or it could be that the portrait of Job in the first two chapters has determined how readers have read the later and quite different portrayal of Job in the rest of the book. But I think it more likely that the misreading of Job as a patient sufferer should be construed as due to readers' resistance to the portrait of Job's intemperate and near-blasphemous speech, to their refusal to accept that the hero of a biblical book could be so hostile to heaven. Whatever the reason, the portrait of Job that I find inscribed on every page of the book except the first is entirely effaced by this interpretational mode. In this case, what the book of Job has done to its readers is less than what the readers have done to the book of Job; or rather, the book has so provoked them to moral outrage that they have felt it necessary to suppress the evidence that has been staring them in the face.

The second strain in interpretation—which sees Job as representing reason and experience over against dogma—has much more grounding in the book of Job itself, but it nevertheless represents a projection of the interpreters' self-understanding upon the book, and is a distortion (as I think it) of the book itself. For, on the one hand, it minimizes Job's attachment to the conventional theology of his age; for the fact is that although he dissents from the friends' views of exact retribution, he nevertheless believes in retribution of some kind (for he believes that an innocent man like himself should *not* suffer), and in every other regard he stands for the religious dogma of his time rather than for unfettered rationality. And, on the other hand, such a reading turns the book of Job into nothing but a collection of Joban speeches, a vehicle for Job's ideas—and so must systematically write the prologue, the friends' speeches, the divine speeches and the epilogue out of the book. In this case, what the book has done to its readers is to so engage their sympathies with the character Job as to make them lose sight of the book as a whole.

The third strain in interpretation—which reads Job as representing humanity as the victim of an absurd universe—does indeed take the divine speeches into consideration, making them an affirmation of the irrationality (from the human perspective) of the divine activity. But it too, like the second strain, essentially makes the book of Job a collection of speeches by Job and negates the book as a whole, with its prologue, its epilogue, and the speeches of the friends.

As for the fourth strain in interpretation, the categorization of the book of Job as 'wisdom' has functioned to protect the argument of the book and its assumptions from criticism. True, in scholarly language the term 'wisdom' means, properly speaking, 'Israel's wisdom tradition' and it does not imply the critic's assent to its validity. Yet in practice the stance taken by virtually all scholarly readers of the book is complicity with the text. The book of Job is said by all those who write commentaries on it to be a masterpiece of world literature and to express profound insights into the human condition. The result has been that Job himself or the book as a whole has become virtually immune from criticism—even though the book itself makes it crystal clear that Job's whole argument in defence of his innocence results from his ignorance of the reasons for his suffering, and even though the speeches of the friends, which form the bulk of the book, are said by the most authoritative voice in the book, God's, to be in the wrong. If Job is entirely under a misapprehension and the friends have not spoken what is right, where is the 'truth' in the book of Job? No one seems to have seen it this way, no one seems to have been troubled about regarding as 'wisdom' a book that—by its own admission—is mostly wrong. The history of the interpretation of the book, I conclude, shows that what the book does to you is suppress your critical instincts and persuade you to adopt the book's implicit ideologies.

b. *The Effects of the Text on its Modern Readers*
As with the chapter on the Song of Songs, I acknowledge that this part of the study would have been better if I had carried out in-depth interviews with many readers of our own time. Not inclined to the privations attendant on rigorous fieldwork, I decided rather to offer my own reactions to the book, inasmuch as I could reconstruct them from a time before I thought as I do now, as the sample from which I could extrapolate to other readers.

1. The book of Job persuades its readers that there is a causal relation between piety and prosperity, and that that relation is unproblematic.

I mean to say: the hero of the book is a pious and prosperous man, whose prosperity is the consequence of his piety. That is a given of the story, and it is never challenged. God has blessed Job and all that he has, and there is no mistake about that. What the book raises as an issue is not whether prosperity should indeed ever be regarded as sa consequence of piety, but the question whether a poor and suffering man, as Job has ostensibly become, can be pious. In focusing upon the piety or otherwise of this most untypical poor man, Job, the book deflects attention from the deeper and prior question, why anyone should imagine there is any connection at all between wealth (or poverty) and godliness.

In short, while the problem *raised by* the book is whether a suffering man can be an innocent one, the problem of the book (i.e. the problem constituted by the book) is a different one. And it is inscribed, though silently, in its first *waw* consecutive: Job was a perfect man *and* he had seven thousand sheep (1.1-3). In the *faux-naïf* style of the narrative,[3] that *and* means to say *and so*: his great riches are a consequence of his perfect piety. That is the point at which the real problematic of the book is embedded— but the narrative craftily persuades readers that in v. 2 of the first chapter we are still seeing the stage set, and that the real action, the real problematic, has yet to be developed and unfolded.

Consider how fundamental that *waw* consecutive is for the book as a whole, how that *waw* or 'pin' is the linchpin for the work. If there never was, or if no one had imagined there was, a causal connection between piety and prosperity, the Satan could never have asked his question, God could not have authorized the testing of Job, Job could not have suffered, and there could have been no book of Job. For the Satan's question asks God to remove the prosperity to see whether piety collapses—and *that* question hangs upon the assumption that there is a relation of cause and effect between piety and prosperity.

3. On which see my paper, 'False Naivety in the Prologue to Job', *Hebrew Annual Review* 9 (1985), pp. 127-36.

What is more, the book as a whole affirms the truth of the doctrine of reward for piety; for Job, the most perfect of humans, ends up the wealthiest. Even if he has been temporarily empoverished, his poverty is only temporary. Once again, however, readers have their attention deflected from this subliminal assertion of the book, for the narrative has convinced us that Job has been unjustly treated—Job himself has made out this case eloquently and persuasively—and the narrative has aroused in us a desire for Job's vindication, which means, in Job's terms, the restitution of his fortunes. When we read at the end of the book that Job becomes wealthy again, we are glad for Job, for we like happy endings and we crave closure; and there is not one in a hundred among us who draws an ideological consequence from the plot and exclaims, Aha! so piety *does* lead to prosperity in the end!

Furthermore, what we are persuaded not to notice, by the flow of the narrative and by the attractiveness of the character Job, is that in fact Job has *not* been treated unjustly—not unless the doctrine of retribution is true. Job's protest against the injustice of his treatment is very *sympathique*, so much so that it is a rare reader who resists him. But unless his piety *should have* been rewarded with wealth and health, there is no injustice in what he suffers, and no deserving in his restoration.

2. The book of Job persuades its readers that wealth is unproblematic, ethically speaking. Who among its readers is unable to sympathize with Job because he is a rich man? Few who read these lines, I should think, for anyone who can afford to buy books or spend non-productive time in public libraries is already a wealthy person, by world standards, and is already, in a way, a member of the social class of Job and his friends.

I am too, and I never raised this question until once, when I was lecturing on Job, I had this response from one of my audience: 'Man, I don't like this dude Job. He is a rich man, and I am not. I have to get up at four in the morning to go to work before I come to school; I have to do three jobs to keep my family and pay for my education. Why should I be interested in the story of this rich man? He has nothing to do with me.'

Now I know that the book of Job takes wealth for granted as a good thing, even representing extreme wealth as going hand in hand with great virtue. It persuades its readers who are wealthy that it is perfectly all right to be wealthy, that they should not feel bad about it, in fact that they should not even stop to think about it. It is a rare reader, one who has not yet been inscribed in the scholarly literature (but I am putting him there at this very moment!), who resists such persuasion, reading from his own place.

3. It persuades readers that explanations of reality, and especially genetic and causal explanations, are worth having. In the story of the book of Job, Job is suffering, and thereupon the primary question on the agenda of the book becomes, *Why* is he suffering? What is the *cause* of the suffering? The book is so structured as to supply an ostensibly complete answer to that question; that is the function of the prologue.

Now it is a typically intellectual attitude, that explanations for states of affairs are worth having. I myself, being an intellectual, naturally think it is good that there are some people in the world who try to *understand* it and *account* for it. So I am by profession very partial to the book of Job. We intellectuals take delight in everything that confirms our own orientation. So we do not question the book in this regard; we do not even notice that it is subliminally supporting us. And, especially, we do not know that this orientation of ours is not natural, not obvious, not obligatory. For *understanding* reality is only one option among many when we are faced with an object or a state of affairs. There are people who think it more important to change the way things are than to understand it, and others prefer to use things or enjoy them than to do either. Faced with a bicycle, we can choose to study how it works, or to discover its prehistory—or to ride it. And there is no reason to think that understanding the origins of the bicycle will be of any use at all in learning how to ride it or in getting from A to B.

Faced with suffering, we have no reason to think that understanding its origin will have much value. Knowing how to handle it, how to behave ourselves while suffering, how to remain ourselves while suffering—these may be much more important. But the book of Job persuades us, and especially because we do not notice it is doing it, that understanding, and understanding origins, is the one thing worth doing.

4. It persuades readers that it somehow answers the problem of suffering. Readers are in fact generally quite content with the conclusion of the book. They do not feel that it raises more questions than it solves, or that its whole approach is wrong-headed. Indeed, throughout the history of interpretation of the book it seems to have been the case that whatever the explanation of suffering that readers have found it to be proffering, the book of Job's explanation has been thought to be the best. Readers of the book of Job, in other words, have almost always agreed with it. It is hard to find a reader who says, I believe I understand what the book of Job is saying, and I don't agree with it.

So successful is the book at persuading readers of the rightness of its position that readers rarely notice the enormous paradox the book presents: the book is generally regarded as dealing with the problem of human suffering in general but the narrative is clearly about a quite exceptional occurrence. For the Job of this book is a very untypical human being, since he is the most perfect and the most wealthy man of all. How can the experience of such a man be characteristic of human experience generally? How, indeed, can his experience have any relevance at all to the rest of us?

And if that conclusion is resisted, and it is claimed that the book is not principally about the man Job but about humans generally, what then? If the testing of Job is meant to establish not just whether Job himself serves God 'for naught' but whether it is possible for human beings in general to do so, then Job's maintenance of his piety under the onslaughts of the Satan has resolved the question once and for all. He has proved the possibility of disinterested piety. If that is so, then the reason for Job's suffering cannot be (or is unlikely to be) the reason for anyone else's suffering, for the highly successful experiment with Job will surely not have to be repeated. The book, however, persuades readers that they are reading about a universal human problem, when in reality they are reading about Job's problem—a problem that is, by the logic of the narrative, no one else's.

What the book of Job does to you if you read it, in short, is to inveigle you into a willing (or unconscious) suspension of disbelief. By its charm and its force, by its rhetoric and its passion, it persuades its readers of ideas that cannot be defended—or should not. It engages our sympathy for a character we know to be labouring under a vast illusion, we ourselves knowing from the prologue how misconceived his complaints against heaven are. It convinces us to pose the problems of suffering in the terms the book itself offers us, and to profess ourselves more or less content with the answers that it gives. That, at any rate, is the testimony of the ages to the book of Job. Unless criticism of it has been suppressed, or self-repressed, it has had its way with readers—which is, no doubt, what we mean when we call it a great and powerful work of literature.

7

Job and the Spirituality of the Reformation*

In the introduction to his excellent anthology of writings on the book of Job, Nahum N. Glatzer comments that, with some notable exceptions, 'Jewish interpreters in the premodern period Judaized Job and Christian expositors Christianized him'.[1] Even in the modern period, he observes, 'the interpreter's intellectual preoccupation still tends to determine his reading of the book and causes an adaptation of Job to his own thinking or needs'.[2] For Glatzer, as for many scholars, such interpretations 'advance our understanding of the book very little' and invite merely the condemnation or the scorn of readers at the ingenuity of older interpreters in 'bypassing the stubborn soil of the book and in fashioning its hero in their own image'. In these postmodern days, however, rather than patronizing our predecessors we might do well to regard it as a tribute to the richness of the book of Job that it is amenable to so many varying readings that have engaged the sympathies and commitments of readers across many cultural divides. It is in that spirit that the present study of Job and the spirituality of the Reformation (by which I mean just Luther and Calvin) is undertaken.

The term 'spirituality', as I am using it in this chapter, can be defined as 'the forms that holiness takes in the concrete life of the

*   An earlier version of this essay was published in *The Bible, the Reformation and the Church: Essays in Honour of James Atkinson* (ed. W.P. Stephens; Journal for the Study of the New Testament Supplement Series, 105; Sheffield: Sheffield Academic Press, 1995), pp. 49-72.

1.   Nahum N. Glatzer, *The Dimensions of Job: A Study and Selected Readings* (New York: Schocken Books, 1969), p. 11.
2.   Glatzer, *The Dimensions of Job*, p. 12.

believer',[3] or as 'the attitude faith should take as it is exercised in the unceasing conflict and contradiction in which a Christian is involved in daily life in the service of Christ'.[4] It is not a term that has always been used in studies of the Reformers, partly because some other term, such as 'the Christian life', has been substituted for it, but partly also because the Reformers' concern with spirituality has often been obscured by an exclusive concentration on their theology. It is nonetheless increasingly being urged today that casting their whole intellectual activity as a quest for a spirituality, for a religious way of being in the world, may in fact be a legitimate way of understanding them. Timothy George, for example, argues that 'Calvin's life's work can be interpreted as an effort to formulate an authentic spirituality, that is to say, a modus vivendi of life in the Spirit'.[5]

However that may be, my specific concern here is with the question how Luther and Calvin invoked the person of Job to express their own perception of spirituality, that is, their understanding of the nature of the believing life. By way of preface to a study of their representations of Job, I shall try to establish some context for their outlooks, both in the exegetical tradition they inherited and in the spirituality of their own time.

1. *The Figure of Job in Pre-Reformation Spirituality*

What is the earliest extant interpretation of the figure of Job? We cannot be sure. It may that of the epistle of James, or that of the *Testament of Job*, a work variously ascribed to the last pre-Christian century or to the early Christian period.[6] In the

---

3.   So Lucien Joseph Richard, *The Spirituality of John Calvin* (Atlanta: John Knox Press, 1974), p. 1.

4.   Ronald S. Wallace, *Calvin's Doctrine of the Christian Life* (Edinburgh: Oliver & Boyd, 1959), p. vii, who does not however use the term 'spirituality'.

5.   Timothy George, *Theology of the Reformers* (Nashville: Broadman Press, 1988), p. 224.

6.   See *Studies on the Testament of Job* (ed. Michael A. Knibb and Pieter van der Horst; Society for New Testament Studies Monograph Series, 66; Cambridge: Cambridge University Press, 1989), esp. pp. 27-32 (in Russell P. Spittler's 'The Testament of Job: A History of Research and Interpretation', pp. 7-32).

epistle of James, Job is known solely as an embodiment of 'patience' or 'steadfastness' (ὑπομονή), and his experience of God is characterized as that of a 'compassionate and merciful' (πολύσπλαγχνος...καὶ οἰκτίρμων) Lord:

> Behold, we call those happy who were steadfast. You have heard of the steadfastness of Job, and you have seen the purpose of the Lord, how the Lord is compassionate and merciful (5.11).

In the *Testament of Job* also, where there is a more developed portrait of Job, Job's perseverance in the sufferings inflicted on him by the Satan is one of its principal themes.[7] Here the patience of Job is expressed with three distinct terms: ὑπομονή, 'standing firm', καρτερία, 'stubbornness, toughness', and μακροθυμία, 'patience' (by which one perseveres and endures).[8]

Few modern readers, left to their own devices, would fix upon 'patience' as the most outstanding characteristic of the biblical Job's personality, or, at least, if they recognize in chs. 1–2 the 'patient' Job who accedes to the divine will, they would soon want to contrast this image with that of the 'impatient' Job in the remainder of the book.[9] No doubt the author of James had no intention of subsuming all the virtues of Job under this single heading, or of headlining the narrative of the whole book with the term. But the mere accident that this is the sole reference to Job within the New Testament ensured that in the history of interpretation this construction of the character of Job remained prominent.[10]

James was not of course the only interpreter of the character of Job available to the Reformers. Among the Christian writers on Job most influential upon them must be counted Gregory the Great, with his *Morals on the Book of Job*, and Thomas Aquinas, with his *The Literal Exposition on Job*.

---

7.   Cees Haas, 'Job's Perseverance in the Testament of Job', in *Studies on the Testament of Job*, pp. 117-54 (117).

8.   Haas, 'Job's Perseverance', pp. 117-54.

9.   Cf. H.L. Ginsberg, 'Job the Patient and Job the Impatient', *Conservative Judaism* 21 (1967), pp. 12-28.

10.   I cite only, by way of example, one of Gregory's first sentences about Job, as a man 'who in a word, we know, received from the Judge of that which is within the reward of the virtue of patience' (*Moralia*, Epistle, 3 [= *Morals*, I, p. 8] [see note 11 below]).

The *Moralia* of Gregory[11] is of course one of the classic works of mediaeval exegesis, expounding the threefold sense of the book,[12] a literal sense (Job is afflicted by God in order to increase his merit[13]), an allegorical sense (Job is the suffering Redeemer[14] and the church in its earthly sufferings[15]) and a moral sense (Job transcends the temporal realm and ascends to the eternal[16]). But, as befits a course of sermons more than a work of academic theology, the issue of the spirituality of the book of Job arises early on in his work when Gregory compares his own physical suffer-

---

11. Gregory I (the Great), *Libri XXXV Moralium, Patrologia Latina* (henceforth *PL*), LXXV, pp. 509-1162; LXXVI, pp. 9-782; *S. Gregorii Magni Moralia in Iob* (ed. M. Adriaen; Corpus Christianorum, Series Latina, 143, 143A, 143B; Turnhout: Brepols, 1979–85); *Grégoire le Grand: Morales sur Job* (Première partie, Livres I–II, ed. Robert Gillet, trans. André de Gaudemaris [2nd edn]; Troisième partie, Livres XI–XVI, ed. Aristide Bocognano [2 vols.]; Sources Chrétiennes, 32 *bis*, 212, 221; Paris: Cerf, 1975, 1974, 1975); *Morals on the Book of Job, by S. Gregory the Great* (A Library of Fathers of the Holy Catholic Church, 18-20; Oxford: John Henry Parker, 1844) (cited below as *Morals*). References below are made to the Sources Chrétiennes edition and to the Parker edition when available, and otherwise to the *Patrologia*.
On Gregory's commentary on Job, see Bertrand de Margerie, *Introduction à l'histoire de l'exégèse. IV. L'occident latin de Léon le Grand à Bernard de Clairvaux* (Paris: Cerf, 1990), pp. 171-81 (I am grateful to Dr Jennifer Dines of Heythrop College for lending me this book); P. Catry, 'Epreuves du juste et mystère de Dieu. Le commentaire littéral du livre de Job par Saint Grégoire', *Revue des études augustiniennes* 18 (1972), pp. 124-44. The pages on Gregory's exposition of Job in Glatzer's handbook (*The Dimensions of Job*, pp. 27-32) unfortunately do not extend beyond a collection of typological and allegorical identifications.
12. The threefold sense is, in Gregory's words, to 'unravel the words of the history in allegorical senses' and 'to give to the allegorical senses the turn of a moral exercise' (*Moralia*, Epistle, 1 [= *Morals*, I, p. 5]).
13. 'While the innocent person is bruised by the blow, his patience may serve to increase the gain of his merits' (*Moralia*, Preface, 5.12 [= *Morals*, I, p. 24]).
14. '[T]he blessed Job conveys a type of the Redeemer... For there never was any Saint who did not appear as His herald in figure' (*Moralia*, Preface, 6.14 [= *Morals*, I, pp. 27, 26]).
15. On Job 19.6 (= *Moralia* 14.31.38–32.39 [*PL*, LXXV, pp. 1059-60]).
16. On Job 7.15 'My soul chooseth hanging', Gregory writes: '[I]n... quitting earthly objects of desire, they raise the mind on high' (*Moralia* 8.25.44 [= *Morals*, I, p. 450]). Cf. also 5.40.72; 7.12.27.

ings with those of Job. He himself, afflicted by 'frequent pains in the bowels' and 'under the influence of fevers... draw[ing] [his] breath with difficulty', thinks that perhaps 'Divine Providence designed, that I a stricken one, should set forth Job stricken, and that by these scourges I should the more perfectly enter into the feelings of one that was scourged'.[17] In so saying, he announces a self-identification with the Job of the book who 'bore the strife of the spiritual conflict'[18] and revealed his virtue and fortitude by his reaction to suffering.[19] '[E]very good man, so long as he is not smitten, is regarded as insipid, and of slight account',[20] Gregory writes, revealing as he does so, no doubt, how he construes his own state of health. Suffering for Job, and hence for himself, is character-forming, but it also brings the sufferer to public attention. '[H]ad [Job] not been stricken he would never have been the least known to us';[21] and Gregory himself, as supreme pontiff, cannot be blind to the analogy between Job and himself.

More important, perhaps, is what is generally acknowledged as a key concept in Gregory's spirituality: that of his antithesis of interiority and exteriority.[22] In the Preface to the *Moralia* he tellingly evokes the tension in his own life between the contemplative and the active life, lamenting that 'now that the end of the world is at hand...we ourselves, who are supposed to be devoted to the inner mysteries, are...become involved in outward cares (*curis exterioribus*)'.[23] But more broadly, and beyond his own personal experience, humanity itself, which was destined for interiority, is imprisoned and exiled in exteriority:

---

17. *Moralia*, Epistle, 5 (= *Morals*, I, p. 10).

18. *Moralia*, Preface, 1.3 (= *Morals*, I, p. 15).

19. '[I]t was by strokes that the report of his virtue was stirred up to fragrance...[W]hen disturbed [he] did scatter abroad the odour of his fortitude... For as unguents, unless they be stirred, are never smelt far off... so the Saints in their tribulations make known all the sweetness that they have of their virtues' (*Moralia*, Preface, 2.6 [= *Morals*, I, p. 18]).

20. *Moralia*, Preface, 2.6 (= *Morals*, I, p. 18).

21. *Moralia*, Preface, 2.6 (= *Morals*, I, p. 18).

22. See especially Claude Dagens, *Saint Grégoire le Grand: Culture et expérience chrétiennes* (Paris: Etudes Augustiniennes, 1977), pp. 133-244.

23. *Moralia*, Epistle, 1 (= *Morals*, I, p. 4).

For man, being created for the contemplation of his Maker, but
banished from the interior (*internis*) joys in justice to his deserts...
undergoing the darkness of his exile, was at once subject to the
punishment of his sin, and knew it not; so that he imagined his
place of exile to be his home... But He Whom man had forsaken
within (*intus*), having assumed a fleshly nature, came forth God
without (*foris*); and when he presented Himself outwardly (*exterius*),
he restored man, who was cast forth without (*foras*), to the interior
life (*ad interiora*), that [h]e might henceforth perceive his losses.[24]

The spiritual life is therefore for Gregory a retreat from the
external to the interior. How does the figure of Job sustain this
position? Not very well, it must be said, and one misses in Gregory a close and systematic parallel of the history of the man Job
with the spiritual experience. But in one respect Job plays out a
key phase in the journey inwards and upwards: suffering, temptation, testing—which Job embodies—are the *flagella Dei*, which
purify the soul and stimulate its desire to arise to God.[25] 'The
soul [= "the interior man"] that lifts itself up toward Him he both
lets loose to wars without, and endues with strength within.'[26]
And 'the more the soul of the just suffers adversity in this world,
the more thirst it has to contemplate the face of its Creator'.[27] Job
as sufferer is thus the model of the believing soul who is driven
by suffering towards the divine.[28]

24.   On Job 6.2-3 (*Moralia* 7.1.2 [= *Morals*, I, p. 366, incorrectly capitaliz-
ing the last 'he' in the quoted text]).

25.   'Les *flagella Dei*, les souffrances, les malheurs de tout genre sont
donc destinés à opérer au cœur de l'homme une sorte de résurrection: la
prosperité extérieure dissimule un effondrement intérieur; ce sont les
épreuves qui, en troublant cette prosperité, inciteront l'homme à se res-
saisir, en vue d'un redressement intérieur. Cette correspondance entre l'af-
faiblissement physique et le progrès spirituel est une des lois de la vie chré-
tienne: c'est ainsi que «par un grand principe d'équilibre, nous comprenons
que nous recevons de Dieu à l'occasion de nos progrès intérieurs, et ce que
nous sommes à l'occasion de nos défaillances extérieures»' (Dagens, *Grégoire le Grand*, p. 188, quoting *Moralia* 19.6.12).

26.   On Job 10.10-11 (*Moralia* 9.53.80 [= *Morals*, I, p. 552]). The translation
in the Parker edition misleadingly has 'the soul that is lifted up'; for the
translation above, cf. Dagens, *Saint Grégoire*, p. 187.

27.   *Moralia* 16.27.32.

28.   Cf. Calvin, *CO* (see note 78 below), XXXV, p. 511: 'When we are
struck down we are the better disposed to aspire to the heavenly life'.

A final note in the spirituality of Gregory is his extreme denigration of human worth. Confronted with Job's affirmation of his innocence, 'I know that I shall be found to be just' (13.18), and his apparent acknowledgment of sins (13.15, 26; 14.17),[29] Gregory concludes that 'in attributing to himself iniquity and to the omnipotent Lord his justification, he recognizes himself as a sinner on his own account (*ex se*) and acknowledges that it is as a divine gift that he has been made just'.[30] This severe disjunction of human sinfulness and divine merit takes rather unattractive form when he comments on Job's final confession of his ignorance: 'All human wisdom, no matter how great its acuity, is folly when compared with the divine wisdom. All things that are humanly just and beautiful, if they are compared with the justice and beauty of God, are neither just nor beautiful—nor are they anything at all (*nec omnino sunt*).'[31] Job becomes here a vehicle for a rather totalitarian impulse that is to be found also in some other forms of spirituality besides Gregory's.

Thomas Aquinas[32] set out, in his commentary on Job, on a path distinct from that of Gregory. 'Blessed Pope Gregory', he wrote, 'has already disclosed to us its mysteries [that is, its mystical senses] so subtly and clearly that there seems no need to add anything further to them.'[33] In fulfilling his own goal, however,

---

29. Gregory takes *vias meas in conspectu eius arguam* in 13.15 as 'I will criticize my ways in his sight' (cf. *Moralia* 11.35.48) whereas the Vulgate may simply mean 'I will defend my ways'—which is what the Hebrew surely means.

30. *Moralia* 11.38.51.

31. *Moralia* 35.2.3 (*PL*, LXXVI, p. 751).

32. Thomas Aquinas, *Expositio super Job ad litteram* (Sancti Thomae de Aquino, Opera Omnia, iussu Leonis XIII P.M. edita, 26; Rome: ad Sanctae Sabinae, 1965). The most recent English translation is: *Thomas Aquinas. The Literal Exposition of Job: A Scriptural Commentary concerning Providence* (ed. and trans. Anthony Damico [translator] and Martin D. Yaffe [Interpretive Essays and Notes]; The American Academy of Religion, Classics in Religious Studies, 7; Atlanta: Scholars Press, 1989). I found useful some comments on Aquinas's treatment of Job by Susan E. Schreiner, '"Through a Mirror Dimly": Calvin's Sermons on Job', *Calvin Theological Journal* 21 (1986), pp. 175-93 (178-79).

33. *Expositio*, Prologue, 99-102 (= Damico and Yaffe, *Aquinas...Job*, p. 69).

to explain merely the literal sense of the book, the sense 'primarily intended by the words, whether they are used properly or figuratively',[34] he does not fail to leave some hints of his estimation of Job and of the role Job played in his image of the spiritual life.

For Thomas, Job is a pious man; indeed, it is fundamental to his understanding of the book that Job is 'perfect in every virtue'. For the book of Job, being intended, as he believes, to show that 'human affairs are ruled by divine providence',[35] must deal satisfactorily with the problem of undeserved suffering, which is 'what most seems to exclude divine providence from human affairs'.[36] Job represents such a case. The only fault that can be ascribed to Job is that in speaking immoderately he provokes scandal in the minds of his interlocutors,[37] and in speaking so strenuously of his own innocence he gives the impression of pride and of doubting the divine judgment.[38] Even Job's curse on the day of his birth (ch. 3) is nothing more than a natural 'sadness' proceeding from the 'lower part of the soul', the upper part of the soul being rationally convinced that some good must rightly be expected from his misfortunes.[39]

Job is then, for Thomas, an exemplar of the pious soul, afflicted by external troubles, including the intellectual challenges of his friends, but free of internal turmoil or doubt of God's benevolence. Even when the Hebrew text seems to have Job directly accusing God of injustice, Thomas interprets the sentence as a mere hypothetical, for it is not possible that a man of Job's piety could utter an accusation against God. Thus at 19.6, for instance, 'God has afflicted me with an inequitable judgment', Thomas's comment is that '[i]f adversities come about only in return for sins, God's judgment...is inequitable'[40]—but of course they do not, he means, and so God is by no means unjust. Other readers may of course find Thomas's reading too bland, and may discern

---

34. *Expositio*, 1.6.233 (= Damico and Yaffe, *Aquinas...Job*, p. 76).
35. *Expositio*, Prologue, 57 (= Damico and Yaffe, *Aquinas...Job*, p. 68).
36. *Expositio*, 1.1.6-8 (= Damico and Yaffe, *Aquinas...Job*, p. 71).
37. *Expositio*, 38.1.10-13 (= Damico and Yaffe, *Aquinas...Job*, p. 415).
38. *Expositio*, 42.1.1-5 (= Damico and Yaffe, *Aquinas...Job*, pp. 469-70).
39. *Expositio*, 3.4.98-99 (= Damico and Yaffe, *Aquinas...Job*, p. 101).
40. *Expositio*, 19.6.45-48 (= Damico and Yaffe, *Aquinas...Job*, p. 264).

a much sharper conflict within Job's own spiritual experience; Job, they may well feel, both believes, on the one hand, that adversities do only come about in return for sins and that God's judgment is inequitable, and on the other, maintains that he is a pious man nevertheless.

2. *The Spirituality of the Late Middle Ages*

The exegetical tradition that is exemplified by Gregory and Thomas and that was inherited by the Reformers is not the whole background to their readings of the figure of Job. Inasmuch as Job was for them a model of Christian spirituality, their construction of the figure of Job has also to be set against prevailing themes in late mediaeval piety in order to be best appreciated. In some respects, of course, their Job marks out new ground in a depiction of Christian holiness, but in others they are conforming their Job to the expectations of a Christian society with its own long history of spirituality. The old conundrum about the Reformation's periodization, whether it belongs best with the mediaeval period or with the modern,[41] though it is generally thought to have been satisfactorily disposed of in favour of linking together Reformation, Renaissance and Enlightenment, comes back into play when we consider the Reformers' spirituality rather than their academic theology.

Among leading themes in the spirituality of the pre-Reformation period, François Vandenbroucke has identified pessimism, 'satanic fever' and popular piety.[42] There was a far-reaching pessimism, he suggests, about the state of the church, the morals of the clergy and the capacity of the church to meet the needs of the new nationalisms. The gloomiest manifestation of pessimism was to be found in the 'macabre sensibility' of the fifteenth

41.   See Ernst Troeltsch, *Protestantism and Progress: A Historical Study of the Relation of Protestantism to the Modern World* (trans. W. Montgomery; London: Williams & Norgate, 1912). See further, George, *Theology of the Reformers*, pp. 15-16.

42.   In Jean Leclerq, François Vandenbroucke and Louis Bouyer, *The Spirituality of the Middle Ages* (A History of Christian Spirituality, 2; London: Burns & Oates, 1968 [French original, 1961], Part 2, Chapter 9 ('Lay Spirituality from the Fourteenth to the Sixteenth Century'), pp. 481-505.

century[43] that gave rise to numerous treatises on the art of dying and to the literature of the *danses macabres*. By 'satanic fever' he means the powerful fascination of the concept of the devil and his works that gripped the popular imagination from the fifteenth to the seventeenth centuries,[44] and that left a permanent mark in the art of Dürer, Bosch and Brueghel. To the repression of satanism the Inquisition turned its attention, while the treatise *Malleus maleficarum*, 'The Hammer of Witches' (c. 1487), sanctioned the persecution of suspected witches and cast women generally in the role of seductresses and potential agents of the devil. Popular piety gave an outlet for the 'subjective and psychological aspects of the Christian life',[45] which was losing touch with the formal Divine Office and developing instead, in the spirit of the *devotio moderna*, its own prayerbooks (*preces devotae*) and Books of Hours. The cult of the Virgin, the rosary and the angelus, together with the rise of charismatic preachers addressing the consciences of their listeners, contributed to what Vandenbroucke calls the 'individualistic tendency' in spirituality.[46] Finally, he finds prominent a pietistic notion of the individual's relationship with God, 'an ear for the psychological overtones of the Christian mysteries' experienced as a 'source of lively emotions'.[47]

Such generalizations cannot of course encompass the whole of Christian spirituality of the period and other, detailed, studies indicate that the 'individualistic tendency' Vandenbroucke has isolated was only one strand. A.N. Galpern, for example, has graphically illustrated, admittedly for one small segment of the Christian world in the sixteenth century, more community-oriented forms of spirituality: the importance of prayer as a social activity, and of commitment to religious solidarity with other Christians in the developing system of confraternities

---

43. Vandenbroucke, *Spirituality*, p. 485.
44. Cf. Heiko Augustinus Oberman, *Masters of the Reformation: The Emergence of a New Intellectual Climate in Europe* (trans. Dennis Martin; Cambridge: Cambridge University Press, 1981), pp. 158-83.
45. Vandenbroucke, *Spirituality*, p. 484.
46. Vandenbroucke, *Spirituality*, p. 497.
47. Vandenbroucke, *Spirituality*, p. 498.

under the aegis of a saint.[48] Marvin B. Becker has similarly anal-ysed for early Renaissance Florence the importance of *caritas* in the sense of civic charity that created hospitals, hospices and orphanages, the role of the confraternities as embodying charity as a collective enterprise, and of a conception of human *dignitas* that did not reside 'in solitary experience or in strategic personal relationships' but in a sense of human solidarity in general.[49]

Against such a background, the present study shows that for both Luther and Calvin the figure of Job models the psychologi-cally oriented, individualistic, pietistic tendencies in their con-temporary spirituality. For both of them, Job is a lone hero of faith, valiantly wrestling with doubt, the devil and uncertainty. It is easy to see how their own psychological proclivities con-tributed to the fashioning of that image, but harder perhaps to admit that it was their tradition, their personalities and the spirit of their age, rather than the text of the book of Job, that deter-mined their configuration of Job. For the biblical Job could just as well have been constructed, for example, as the symbol of human solidarity, as the paterfamilias who gives meaning to his family, as the just magistrate who brings order and security to his society, as the man who himself is formed and sustained by his familial and social relationships, as the representative of human dignity, as the suffering man who is restored not by hav-ing his intellectual problems solved or by experiencing a reli-gious conversion—or even by having his medical condition healed—but by seeing his family renewed and all his acquaint-ances accepting of him. Those were possible constructions of Job in the Reformers' age, but their reading of him did not take up such possibilities.

48.   A.N. Galpern, 'The Legacy of Late Medieval Religion in Sixteenth Century Champagne', in *The Pursuit of Holiness in Late Medieval and Renais-sance Religion* (ed. Charles Trinkaus with Heiko A. Oberman; Studies in Medieval and Renaissance Thought, 10; Leiden: E.J. Brill, 1974), pp. 141-76.

49.   Marvin B. Becker, 'Aspects of Lay Piety in Early Renaissance Florence', in *The Pursuit of Holiness in Late Medieval and Renaissance Religion*, pp. 177-99 (196).

3. *Job in the Spirituality of Luther*

Luther never wrote or lectured systematically on Job, and so his construction of the character of Job has to be gleaned piecemeal from the corpus of his writings.[50] But it is not difficult to discern the main outlines of his view of Job, for there are a few distinctive themes that are constantly recurring. Luther's exegesis in general may well have been, as Jaroslav Pelikan remarks,[51] little more than a product of the exegetical tradition that preceded him, but his Job is different: in many ways Luther's Job is a Luther clone, a model of the Reformer's own self-image.[52]

For Luther, Job is the site of an inner conflict: though he is a saint, he is also a sinner. Sometimes Luther expresses this conflict in objective, externalized language, as when he writes:

> God, who cannot lie, pronounces [Job] a righteous and innocent man in the first chapter (Job 1:8). Yet later on Job confesses in various passages that he is a sinner, especially in the ninth and seventh chapters...(9:20; 7:21). But Job must be speaking the truth, because if he were lying in the presence of God, then God would not pronounce him righteous. Accordingly, Job is both righteous and a sinner (*simul justus, simul peccator*).[53]

But more often Luther is himself identifying with the conflict that Job must feel, caught in this paradox of piety and guilt. How does Job handle this situation?, Luther is asking himself. It is of the utmost importance that Job does not repress the knowledge of the conflict; indeed, his very saintliness consists, in some measure, in his recognition of his own sinfulness and lack of self-worth:

50. See *Luther's Works* (ed. Jaroslav Pelikan; St Louis: Concordia Publishing House, 1957–76), 54 vols. (henceforth abbreviated as *LW*).

51. Jaroslav Pelikan, *Luther's Works*. Companion Volume. *Luther the Expositor: Introduction to the Reformer's Exegetical Writings* (St Louis: Concordia Publishing House, 1959), p. 38.

52. On the spirituality of Luther, see in general A. Skevington Wood, 'Spirit and Spriituality in Luther', *Evangelical Quarterly* 61 (1989), pp. 311-33.

53. On Gal. 2.18 (*LW*, XXVII, pp. 230-31 = WA, II, p. 497). The parallel with Gregory's language, quoted above (cf. note 31) is striking. (The Weimar edition of Luther's works is abbreviated WA from this footnote onward.)

[N]o one blesses the Lord except the one who is displeased with himself and curses himself and to whom alone God is pleasing. So Job cursed the day of his birth (Job 3:1). He who regards himself as anything but completely detestable clearly has praise of himself in his mouth...[W]e never praise God correctly unless we first disparage ourselves.[54]

And he has no confidence in his own merits:

[O]ur total concern must be to magnify and aggravate our sins and thus always to accuse them more and more...The more deeply a person has condemned himself and magnified his sins, the more he is fit for the mercy and grace of God...[W]e should above all and in all things be displeased [with ourselves] and thus with Job fear all our works (Job 9:28).[55]

This last text (Job 9.28) is an especially powerful one for Luther. The Hebrew had read simply 'I fear all my pains', that is, no doubt, in the context, pains yet to come;[56] but the Vulgate has *verebar omnia opera mea*, 'I feared all my works'—which Luther evidently revelled in as an expression of the dangers of works-righteousness, and quoted it over and over again.[57]

Job reflects a deep strain in Luther of self-negation:

54.   On Psalm 34 (*LW*, X, p. 162 = WA, III, p. 191).

55.   On Ps. 69.16 (*LW*, X, p. 368 = WA, III, p. 429).

56.   I have translated 9.27-28 thus: 'If I say, I will forget my moaning, I will lay aside my sadness and be cheerful, I become afraid of all I must suffer, for I know you do not hold me innocent' (*Job 1–20* [Word Biblical Commentary, 17; Dallas: Word Books, 1989], p. 214).

57.   For example: '[O]ut of a contrite and troubled heart...[Abimelech, the Canaanite king of Gerar] is complaining in utmost humility about such a great misfortune. He is one of those who say with Job (23:15): "I took fright at all my deeds"' (on Gen. 20.9 [*LW*, III, p. 348 = WA, XLIII, p. 125]); 'The godly, like Job, fear for all their works. They trust in no righteousness of theirs and consider their sanctity as dung' (on Ps. 1.1; *LW*, XIV, p. 292 = WA, V, pp. 30-31). Gregory found Job's fear to be of what his inner motives for his good works might have been (*Moralia* 9.34.53 [= *Morals*, I, p. 535]). Another text Luther uses against works-righteousness is Job's denial that he has 'kissed his hand' (31.27-28); that would be the act of a 'man who trusts in his own works and glories in a righteousness that does not come from Christ but is produced through his own strength' (on Ps. 2.12 [*LW*, XIV, p. 348 = WA, V, p. 73]).

> Do not permit me to regard anything carnal as pleasing to Thee...
> Thus in Job 3:1f. the flesh is cursed, and Job prays that it may not
> be numbered with his senses, so that the spirit may be saved.[58]

This self-negation goes much deeper than a conventional acknowledgment that no human being is perfect. Luther indeed refers to such statements in the book of Job: 'So Job says [it is Eliphaz and Bildad, actually], "The heavens are unclean in his sight" (Job 15:15) and "the stars are unclean before Him, and the moon does not shine", that is, the saints are not saints before Him (Job 25:5)'.[59] But these are no more than conventional statements of the perfect holiness of God, and Luther's exposition of the self-consciousness of the pious man derives not from such rhetorical generalizations but from the narrative itself. For Luther, Job is not someone who is almost perfect, or one who to some degree falls short of true piety; he is, through and through, a saint—who is at the same time also a sinner:

> [E]veryone can be bewitched by Satan. None of us is so vigorous
> that he can resist Satan...Job was a blameless and upright
> man...But what could he do against the devil when God withdrew
> his hand? Did not that holy man fall horribly?[60]

Job suffers from the vices of his virtue; the conflict within himself is specific to his saintliness:

> [J]ust as sexual desire is powerful in the body of the young man...
> so in the saintly man impatience, grumbling, hate, and blasphemy
> against God are powerful.[61]

Sometimes the inner conflict that Job, as the model of the godly man, endures has external causes—for example, the temptations of the devil:

> [O]ne must be carefully fortified and strengthened against the dis-
> pleasure of the flesh, which fights against faith and the spirit..., as
> that murmuring is described in the examples of two wives: the wife

---

58.   On Ps. 69.27 (*LW*, X, p. 381 = WA, III, p. 439).
59.   On Ps. 51.4 (*LW*, X, p. 239 = WA, III, p. 290).
60.   On Gal. 3.1 (*LW*, XXVI, pp. 193-94 = WA, XL, p. 318).
61.   On Gal. 3.23 (*LW*, XXVI, pp. 340-41 = WA, XL, p. 524).

of Tobias and the wife of Job...These are the flaming darts of the devil with which he tries to overthrow us in order that we may despair and fall away from God.[62]

There is indeed some uncertainty in Luther over the question of the cause of his sufferings. At times, it seems that they are simply to be ascribed directly to the devil—and not to God:

God does not afflict the godly; he permits the devil to do this, as we see in the case of Job, whose children are killed by fire and his cattle by storms, not because God was angry with him, but because Satan was.[63]

But at other times, the devil is no more than an agent of the divine intentions:

The devil at first takes all his property from him with his children and leaves him a peevish, irksome, and abusive wife...[E]xamples of this kind teach us that all the malice and vexation of the devil is only instruction and chastisement, by which we are aroused so that we do not snore and become listless.[64]

The good God permits such small evils to befall us merely in order to arouse us snorers from our deep sleep and to make us recognize, on the other hand, the incomparable and innumerable benefits we still have. He wants us to consider what would happen if he were to withdraw His goodness from us completely. In that spirit Job said (2:10): 'Shall we receive good at the hand of God and shall we not receive evil?'... [H]e did not simply look at the evil, as we would-be saints do; he kept in sight the goodness and grace of the Lord. With this he comforted himself and overcame evil with patience.[65]

62. On Gen. 28.10-11 (*LW*, V, p. 203 = WA, XLIII, p. 568). Elsewhere, however, Job's wife, like Isaac's wife Rebekah, is a saintly woman, though 'not without trials' (on Gen. 26.1; *LW*, V, p. 14 = WA, XLIII, p. 438). Similarly *LW*, V, p. 30 = WA, XLIII, p. 449 on Gen. 26.8. On the ambivalence of Luther's attitude to women, see Jonathan W. Zophy, 'We Must Have the Dear Ladies: Martin Luther and Women', in *Pietas et Societas: New Trends in Reformation Social History: Essays in Memory of Harold J. Grimm* (ed. Kyle C. Sessions and Phillip N. Bebb; Kirksville, MO: Sixteenth Century Journal Publishers, 1985), pp. 41-50.

63. On Gen. 19.10-11 (*LW*, III, p. 264 = WA, LXIII, p. 64).

64. On Gen. 32.3-5 (*LW*, VI, p. 95 = WA, XLIV, p. 70). For Job's sufferings as a trial by God pure and simple, see also *LW*, X, p. 159 (= WA, III, p. 189).

65. On Ps. 118.1 (*LW*, XIV, pp. 49-50 = WA, XXXI, p. 74).

The same adversity can then function both as an instance of satanic temptation to despair and loss of faith and as an example of divine testing:

> Sometimes God sends punishments, not because he finds in the man a sin that deserves such a punishment but because he wants to test his faith and patience. Job did not deserve such punishments...
> It tends to instruct and comfort us when we learn that God often causes even the innocent to experience the most serious misfortunes and punishments, merely in order to test them.[66]

But most often, in Luther's expositions, it is the devil with whom Job has to do—and, in so saying, we cannot help but observe how Luther is addressing a fundamental concern of the spirituality of his own time. Luther's Job is at his most Luther-like when he experiences the assaults of the devil. Every protestation he makes against his trials is the language of the man of faith confronted by satanic persecution. What is more, the book of Job constitutes for Luther an unparalleled sourcebook for language about the devil, being pictured as Behemoth in ch. 40 and as Leviathan in ch. 41.[67] Luther turned to the book of Job more often to read about the devil than about any other topic, it seems: one quarter of his citations from Job in the first volume of his First Lectures on the Psalms, for example, are to these chapters. Here Luther reads that

> [T]he devil ridicules the preachers of the Word, as it is written in Job 41:20 [Vulgate, *Quasi stipulam aestimabit malleum, et deridebit vibrantem hastam*, 'He will think a hammer a reed, and will mock at him who shakes the spear']. But if you take sword in hand, he will see that the matter is serious.[68]

---

66. On Gen. 12.18-19 (*LW*, II, p. 319 = WA, XLII, p. 490).

67. Aquinas had indeed seen in these chapters a description of the devil by analogy with Behemoth and Leviathan, but his primary interest was in the identification of them with the elephant and the whale, quoting Aristotle, Albertus Magnus, Pliny and Isidore on their natural history (*Expositio*, 40.10.221–41.25.457 [= Damico and Yaffe, *Aquinas...Job*, pp. 447-68]; Luther has no interest in anything but their symbolic values.

68. On Ps. 40.2 (*LW*, X, p. 189 = WA, III, p. 228).

'He [namely the devil or a stubborn Jew] will ridicule him who shakes the spear' [Job 41.20], that is, the threatening Word of God.[69]

Job embodies all the virtues of the pious person. His reaction to adversity is exemplary: 'Hope is easier in good times but more difficult in bad times. Therefore only a saint always hopes, always blesses, like Job.'[70] His suffering results from his identification with the sufferings of Christ, for which, incidentally, he is scorned by the Jews. The Christians are the

> wounded of Christ...because they carry His cross. Tropologically, they have been wounded by the word of the Gospel and smitten by the Lord (as their head) according to the flesh. For they mortify themselves, they chastise and afflict themselves perpetually...The Jews, however, not only had no pity on such as were in this way the afflicted, humbled and wounded of Christ...but they persecuted them in addition, adding furthermore that God was persecuting them. So Job says: 'Have pity on me, at least you, my friends, because the hand of the Lord has touched me. Why do you, like God, persecute me...?' (Job 19:21-22).[71]

Job's piety is not simply that of the person who is justified by faith without works. For Job is an exemplar of the doer of good deeds. And 'those who are Jobs, that is, truly good and active people, who busy themselves with good works, are wiser than the devil. For works bear a true witness of the presence of the Holy Spirit.'[72] The prince of Tyre, who is the devil, may be wiser than Daniel (Ezek. 28.3), and he certainly 'knows all mysteries... and he is more brilliant than we'.[73] But he is not more wise than Job; for Job's wisdom consists in his good works.

And because Job is a saint, even expressions of his that we might regard as world-weary or bitter become models for the pious life. Thus Job's 'empty months' and 'wearisome nights', of which he complains in 7.3, are entirely appropriate for the pious man, for his days have not been fulfilling the lusts of the flesh and his nights have been wearisome because 'they have been

---

69. On Ps. 35.2 (*LW*, X, p. 165 = WA, III, p. 195). The reference is to Leviathan.
70. On Ps. 71.14 (*LW*, X, p. 398 = WA, III, p. 455).
71. On Ps. 69.26 (*LW*, X, p. 380 = WA, III, p. 437).
72. On Ps. 68.35 (*LW*, X, p. 348 = WA, III, p. 408).
73. On Ps. 68.35 (*LW*, X, p. 347 = WA, III, p. 408).

occupied with the exercise of the spirit'.[74] Even Job's wish to be dead is, spiritually speaking, a yearning only to be free of earthly constraints. So when he says, 'My soul chooses hanging' (7.15), he is crying out for 'evangelical teaching' which 'does not rest on the earth or on human wisdom, but it arches overhead and takes every understanding captive to the obedience of Christ (2 Cor. 10:5)'.[75] 'Hanging' in fact means being lifted up from the earth and not resting on earthly things, that is to say, 'hanging' is the spiritual language for 'faith in Christ and contempt for visible things'.[76]

For Luther, then, Job is nothing other than a representative believer, justified in the sight of God while still conscious of his own ineradicable sinfulness, perpetually subject to onslaughts of the devil that nevertheless in some way serve the purposes of God, and prey to temptations of impatience and self-righteousness. As the site of inner conflict, Job models Luther's own experience of tension and paradox.

4. *Job in the Spirituality of Calvin*

Calvin has left a very much more considerable legacy of writing on Job than has Luther, namely his 159 sermons on Job preached in Geneva in 1554–1555,[77] and now to be found in their original French in the corpus of his works.[78] Only a selection has

---

74. On Ps. 73.10 (*LW*, X, pp. 426-27 = WA, III, pp. 484-85).

75. On Ps. 42.7 (*LW*, X, pp. 201-202 = WA III, p. 240). This is the exegesis of Gregory, as has been noted above (note 16).

76. On Ps. 36.5 (*LW*, X, p. 170 = WA, III, p. 201).

77. For a vivid account of the transformation of the oral sermons into print, see T.H.L. Parker, *Calvin's Old Testament Commentaries* (Edinburgh: T. & T. Clark, 1986), pp. 9-12. The earliest publication of the sermons on Job was entitled *Sermons de M. Jean Calvin sur le livre de Job, recueillis fidelement de sa bouche selon qu'il les preschoit* (Geneva, 1563). See, on this edition, T.D. Smid, 'Some Bibliographical Observations on Calvin's Sermons sur le livre de Job', *Free University Quarterly* 7 (1960–61), pp. 51-56.

78. *Joannis Calvini opera quae supersunt omnia* (Corpus reformatorum, 61-63; ed. G. Baum, E. Cunitz and E. Reuss; Braunschweig: C.A. Schwetschke, 1887), XXXIII-XXXV (abbreviated below as *CO*; the translations are my own). On Calvin as an Old Testament commentator, see Parker, *Calvin's Old Testament Commentaries*; John Walchenbach, *John Calvin as Biblical Com-*

ever been translated into English.[79]

The difference in the personality—and so, to a large degree, in the spirituality—of Luther and Calvin is well illustrated in a pair of quotations Suzanne Selinger has illuminatingly set side by side.[80] Luther: 'It is by living—no, rather, by dying and being damned—that a theologian is made, not by understanding, reading, or speculating'.[81] Calvin: 'I count myself one of the number of those who write as they learn and learn as they write'.[82]

If for Luther the man Job is the site of conflict between Satan and God, between self-disgust and a consciousness of innocence, for Calvin Job seems rather to exemplify humanity in its 'perceptual agony', to use Susan Schreiner's term, its incapacity to fathom the workings of providence and the pattern in human affairs.

> Central to [Calvin's] exegesis is the recognition of the noetic or perceptual limitations of the human mind trapped in the disorder of human history. Calvin's constant concern with the failure of the mind to know God, which dominates the first book of the *Institutes*, permeates his sermons on Job. Confronted with the disorder of

mentator: An Investigation into Calvin's Use of J. Chrysostom as an Exegetical Tutor (PhD Pittsburgh, 1974); Anthony G. Baxter, *John Calvin's Use and Hermeneutics of the Old Testament* (PhD Sheffield, 1987); J. Haroutunian, 'Calvin as Biblical Commentator', in *Calvin: Commentaries* (Library of Christian Classics, 23; trans. and ed. J. Haroutunian; London: SCM Press, 1958), pp. 15-50; Hans-Joachim Kraus, 'Calvin's Exegetical Principles', *Interpretation* 31 (1977), pp. 8-18.

79.   But I have been unable to trace the volume edited by Leroy Nixon and entitled *Sermons from Job* (1952). Nor have I seen the volume, *Sermons upon the booke of Job, translated out of French* (trans. A. Golding; London, 1584), and so cannot tell if it was a complete translation.

80.   Suzanne Selinger, *Calvin against Himself: An Inquiry in Intellectual History* (Hamden, CT: Archon Books, 1984), p. 16. Cf. George, *Theology of the Reformers*, p. 204: 'If Luther was preoccupied with the anxiety of guilt... Calvin was haunted by the specter of the apparently haphazard and meaningless course of existence'.

81.   WA, V, p. 163.

82.   John Calvin, *Institutes of the Christian Religion* (Library of Christian Classics, 20; ed. John T. McNeill and trans. Ford Lewis Battles; Philadelphia: Westminster Press, 1960), p. 5. Calvin is citing Augustine, as it happens (*Letters* 143.2 [= PL, XXXIII, p. 585]).

history, the mind's eye squints and strains to see divine justice but cannot penetrate or transcend the present confusion which hides providence from its limited and fallen view. Calvin finds the heuristic key to the book of Job in 1 Corinthians 13:12 ['Now we see in a mirror, dimly']. He repeatedly cites this verse to describe the difficulty of perceiving providence in the midst of history...Caught within the turmoil of earthly events, the believer now sees God's providence only as through a mirror dimly...[83]

For the spirituality of Calvin,[84] then, Job represents the believer's recognition of incapacity to comprehend the divine. The crisis of Calvin's Job is an intellectual crisis; experientially, the crisis is known as a sense of confusion and as a commitment to living in a state of uncertainty, with only a hope, and not an assurance, that the uncertainty will some day be dispelled. Knowing that God has his purposes, though they have not been disclosed, may prevent the experience being one of complete *anomie*. But the experience itself is of the provisionality of human existence, and of the recognition that humans are not in control of their universe. The crisis of knowing is a theme announced early in the *Sermons*:

> [Job] knows that God does not always afflict men according to the measure of their sins, but that he has his secret judgments, of which he gives no account to us, and, nevertheless, that we must wait until he reveals to us why he does this or that.[85]

True knowledge of God for Calvin is not simply an intellectual virtue; it is of the essence of piety itself:

> [W]hoever have been endowed with this [true] piety dare not fashion out of their own rashness any God for themselves. Rather, they seek from Him the knowledge of the true God, and conceive Him just as He shows and declares Himself to be.[86]

83. Schreiner, '"Through a Mirror Dimly"', p. 179.

84. See especially Ford Lewis Battles (translator and editor), *The Piety of John Calvin: An Anthology Illustrative of the Spirituality of the Reformer* (Grand Rapids: Baker Book House, 1978), especially 'Introduction: True Piety according to Calvin', pp. 13-26, and 'Calvin on the Christian Life', pp. 51-89. See also Ronald S. Wallace, *Calvin's Doctrine of the Christian Life* (Edinburgh: Oliver & Boyd, 1959), and Richard, *The Spirituality of John Calvin*, esp. pp. 116-29 ('*Pietas* as the Essential Expression of Calvin's Spirituality').

85. On Job 1.1 (*CO*, XXXIII, p. 23).

86. John Calvin, *First Catechism* (ed. Ford Lewis Battles; Pittsburgh:

There is another conflict also in the person of Job: it is between the 'good cause' and the 'bad consequences'.[87] For Calvin, Job is essentially in the right; he does not deserve what is happening to him:

> Here is a cause that is good and true, though it is badly handled (*deduite*), for Job here loses his temper (*se iette ici hors des gonds*, lit. here throws himself off his hinges) and employs such excessive and terrible speeches that he shows himself in many places to be a man in despair. He even becomes so excited (*s'eschauffe*) that he seems to be wishing to resist God. So this a good cause that is badly handled (*conduite*).[88]

The friends, on the other hand, are in the wrong about the reasons for Job's suffering, and so they have a 'bad cause', even though they speak in fine and holy sentences and 'there is nothing in their speeches that we may not receive as if the Holy Spirit had spoken it'.[89] Job is in the right, but his experience of righteousness is of an unsettling and anxiety-inducing state of being. His experience is thus a revealing expression of Calvin's own personal spirituality.

Job furthermore represents the tension between pious convictions and human weakness. For Calvin, the Old Testament in general serves as a mirror of Christian life and experience, and Job in particular mirrors 'how (good) men often act under severe trials. He desires to obey God but his emotions and sufferings get the better of him...Job, under Calvin's hand, becomes a mirror of our own weakness.'[90] When he curses the day of his birth, Calvin writes,

Pittsburgh Theological Seminary, 1972), p. 2; cf. Richard, *The Spirituality of John Calvin*, p. 119: 'The whole notion of *pietas* is dominated by the reality of the knowledge of God'.

87.   Cf. David F. Wright's characterization of Calvin's key distinction between 'laudable ends and reprehensible means' ('The Ethical Use of the Old Testament in Luther and Calvin: A Comparison', *Scottish Journal of Theology* 36 [1983], pp. 463-85 [466]).

88.   On Job 1.1 (*CO*, XXXIII, p. 23). Similar language is used on Job 32.1 (*CO*, XXXV, p. 7).

89.   On Job 1.1 (*CO*, XXXIII, p. 23).

90.   Baxter, *Calvin's Use and Hermeneutics*, p. 42. On the image of the 'mirror', see Heinrich Bornkamm, *Luther and the Old Testament* (trans. Eric W. and Ruth C. Gritsch; Philadelphia: Fortress Press, 1969). See also

> There is a conflict here, in which on one side the weakness of the
> man is revealed, and on the other we see that he still has some
> strength to resist temptation... Job has no longer the same
> complete perfection as before... he has wished to obey God; but
> nevertheless he has not accomplished the good that he desired.[91]

Nevertheless, Job is also for Calvin, as for his exegetical predecessors *en masse*, the embodiment of piety, and not simply the
believer under stress. Not surprisingly, therefore, we find in the
Sermons some very conventional moral exhortations being drawn
from the character of Job. For example, on Job 1.2:

> We see here the praises that the Holy Spirit gives Job, not so much
> for his own sake as for our instruction, so that we may know how
> we are to govern our lives, that is, that we should walk in frankness
> (*rondeur*) of heart, that there should be no falseness (*fiction*) in us,
> but that our lives should give testimony of such simplicity.[92]

Or, on the wealth of Job reported in 1.3:

> We see the character of Job's virtue in that riches have not blinded
> him with pride, and have not made him too much attached to the
> world or led him to abandon the service of God... By his example
> the rich of this world are admonished in their duty.[93]

Likewise, anger at suffering is bad: it shows lack of gratitude for
God's mercies.[94] Praying for your enemies is good, as Job did in
ch. 42.[95] And so on.

But the virtue of Job that strikes one most forcibly in Calvin is
his obedience and acceptance of the divine will:

> The history written here shows us how we are in the hands of God,
> and that it is for him to order our life, and to dispose of it according
> to his good pleasure, and that our duty is to make ourselves subject
> to him in all humility and obedience; that it is right that we are
> entirely his, whether to live or to die; and that, even when it

Schreiner on the contrast with the concept of nature as a mirror of the providence and control of God ('Calvin's Sermons on Job', esp. pp. 181-89).

91.   On Job 3.1-10 (*CO*, XXXIII, pp. 140, 142).
92.   On Job 1.2 (*CO*, XXXIII, p. 33).
93.   On Job 1.2 (*CO*, XXXIII, p. 34).
94.   On Job 29.1-7 (*CO*, XXXIV, p. 534): 'We are ungrateful to God, if the
memory of his benefits does not soften all our angers (*fascheries*), when it
pleases him to exercise us and to humble us'.
95.   On Job 42.10 (*CO*, XXXV, p. 507).

pleases him to lift his hand against us, even when we do not understand for what reason he does so, nevertheless we should glorify him always, confessing that he is just and fair; and that we should not murmur against him, that we should not enter into dispute with him, knowing that we would always be overcome in any contest with him.[96]

Whether we like it or not, this is the expression, if not the encapsulation, of a comprehensive spirituality on Calvin's part; it is the spirituality of obedience, an obedience that is both mindless ('even when we do not understand') and prudential ('knowing that we would always be overcome'). It by no means does justice to the subtlety and intellectual force of Calvin's thought—nor to his humanity—and will seem to many nothing but naked 'Calvinism' of the least agreeable kind. The worry is that this is what the grand scope of the *Institutes* and the sweep of the Commentaries all boil down to; when the question becomes one of spirituality—no longer 'What shall I believe?' but 'How shall I live, as a believer?'—the book of Job appears, in Calvin's hands, to lead to nothing more inspiriting than recommendation to a quietism that does not doubt or struggle.

5. *Conclusion*

It is nothing surprising, and no criticism of the interpreters of Job, that they have made him to some degree or other in their own image. While characters in literature are inevitably paper-thin when compared even with the dullest of real-life humans, a characterization like that of Job has a huge potential for readers of different centuries to discern divergent and distinctive elements. The question that in most cases needs to be addressed to interpreters of the past, as well as to those of our own age, is not so much whether they have mistaken or misread their text, but how far their own creative engagement with the text has ignored or marginalized other elements or other readers.

So the question I would address to the Reformers and their

---

96. On Job 1.1 (*CO*, XXXIII, p. 21). God, after all, is a patriarch: he 'knows what is proper for each one, and we should be willing to receive whatever portion he pleases to allot to us, just as a *paterfamilias* knows well what is useful for his household' (on Job 42.12 [*CO*, XXXV, p. 510]).

forebears is not whether their depiction of Job as a pious man or
as the site of spiritual conflict is in order, but what dimensions of
the book are being ignored by the inherited framework within
which they read the book. I identify two primary arenas in
which a reader of today might take issue with them.

a. The first is the way in which the speeches of the friends are
treated. The tendency, not only among the Reformers, but generally in the history of exegesis, has been to disregard the radical
conflict between Job and the friends. True, the 'friends' are
always seen as hostile to Job and as contributory to his suffering,
as Thomas says; and Gregory finds in them a figure of the
heretics, who 'mix good and evil'.[97] But their arguments and
aphorisms are regularly treated as if they were on the same level
of authority (religious or literary) as the speeches of Job or the
depictions of the narrator; and the book as a whole—not just the
speeches of Job or of God—is regarded as a repository of wisdom. Luther, for example, not infrequently quotes sentences of
the friends as sayings of Job.[98] The commentators occasionally
show an awareness of how odd their own approach is, treating
as wisdom both Job's words and his opponents' words; but Gregory, for example, argues that since Paul quotes Eliphaz[99] 'some
things contained in their sayings were right', and 'many things
that they say are admirable, were they not spoken against the
afflicted condition of the holy man'.[100] Calvin, as we have seen,
has recourse to the distinction between their 'bad cause' and
their 'fine and holy sentences'—a doubtful one, for though 'fine'
sentences may be used in a 'bad cause', could 'holy' ones be so
used and still remain 'holy'?[101]

As against the praxis of the Reformed commentators, however,
I would argue that the dynamics of the book require us to do
more than read each sentence atomistically. For the book itself
offers us several totalizing perspectives, and from each of them
the friends' positions are in the wrong. If it is Job's perspective
that we adopt, the friends' speeches are entirely misconceived. If

97. *Moralia* 5.11.28 (= *Morals*, I, p. 262).
98. See, for example, note 59 above.
99. 1 Cor. 3.19, citing Job 5.13.
100. *Moralia* 5.11.27 (= *Morals*, I, p. 261).
101. See note 89 above.

it is the Lord's perspective in the final chapter that we adopt, the unambiguous judgment upon the friends' arguments is that they 'have not spoken of me what is right' (42.7).[102] And if it is the narrator's perspective that we adopt, then everyone is in the wrong, for Job as much as the friends has been labouring under the illusion that his sufferings must have something to do with his sinfulness, real or alleged—whereas the prologue to the book has made it clear that it is solely for his piety, and not for any wrongdoing, that Job is suffering.

In short, the narrative of the book represents the friends as Job's enemies and wrongful accusers; but the Reformers, like most traditional commentators, were unable to jettison the speeches of the friends—as the narrative logic demands—because they found too much congenial and conventional 'wisdom' in them.

b. It has proved exceedingly hard for exegetes to take the ending of the book and therewith Job's restoration to wealth and influence, seriously—principally, I suppose, because the ending so evidently seems to undermine the thrust of all that precedes. According to the first 41 chapters, that is to say, wealth and poverty have nothing to do with innocence and piety, and according to ch. 42 they have.[103] In other words, in the bulk of the book the rich man, who is also the empoverished man, is consistently righteous; his wealth neither brings about nor sabotages his piety. And that has been the very point that the narrative has been set up to solve: the original question that set the whole story in train was, 'Does Job serve God for nothing?' (1.9). And yet in the last chapter his restored wealth is evidently a reward for his piety, and the result of his maintaining his integrity.

102. Gregory's explanation, that the following words, 'as my servant Job has spoken', prove that some things they said were right but 'they are overcome by comparison with one who was better', will not convince (*Moralia* 5.11.27 [= *Morals*, I, p. 261]).

103. On the 'deconstruction' of the book by its last chapter, cf. my essay, 'Deconstructing the Book of Job', in *What Does Eve Do to Help? and Other Readerly Questions to the Old Testament* (Journal for the Study of the Old Testament Supplement Series, 94; Sheffield: JSOT Press, 1990), pp. 106-23 (previously published in *The Bible as Rhetoric: Studies in Biblical Persuasion and Credibility* [ed. Martin Warner; Warwick Studies in Philosophy and Literature; London: Routledge, 1990], pp. 65-80).

Luther, not having written a commentary on Job, is under no obligation to deal with the ending of the book, and it is not surprising that he completely ignores it. Calvin, on the other hand, preaching his way systematically through the book, is under some compulsion to treat it—and treat it in conformity with his theology and his spirituality. His intention, it must be said, seems to be to deflect the implication of the final chapter—which can only be that suffering saints may expect to regain their wealth or health—by claiming (though not from the text) that the doubling of Job's goods does not always happen to saints, 'for God does not treat us with an equal measure; he knows what is proper to each one'.[104] And as for 'temporal blessings', says Calvin, by all means let us seize them if God sends them, but let us recognize that the main thing, and the real profit, is that we have been delivered and our faith has been strengthened.[105] Furthermore, he argues, material prosperity was the only way God could reward a saint of Old Testament times, for 'then there was no such revelation of the heavenly life as there is today in the Gospel'.[106] Job may have lived a long life, but longevity is a mixed blessing since there are many unbelievers who live long, and in any case the shorter life span today is more than compensated for by the afterlife that New Testament believers, unlike Job, have to look forward to. And what is more, God had to prolong the life of the ancients in order to give them more opportunity to experience his goodness; for us, three days in this world would be enough to experience the goodness of God.[107]

The very multiplicity of Calvin's arguments warns us that something is amiss. He needs to convince himself that the text does not carry the implications it seems to. It is especially revealing that throughout the *Sermons*, so long as Job has been suffering, he has been 'we'; the moment he is prosperous again he is not 'we'. Of his restoration Calvin says calmly, *Cela donc ne se verra tousiours*, 'But that will not always happen'.[108] There is

104. On Job 42.12 (*CO*, XXXV, p. 510).

105. On Job 42.12 (*CO*, XXXV, pp. 510-11).

106. On Job 42.15 (*CO*, XXXV, p. 512).

107. On Job 42.16-17 (*CO*, XXXV, pp. 512-13).

108. On Job 42.10 (*CO*, XXXV, p. 510). There may be a parallel to the exegetical move of Calvin that William McKane has commented upon, that

something a little disingenuous here. And the issue is by no means a marginal one. For if Job in his restoration is not the image and model of the saint, by what reckoning is the suffering and maltreated Job a mirror of Christian spirituality? To view the Job of conflict as the model of Christian spirituality, but not the Job of success, is perhaps to cast spirituality in too negative a mode—or perhaps even to call into question the validity of the whole idea of Job as a model.

There are loose ends in the Reformers' readings of Job, loose ends perhaps that threaten to trip them up quite disastrously. But that is not the sum and substance of their engagement with the figure of Job, nor even its end result. Creatures of their time, and creating a Job in their own image, the Reformers nevertheless honoured the biblical Job by pressing him into the service of their own distinctive spirituality.

'Calvin has a general principle of interpretation that the content of weal or bliss in these [Davidic and Messianic] oracles can never be satisfied by referring them to historical kings of David's line or to any this-worldly polity' ('Calvin as an Old Testament Commentator', *Nederduitse Gereformeerde Theologiese Tydskrif* 25 [1984], pp. 250-59; I am grateful to Professor McKane for letting me have a copy of his paper).

8

A World Established on Water (Psalm 24)
Reader-Response, Deconstruction and Bespoke Interpretation[*]

Let's talk of readers' response. Or, since I am doing the talking, let me talk of *this* reader's response.

There are things about this fine and famous psalm a reader like me cannot swallow. There is, for instance, the idea of the world being founded upon seas and rivers. The poet, for his part, actually believes (does he not?) that underneath the rocks and dirt of the earth's surface there is an underworld sea, fed by rivers, upon which the world floats. And I do not believe that. Or rather, to put it more strongly but more exactly, I *know* that that view is wrong.

But this is not the only point on which I cannot buy the ideology of the psalm. For me, this cosmological misapprehension is only the outcropping of a larger seismic fault that runs hidden beneath the whole surface of the psalm.

I will be arguing that the psalm is riddled with religious ideas as unacceptable as its cosmology, and further, that it is not even internally coherent. At the end I will suggest an answer to the question of what is to be done with a piece of sacred literature that is so ideologically and religiously alien today even to a person of goodwill toward it (like myself), and that speaks with so uncertain a voice. I will, in other words, deploy three strategies: an ideologically slanted reader-response criticism, a deconstructionist critique, and a new proposal for a goal-oriented

[*]   An earlier version of this essay was published in *The New Literary Criticism and the Hebrew Bible* (ed. J. Cheryl Exum and David J.A. Clines; Journal for the Study of the Old Testament Supplement Series, 143; Sheffield: JSOT Press, 1993), pp. 79-90. The essay was originally delivered as a paper in the Rhetorical Criticism Section, Society of Biblical Literature, Annual Meeting, New Orleans, November, 1990.

hermeneutic, which I call 'bespoke' or 'customized' interpretation.

1. *A Reader-Response Criticism*

Let me first speak of the reader that I am. Toward the poem as a whole I find myself ambivalent. All my life I have found the poem powerful and uplifting. This is partly due to the background music I inevitably hear when I read the poem, the singing of it by the Scottish Male Voice Choir, all the vogue in my religious neck of the woods in the fifties. But there is also something grand and elevated about its tone that attracts me—at least, that attracts a romantic and soulful part of me.

I also recognize and accept that the poem has been, and still is, a vehicle for worship in Jewish and Christian communities for two and a half millennia or more; and however unlovely those communities may have been, I have no urge to sniff at their religious experience. In short, I want to be able to say something positive about this poem.

The other side of it is that the poem is built upon two ideologies that I deplore: the first a notion that 'holiness' attaches to places, the second an idea of victory in war as glorious.

a. *Holiness*

According to the poem, only those who live blameless lives are entitled to enter the temple of the Lord—it is those who have clean hands and a pure heart who 'shall', or 'should', ascend the hill of the Lord and stand in his holy place (vv. 3-4).[1] No doubt there is a sense of fit here, an idea that pure people and things belong in holy places, and that outside the temple, *pro fano*, is the place for the profane. But there is equally plainly a sense that the holiness which exists in the 'holy place' is in need of protection from the impure, that it is open to contamination by unholiness.[2]

---

1.   Is this a prediction of who in fact *shall* enter the holy place, or who it is who is *entitled* to enter it?

2.   Holiness is 'defined on the one hand as that which is consistent with God and his character, and on the other as that which is threatened with impurity' (David P. Wright, 'Holiness (OT)', in *The Anchor Bible Dictionary* (ed. David Noel Freedman; New York: Doubleday, 1992), III, pp. 237-49 (237).

In such an account, holiness is being understood both in a religious-cultic and in an ethical sense: holy places clearly cannot be holy in an ethical sense, but are holy only because they have been marked out as such by a divine signal.[3] Humans, on the other hand, need to match the holiness of the holy place by the kind of holiness that they can acquire, which is ethical purity (and not, of course, a religious-cultic designation, unless they happen to be priests). In the language of the poem, the place is 'holy' and the entrants to it are 'clean'. Ethical 'uncleanness' is unsuitable for a 'holy' place.

My question to myself, as a reader checking all the time on my responses to texts, is: Can I tolerate a notion of holiness that sees it as contaminatable? If the world contains relatively small pockets of holiness, like a hill of the Lord or a temple, surrounded by vast areas of unholiness, like (presumably) everywhere else, and if the unholy has the power to contaminate the holy but the holy does not have the power to infect the unholy, what future, I ask myself, is there for the holy? The holy is rather under threat, is it not, if it has to be protected from the unholy by the exclusion of unrighteous people from visiting the sanctuary. For if impure people are supposed to be kept out of the shrine, or keep themselves out, in order to protect its holiness, what happens if impure people are inadvertently allowed in? Does the holy thereby become unholy?

In a word, Is the holy to be at the mercy of doorkeepers? Would it not be better, I say to myself, to think of holiness, as a symbol of the divine, as incapable of being damaged by humans? If it is worth the name of holy, must it not in any case be more powerful than its opposite, whatever *its* name? Why not

---

3.   'We cannot make shrines and cannot select their "positions", but can never do more than merely find them' (G. van der Leeuw, *Religion in Essence and Manifestation* [trans. G.E. Taylor; New York: Harper & Row, 1963], p. 398). Typically the holy place in Israelite religion is 'the place that Yahweh your God shall choose to put his name there' (Deut. 12.5), that is, the place of theophany. And Israel is to 'take care' that it does not choose its own holy places (Deut. 12.13). Cf. also my paper, 'Sacred Space, Holy Places and Suchlike', in *Trinity Occasional Papers: Essays Presented in Honour of Revd Professors Hans Spykeboer and Bruce Upham* 12/2 (November, 1993), pp. 19-30.

think of the divine presence as a powerful purifying influence that can quite easily cope with sinners and can in some way annihilate their impurity? A temple, then, if it is to be conceived of as a dwelling of the divine presence, would be a place where the unrighteous were confronted by the contrast between their badness and divine goodness, and thus it would function as a locus of ethical transformation. Holiness would be viewed, not defensively as it is here, as a substance in need of protection, but as a force for positive change in the community.

But if I 'buy' the psalm, I 'buy' its ideology of holiness, and I had better be aware of what I am doing.

b. *War*
The second ideology sustaining this poem which I find myself unable to accept is of the glory of war, or rather, of victory in war. It is not that the humans are warlike, but that the deity himself is. This only makes it worse, from my ethical perspective at least.

It comes, in fact, as something of a shock to the first-time reader of the poem (or, shall we say, to the curious and close reader) that it moves in that direction. For in its first strophe the poem has breathed a pacific air of stability and constructiveness. At its beginning, what is reported is a creative act of 'founding' and 'establishing' that has overridden any cosmic tendency to instability, and there is not a hint of conflict in the world order that results. And in the second strophe, there are no real villains nor any sign of organized opposition to the forces of good that needs to be put down by force. It is in this context of world stability and personal goodness that we encounter what is the principal truth, for this poem, about the God who dwells on the holy hill and whose face the generation of the righteous are seeking. This God is celebrated, not for his creative powers (strophe 1) nor as the fount of human goodness (strophe 2), but because he is 'mighty in battle' (v. 8) and 'Yahweh of armies' (v. 10). What makes him 'glorious' is that he is 'strong and mighty' enough to achieve military victories. There is no glory, in this poem, in creating the world, there is no glory in being the object of worship by clean-living toilers up the steep ascent of Zion. The glory that gains him the right of access through the ancient gates is his glory gained on the field of battle.

Now, as we all know, glory and honour in war is nothing other than victory. The victors always retire in honour, the defeated in disgrace. But what makes victory, and what makes defeat? Not the rightness of the cause, not the gallantry of the combatants, not the prayers of the faithful. Victories are won by superior numbers, by alliances, by tactics, and by chance. And a victor deserves praise for nothing other than winning. This is not my idea of glory, and the fact that someone says military prowess is what makes God glorious does not impress me.

We had better know what we are doing. In subscribing to Psalm 24, we are writing a blank cheque for war, for the validity of war imagery to describe the deity's activities, and for the unexamined assumption that war solves problems. If I 'buy' the psalm, I 'buy' its ideology of war.

So, a reader-response approach to this psalm highlights elements in it, quite fundamental elements, that raise uncertainties, if not hostilities, in the mind of the modern reader, this one at least. These have proved to be uncertainties about whether *we* can affirm what it is the psalm seems to be affirming.

2. *A Deconstructive Critique*

The problems with this psalm are greater than those, however. We next must consider, not whether *we* can affirm the psalm, but, whether the *psalm itself* affirms what it affirms. Are there aspects in which it is at odds with itself, perhaps even to the extent of undermining what it is professing? Does it deconstruct itself at all?

Yes, in these four respects.

1. *Although the whole world belongs to the Lord (v. 1), it is not all 'holy'.*
Now according to the cultural conventions in which our text participates, the 'holy' is generally defined as what belongs to the deity. In the Hebrew Bible, a temple, heaven and priests are 'holy' because of their attachment to the deity. It follows that if the whole earth is 'the Lord's', the whole earth is 'holy'.

This view affirmed by the poem in its opening lines is subsequently undermined by the reference to the 'holy place' belonging to the Lord, presumably upon the 'hill of the Lord' (v. 3). If all the world belongs to the Lord, in what sense can *one hill* 'belong' to the Lord? And if all the world is holy by virtue of his possession of it, in what sense can *one* place be 'holy'?

I conclude that while the poem wants to maintain that the world as a whole is undifferentiatedly the Lord's possession, it cannot sustain this view, but allows v. 3 to deconstruct v. 1.

2. *Although all those who live on the earth 'belong' to the Lord (v. 1), some of them must be his enemies.*

Again, the two affirmations undermine one another. For in what sense could it be said that the deity 'owns' his enemies? If he finds it necessary to engage them in battle, and if battle against them is so difficult that any victory over them is 'glorious', how could they already be said to be 'his'?

So the reference to warfare deconstructs the assertion of Yahweh's ownership of and lordship over all the earth's inhabitants—and vice versa.

3. *Although ascending the hill of the Lord proves one's innocence, those who who ascend are in need of 'vindication' from God.*

Those who ascend the hill of the Lord are promised 'vindication' from God. The implication is that at present they lack such vindication and stand in need of it.

In the eyes of whom do they stand in need of vindication? Presumably both God and themselves are well aware of their moral virtue, so it must be in the eyes of others that they need to be vindicated. But where are the people who are refusing them recognition, and before whom their virtue must be demonstrated? There is nothing in this poem about any assaults on the integrity of the righteous by the wicked, nor any complaint that these people of clean hands and pure hearts are being persecuted or otherwise maltreated by those less upright than themselves.

So the poem craves vindication for the innocent worshippers, but, deconstructively, cannot find any respect in which they might need it.

Furthermore, since it is only those of clean hands that are permitted to ascend the hill of the Lord, the very act of participation in worship is sufficient testimony of their uprightness. They already have their vindication, and so the promise of a future vindication becomes nugatory.

4. *Those who worship on the hill are expected to have clean hands and not to have lifted up their soul to vanity. But the deity is not.*

A double standard in ethics is in operation here.

The worshippers must have clean hands or they will contaminate the holiness of the hill. But the deity ascends it straight from the battlefield, his hands dripping with blood. Does 'lift up your heads, O gates' perhaps then mean 'Look the other way'?

The worshippers must not have lifted up their souls to vanity, but the deity has been soldiering away, seeking the bubble reputation even in the cannon's mouth. 'Reputation' is nothing but Shakespearean for 'glory', and the quest for glory in war is surely a quintessential lifting up of the soul to vanity.

In short, the qualities demanded of the worshippers are deconstructed by the qualities praised in the deity they worship. And vice versa.

These are not the only places in which this poem deconstructs itself, but they are pretty central. The question arises: What is to be done with such a text?

3. *Bespoke Interpretation*

In the rest of this chapter I want to offer a framework for dealing with such a question. I call it a goal-oriented hermeneutic, an end-user theory of interpretation, a market philosophy of interpretation, a discipline of 'comparative interpretation'. This framework has two axes.

First, there is the indeterminacy of meaning. Second, there is is the authority of the interpretative community.

First, then, comes the recognition that texts do not have determinate meanings. Whatever a text may mean in one context, it is almost bound to mean something different in a different context. 'Bus stop' will mean one thing when attached to a pole at the side of the road, another thing when shouted by an anxious parent to a child about to dash into that road.

We may go further. Nowadays we are recognizing that texts not only do not have determinate meanings, they do not 'have' meanings at all. More and more, we are coming to appreciate the role of the reader, or the hearer, in the making of meaning, and recognizing that, without a reader or a hearer, there is not a lot of 'meaning' to any text. Psalm 24 means whatever it means to its various readers, and if their contexts are different, it is likely that it will mean different things to different readers. There is no one authentic meaning which we must all try to discover, no matter who we are or where we happen to be standing.

The second axis for my framework is provided by the idea of interpretative communities. If we ask who it is that authorizes or legitimates an interpretation, who it is that says something may count as an interpretation and not be ruled out of court, the answer can only be: some group, some community. Solipsistic interpretations may be fun for their inventors—you meet a better class of reader that way—, but if there is no group who will accept them, they don't survive. Some interpretations are authorized by the Society of Biblical Literature, some by the ecclesiastical community, but most by little sub-groups within these communities, the Intertextuality in Christian Apocrypha Seminar and the like. The market for interpretations is getting to be very fragmented these days, and I sometimes count myself lucky if I can sell an interpretation to six people.

What we call legitimacy in interpretation is really a matter of whether an interpretation can win approval by some community or other. There is no objective standard by which we can know whether one view or other is right; we can only tell whether it has been accepted. What the academic community today decides counts as a reasonable interpretation of Psalm 24 *is* a reasonable interpretation, and until my community decides that my interpretation is acceptable, it *isn't* acceptable.

Of course, what one community finds acceptable, another will find fanciful or impossible. A faculty of theology in a modern university will not approve of the interpretations of our psalm made by St Augustine and his community, for example, neither would St Augustine think much of the interpretations of the faculty of theology. There are no determinate meanings and there are no universally agreed upon legitimate interpretations.

What are we exegetes then to be doing with ourselves? To whom shall we appeal for our authorization, from where shall we gain approval for our activities, and above all, who will pay us?

The simplest answer for academics has long been that we will seek the approval of no one other than our fellow academics. If our papers get accepted by *Vetus Testamentum* and *New Testament Studies* they are valid, and if they don't they're not.

This safe answer has started to fall apart, though. We are beginning to realize that what counts as a valid interpretation in Cambridge, England does not necessarily do so in Cambridge, Massachusetts, and even less so in Guatemala City or Jakarta or Seoul. The homogeneity of the 'scholarly world' is proving fissiparous, and many smaller interest groups are taking the place of a totalitarian Bibelwissenschaft. More and more scholars are seeking their legitimation from communities that are not purely academic.

Where does that leave us?

If there are no 'right' interpretations, and no validity in interpretation beyond the assent of various interest groups, biblical interpreters have to give up the goal of determinate and universally acceptable interpretations, and devote themselves to producing interpretations they can sell—in whatever mode is called for by the communities they choose to serve.

This is what I call 'customized' interpretation. Like the bespoke tailor, who fashions from the roll of cloth a suit to the measurements and the pocket of the customer, a suit individually ordered or bespoken, the bespoke interpreter has a professional skill in tailoring interpretations to the needs of the various communities who are in the market for interpretations. There are some views of Psalm 24 that churches will 'buy' and 'wear', and others that only paid up deconstructionists, footloose academics and other deviants will even try on for size.

There is nothing unethical in cutting your garment not only according to your cloth but also according to your customer's shape. Even in a market economy, no one will compel you to violate your conscience, though it may cost you to stick to your principles. As a bespoke interpreter responding to the needs of the market, I will be interested, not in the 'truth' about Psalm 24, not in a universally acceptable interpretation of it, but in eradicating shoddy interpretations that are badly stitched together and have no durability, and I will be giving my energies to producing attractive interpretations that represent good value for money.

In such a task interpreters of today do not have to start from scratch. For this programme has a green angle too.[4] It is ecologically sound, because it envisages the recycling of old waste interpretations that have been discarded because they have been thought to have been superseded. In this task of tailoring to the needs of the various interpretative communities, interpreters can be aided by the array of interpretations that have already been offered in the course of the history of the interpretation of the Bible. In fact, what has usually been called the 'history of interpretation' is ripe for being reconceived as a discipline of 'comparative interpretation',[5] providing raw materials, methods, critiques and samples for the work of designing intelligible and creative interpretations for end-users. For too long the interpretations of the past have been lumped together under the heading of the 'history' of interpretation, with the unspoken assumption that what is old in interpretation is out of date and probably rotten and the hidden implication that what is new is best.

It would be far more modest to allow that anyone who has had serious thoughts about our text at any point in history may have something to contribute to someone's understanding today, and to put on our shelves beside Weiser and Dahood the commentaries of Origen and Augustine, Rashi, Aquinas, Luther and Calvin. So long as their books survive, they are our con-

---

4.   'Green' interpretation has already a long history, as Mark Love and Ruth Anne Reese, Sheffield graduate students, pointed out in their study of inner-biblical exegesis, '"Green" Texts: Recycling in Jude and Zechariah', a paper in the Literary Approaches to the Bible Section, Society of Biblical Literature International Meeting, Budapest, July, 1995.

5.   On this concept, see also *Telling Queen Michal's Story: An Experiment in Comparative Interpretation* (ed. David J.A. Clines and Tamara C. Eskenazi; Journal for the Study of the Old Testament Supplement Series, 119; Sheffield: JSOT Press, 1991), esp. pp. 7, 61-63.

temporaries, and their writings provide alternate raw data for our business of interpretation.

In conclusion, I offer some samples of Christian interpretation (by way of example) of the last verses of the psalm, the entry of the King of Glory through the ancient gates.

Let us suppose—as all the modern commentaries would have us do—that in ancient Israelite times the poem celebrated the transfer of the Ark to Jerusalem for the first time, or perhaps, accompanied an annual ritual in which the Ark, symbolizing the presence of Yahweh, was taken out of the city and then restored to the temple amid festal rejoicing. This may or may not be true. Is it treasonable to say, as a reader of the Bible, Who wants to know this? Must I, as a Christian of the last decade of the twentieth century (if that is what I am), care so much about ancient Israelites, dead every one of them, that I must forever read this psalm, in my own Bible for which I paid good money, as somehow belonging to them more than to me?

May I not ask, Who for me is the King of Glory? What have these words to do with me and with the central figure of the Christian faith? And if you, interpreter of the Old Testament, cannot tell me that, or if you think my question illegitimate, will you kindly tell me what you are doing with my money from the church collection plate?[6]

Suppose that I say, For me, for my interpretative community, the king of glory is Jesus Christ, as the centre of my religious devotion. The question that then arises as I read Psalm 24 is this: To what moment in the story of Jesus Christ do these words attach themselves? What is this psalm telling me of the character about whom my principal interest revolves? J.M. Neale, in his *Commentary on the Psalms from Primitive and Mediaeval Writers* (1869),[7] mentions seven interpretations that have been offered by

6. I am assuming here that most interpreters of the Old Testament are paid by the church rather than the state.

7. J.M. Neale and R.F. Littledale, *Commentary on the Psalms from Primitive and Mediaeval Writers, and from the Various Office-Books and Hymns of the Roman, Mozarabic, Ambrosian, Gallican, Greek, Coptic, Armenian, and Syriac Rites* (London: J. Masters, 1860–74). See also Louis Jacquet, *Les Psaumes et le coeur de l'homme: Etude textuelle, littéraire et doctrinale* (Gembloux: Duculot,

ancient writers that are suitable for a Christian reader of that type; three or four of them will do for the present.

Most common among the Latin church was the view that here are the gates of Hades which Christ triumphantly enters in his descent into Hell, in the days between his death and his resurrection. For example, in the *Gospel of Nicodemus* (not later than the mid-fourth century CE)[8] we are transported to the scene at Hell gate. Satan, who has successfully had Jesus crucified, now expects to keep him fast bound in the underworld. The personified Hades, however, is afraid of the arrival of Jesus, since he knows of the raising of Lazarus, and fears that Jesus may now be about to perform a similar miracle on all the inhabitants of the underworld. Thereupon, we read, '[T]here came the voice of the Son of the most high Father, as the voice of a great thunder, saying: Lift up, O princes [which is how the Vulgate reads], your gates, and be ye lift up, ye everlasting doors, and the King of glory shall come in'. Hades replies, 'Who is this King of glory?', and the voice sounds again, 'The Lord strong and mighty, the Lord mighty in battle'. Thereupon the gates and bars of hell are suddenly crushed, and the King of Glory enters hell in human form. Satan is bound in chains, while Adam, the patriarchs, the prophets and the martyrs ascend to heaven following Jesus. Hell has been harrowed.

Another interpretation sees here—not the harrowing of hell, but—the ascension of Christ. The gates become the gates of heaven, the voices are of angels addressing one another, the King of Glory is ascending to the heavenly Mt Zion, and the scene is one of welcome. Says Augustine,

> The heavenly spirits beheld Christ all-glorious with his wounds; and bursting into admiration at those glittering standards of divine

---

1975), I, p. 577, and Jean Daniélou, *The Theology of Jewish Christianity* (The Development of Christian Doctrine before the Council of Nicaea, 1; London: Darton, Longman & Todd, 1964), pp. 83-84, 210, 259-63, for bibliographical references to the use of Psalm 24 in the Christian tradition.

8.   *Gospel of Nicodemus* (*Acts of Pilate*), II.5 (21).1 (Greek version), in Montague Rhodes James, *The Apocryphal New Testament, Being the Apocryphal Gospels, Acts, Epistles, and Apocalypses* (Oxford: Clarendon Press, 1924), p. 132.

virtue, they poured forth the hymn, *Quis est iste Rex Gloriae*? They called him not King of Glory because they saw him glorious, but because they saw him wounded.[9]

There is no need to stop there. There is no right interpretation, though there may be bad ones. Gregory of Nyssa finds in the two challenges, 'Who is the King of Glory?', two separate scenes: for him, the first ocasion is the descent of Christ to earth, where-upon the heavenly powers 'inform [the gatekeepers] that it is he who is strong and mighty in battle, who is going to battle with the one who has reduced mankind to servitude'; the second occasion is the return of Christ to heaven as the Lord of hosts who has obtained power over all things.[10]

At such a point we have only begun to enter upon the meta-phorical meanings of 'gates' and 'entry' and 'raising up'. The Mozarabic Missal uses the words in yet another sense, in the course of a collect said just before the consecration of the ele-ments into the body and blood of Christ. And so on. The poem has, in its Christian interpretation, then, transcended its original significances in the history of ancient Israel, whatever they were, and has become multivalent.[11]

Every new interpretation creates an access of meaning for the poem. There are no barriers to the development of fresh inter-pretations, since every new group of readers creates a new reading location. Your place or mine? becomes the question for bespoke interpreters, who will always have on hand a clutch of

9.   I have not been able to trace this quotation.

10.   Gregory of Nyssa, *Patrologia Graeca*, XLIV, col. 693. Similarly Gregory Nazianzus, *Patrologia Graeca*, XXXVI, col. 657; Ambrose, *De mysteriis*, 35.

11.   The Mozarabic Missal is contained in *Patrologia Latina*, LXXXV. For the interpretation that the moment in view is the descent of Jesus to earth for the incarnation, see, for example, the charming little book of the third or fourth century, *Physiologus*, ancestor of the mediaeval bestiaries; in its first chapter, on Christ as the lion, we learn that '[T]hose that are on high not knowing him as he descended and ascended said this, "Who is this king of glory?" And the angels leading him down answered, "He is the lord of virtues, the king of glory"' (translation by Michael J. Curley, *Physiologus* [Austin: University of Texas Press, 1979], p. 4). In the Apocalypse of Peter, the opening of the gates of heaven is referred to the moment of the transfiguration (James, *The Apocryphal New Testament*, p. 519).

ready-made interpretations but will do their best work when making house calls, fired up by the challenge of a new market.

Here now is a brand-new interpretation, fresh from your friendly corner bespoke interpreter. Come and buy. It is not a Christian interpretation, but rather a non-religious interpretation that attends to the connotations rather than the denotations of the language, and, since the language of the psalm is so over-determined anyway, it doesn't require you to give up any other favourite interpretation you may already have.

Let's say Psalm 24 is about world-building and world-orienting, about locating oneself at the centre (the Lord's hill), up it (ascending) and in it (entering the gates). And let's say the world that is being built is the world of meaning, and the poem concerns making a world of meanings, meanings secure enough to be going on with. So in Psalm 24 we are celebrating a world that is founded, established—a world where we can find the direction to the Lord's hill, for example, a world where Wittgenstein could say, Now I can go on. It has orientation and it has elevation: it is three-dimensional space—which is to say, a world for living in.

Now in the world of meaning there is undifferentiated space—the earth at large—and there is a particularity of space—a specific hill, the hill we seekers for meaning are interested in ascending. To ascend the mountain of particular meaning, we need a pure heart, of course, because purity of heart is to will one thing—and no swearing deceitfully by the false gods of theory. Now each of us sets out on the quest for meaning alone: 'who (singular) shall ascend the hill of the Lord?... The one that has clean hands... We ascend the mountain in our singularity; but when we attain the blessing, which is the vindication of our quest, we find ourselves in the company of a whole generation of seekers for meaning, a veritable Fishian interpretative community: 'This is the generation of those who seek your face...'

The one who ascends the hill is, himself or herself, personally a king of glory. There is nothing glorious in itself; glory signifies the esteem of others. Glory is the recognition by a public who acclaim success in the quest for meaning. Yes, it *is* a struggle, though a demilitarized one, against the intractability of experience and the bewildering array of interpretations already in the field.

Centring ourselves, knowing which way to turn, is a construction of a reality, a world-ordering enterprise. But if we even ask for a moment how firm a foundation we saints of the Lord have laid for ourselves in this world-ordering enterprise, we recognize that the world we have established is founded not upon pillars but upon seas and rivers. We float on a raft of signifiers under which signifieds slide playfully like porpoises; but we have to live *as if* the foundations were solid all the way down to bedrock. We cannot peer too long into the deconstructive underworld waters.

I have often wondered what one should do after deconstructing a text. A true deconstructionist would say, Start deconstructing the deconstruction. But there is another answer, which is truer, I think, to the experience of readers who have performed, or witnessed, a deconstruction. It is very difficult to forget a deconstruction; it is hard to get it out of your head. But the mind demands more order than deconstruction will leave us with, and will go on wilfully constructing, inventing new connotations, new contexts, new interrelationships which will shore up the text, even if only temporarily.

That is what I feel the course of this essay has done. I wanted to expose the fragility, the volatility of the text, its weakness and its incoherence. It was not in order to recommend its abandonment or replacement by some other stronger and less questionable text, but to point up the fragility of texts in general, the inconclusiveness of interpretations, and the impulse nevertheless to stitch them together again no matter how. Weaving and interweaving of interpretations that mean something to someone, that meet with a cry of recognition or at least a grudging assent from some interpretative community—that resolidifies texts. It is the best we can hope to do. It is something like building a universe, intelligently knit together but resting ultimately on unpredictable and ever shifting underground waters. Which was itself an interpretation of Psalm 24.

9

God in the Pentateuch:
Reading against the Grain[*]

1. *Preliminaries*

a. *Method*
There seem to me to be three kinds of data we could use in constructing a picture of God in the Pentateuch. The first is what the character God says about himself, the second is what the narrator says about him, and the third is what the narrator depicts him as doing and saying.

The first kind of data might seem to some readers a very reliable type of information; for here it might appear that it is God himself who is talking about himself. But we need to realize that when the narrative says, 'The LORD...proclaimed, "The LORD, the LORD, a God merciful and gracious, slow to anger, and abounding in steadfast love and faithfulness"' (Exod. 34.6), this self-description does not consist of the words of God himself (what language does *he* speak?) but of the words of the narrator (in Hebrew). These are no more than words put in the mouth of the character God by the narrator, and, behind the narrator, by the author. Such sentences of self-description contribute to our overall picture of the character God, of course, but the words in the mouth of God have no privileged status compared with words spoken directly by the narrator in describing God's motives and actions.

Perhaps the second kind of data will be more useful. They will

* An earlier version of this essay was published in *Studies in Old Testament Theology: Historical and Contemporary Images of God and God's People* (Festschrift for David L. Hubbard; ed. Robert L. Hubbard, Jr, Robert K. Johnston and Robert P. Meye; Dallas: Word Books, 1992), pp. 79-98, and is reprinted by permission. The essay was also delivered as the Peake Memorial Lecture, Leeds, June, 1994.

at least be words that the narrator is committing himself to,
being his own words, and not words he is ascribing to one of his
characters. Assuming that the narrator is a reliable one—which
is not always a safe assumption even in biblical texts, for the
narrator is sometimes ironical and sometimes extremely reticent, and in those respects at least not to be relied on in any
simplistic fashion—we can take it that the descriptions the narrator gives us of the character God are material for our construction of a picture of God in the Pentateuch. The only problem here is that there are not many such descriptions of God on
the part of the narrator. We learn from the narrator in Gen. 6.6
that Yahweh was 'sorry that he had made man on the earth, and
it grieved him to his heart', and we find in Exod. 24.17 that 'the
appearance of the glory of the LORD was like a devouring fire'—
but there are very few sentences like these, describing his
appearance, his feelings or his character, in the whole of the
Pentateuch. We could hardly construct a very rounded picture of
God on the basis of what the narrator tells us directly and
descriptively about him.

There is a third kind of data, the account of what God does
and says throughout the narrative. Here we have a much more
plentiful source of knowledge about the figure of God in the
Pentateuch. The problem with this source, however, is that its
significance for the picture of God is at times far from clear. It is
a risky business even in everyday life making inferences from a
person's actions to their character; but in everyday life we usually have the possibility of cross-checking our provisional con-
clusions with the person himself or herself, of approaching other
people for other points of view, and of seeing many repeated or
similar actions. In the case of the character God—as of *characters* everywhere—all these possibilities are foreclosed to us. If
we are to consider the character 'God in the Pentateuch' we
shall be shut up to the evidence that the Pentateuch provides. We
shall not be thinking about a real 'person', and we shall not be
able to check our evidence from the Pentateuch with other evidence. The picture that results will be at times tantalizingly
ambiguous, and there will be tensions and incompatibilities in it
that cannot be thoroughly resolved. It is simply impossible, for
example, to say why it is that the character God does not allow

Moses into the promised land,[1] or indeed what most of the motives and intentions of the character are.

The thrust of the present essay must in consequence be not toward developing some unified and coherent portrait of the God depicted in the Pentateuch, but to bring to the surface some of the materials, contrasting and inconclusive though they may be, that contribute to the portraiture.

b. *The Pentateuch as a novel*

Let us think of the Pentateuch as a novel.[2] Not that it is a work of fantasy, and not that it must be declared 'untrue' if it does not at every point report historical actuality with the utmost fidelity. Like *War and Peace* and *Adam Bede*, the Pentateuch has its own truth and its own credibility even when it recounts events we perhaps do not think actually happened, like a snake talking or a universal flood. Like a novel, it reports the inner thoughts of its characters, which no one else could ever have heard, and it recounts the dialogue of persons whose actual words had been long since forgotten when the author was writing. Like a novel, it transports its readers through space and time, makes them witnesses to the behaviours and changing motivations of its characters, and, on the whole, avoids the didactic and the dog-matic, insisting that its readers judge for themselves the persons and the acts they encounter in its pages.

Above all, the Pentateuch is a novel in that it is a machine for generating interpretations, to use Umberto Eco's phrase. There

---

1.   Num. 20.12 says it is because Moses 'did not trust' in the Lord; but it proves impossible to tell how his action of striking the rock evidenced a lack of trust.

2.   The 'novel' is not just a modern genre, of course, for the ancient novel is well attested; see Graham Anderson, *Ancient Fiction. The Novel in the Graeco-Roman World* (London: Croom Helm, 1984); Tomas Hågg, *The Novel in Antiquity* (Oxford: Basil Blackwell, 1983); Ben Edwin Perry, *The Ancient Romances: A Literary-Historical Account of their Origins* (Stather Classical Lectures [1951], 37; Berkeley: University of California Press, 1967). I am grateful to my colleague Loveday Alexander for these references. I am not arguing that the Pentateuch *is* a novel of this kind from the point of view of its genre, but only that it is not improper to regard it as having some elements in common with the novel.

are so many complex strands in it, so many fragmentary
glimpses of its personalities, that we cannot reduce it to a single
coherent graspable unity that all readers will agree upon.[3] This
chapter will therefore do no more than develop some possible
readings of the Pentateuch. And these variant readings will not
be just the result of the wilful imposition of readers' prejudices
upon the text, for, like all texts, the Torah has, as Rabbi Ben Bag
Bag long ago said, all its interpretations enshrined within it:
'Turn it and turn it again, for everything is in it'.[4]

c. *God as a character*

Let us next recognize that the God in the Pentateuch is a character in a novel. God in the Pentateuch is not a 'person'; he is a
character in a book. And there are no people in books, no real
people, only fictions; for books are made, not procreated. Even
when the characters have the same name as real people and
remind us vividly of the real people whose names they bear, they
are still made of paper. Even if I should write my autobiogra-
phy, the readers of my book will not be encountering me, but
only the fictive character I have chosen to create in my writing.[5]

The point, obvious though it is, is worth making in this connection if we are to speak honestly about the God in the Pentateuch. For if we were to imagine that the God of whom it speaks
so extensively is identical with the 'true God'—the God who is
worshipped and theologized about—we might have some serious theological problems on our hands, and at the very least we
should be tempted to modulate what we read in the text of the
Pentateuch in order to harmonize it with what we already

3. The reader may wonder how this squares with the claim implied
in the title of my book, *The Theme of the Pentateuch* (Journal for the
Study of the Old Testament Supplement Series, 10; Sheffield: JSOT Press,
1976). It does not. I now think that there there is more than one way of
saying 'what the Pentateuch is all about', though I still think that the
theme of the fulfilment and non-fulfilment of the threefold promise is
one fruitful way of talking about the Pentateuch.

4. *Pirqe Aboth* 5.22.

5. The point is further helpfully developed by Dale Patrick in his
The Rendering of God in the Old Testament (Overtures to Biblical Theology, 10; Philadelphia: Fortress Press, 1981), Chapter 1 'The Characterization of God' (pp. 13-27).

believe we know of the 'true God'. No doubt there is a serious question here, namely what the relation is between the God who is a character in the book and the 'real God', but we cannot begin to address it until we have systematically made a distinction between the two. How else could we approach the issue of their relationship?

d. *Reading with and against the grain*
Most readers of the Pentateuch, the Jewish and Christian communities especially, approve of the story the Pentateuch tells. They think it was a good idea to create the world, to destroy it with a flood, to choose one family and nation as the principal object of divine blessing, and to give to that nation the land of Canaan as their homeland. They are in general sympathetic to the Hebrew people, and tend to believe that what was good for the Hebrews is what should have happened. In short, most readers of the Pentateuch have subscribed to the ideology of the text; they have read with the grain of the text.[6]

But it is not difficult to think how different the narrative could sound if one read *against* the grain, from the viewpoint of an Egyptian or a Canaanite, for example, or even from the perspective of a Jewish or Christian reader who was squeamish about killing or held very strict views about lying. Since the text itself offers very many *points d'appui* for such readings, it is hard to think of a reason why we should *not* make reading against the grain one of our normal strategies for approaching the text. It may be a way of disclosing to us a wider range of possibilities in the text.

6.   I have used the image (which I did not invent; cf. Terry Eagleton, *Against the Grain: Essays 1975–1985* [London: Verso, 1986]) of reading with and against the grain in my paper, 'The Story of Michal, Wife of David, in its Sequential Unfolding', in *Telling Queen Michal's Story: An Experiment in Comparative Interpretation* (ed. David J.A. Clines and Tamara C. Eskenazi; Journal for the Study of the Old Testament Supplement Series, 119; Sheffield: JSOT Press, 1991), pp. 129-40 (129-30). The reader might consider also the image of moiré, 'the meaningful but unstable and reticulating patterns in shot silk' (George Steiner, in *On Difficulty and Other Essays* [Oxford: Oxford University Press, 1978], p. 40). The phrase 'against the grain' goes back at least as far as Dryden (1694), according to the Oxford English Dictionary.

We need not suppose that reading against the grain of the text is a sign of disrespect for the text. What is disrespectful to the text is to assume that it will say what we would like it to say. Nor is it harmful to the church or the synagogue to hear of readings against the grain. We should not assume that 'believing communities' always want to hear, or should hear, only the ideology of the text being rehearsed. Perhaps they also need to know what their texts are capable of, what unorthodox and unconventional meanings they can suggest, and what a large element of choice there is in any decision to take the text's perspective as the definitive word.

e. *The dialectic of the text*
I have just now been describing a dialectic that we can set up between the text and the reader, when the reader takes up a position, or starts out from a position, that is not shared by the text. There is another kind of dialectic we can pay attention to, however. It is a dialectic that is immanent in the text, a dialectic between the elements of tension in the text itself. In the Pentateuch such a dialectic comes to expression in the questions, Is God merciful or vengeful? Does God wish to reveal himself or conceal himself? Is God directing the course of human history or not? Without probing very far beneath the surface of the text of the Pentateuch, we soon form the impression that the text says quite different things on these subjects at different moments, that there is at the very least a tension in the text and at the most there is irreconcilable conflict.

The possibility of such dialectical relations in our texts needs to be in our mind when we address the issue of 'God in the Pentateuch'. Perhaps we will at the end of the day uncover some grand harmonizing truth that brings the poles of tension together and enables us to create some unitary vision of our topic. But even if that should happen 'at the end of the day', we shall have in the meantime to give weight to elements that pull apart from one another, or else we shall never know that there is any unitary statement to be sought for.

2. *Dialectic Readings*

a. *God and Noah*

Here is a very simple example of the dialectic readers may find themselves involved in with their text. The issue can be framed in this way: Is the story of Noah a story of God as saviour or of Noah as saviour?

The ideology of the text has some plain outlines. According to the text, all humans deserve to be wiped out by a flood because of their wickedness, but Noah finds favour in the eyes of Yahweh (Gen. 6.8). God tells Noah how he can escape the flood, God commands him to make an ark, God sends him into the ark, God shuts him in, God remembers him, and God tells him to leave the ark when the waters have subsided. In short, God saves Noah (and, with him, humanity) from the flood.[7]

Readers, however, might well find themselves asking, But what does God actually *do* to save Noah from the flood? If this is a story of some 'saving act' of God, let us say, how exactly does God act in order to save Noah? The answer has to be that God merely tells Noah what to do. God does not do anything himself to save Noah, he tells Noah how to save himself. Compared with some of the 'mighty acts of God' in the Pentateuch, such as the exodus from Egypt when Yahweh fights for the Hebrews and they have to do nothing but 'only to keep still' (Exod. 14.14), there is no saving act of God at the flood at all. So is it a story about God at all, if it is not about anything he does? Is it perhaps a story about the achievement of a great hero, who saves humanity from extinction by keeping alive his family in a boat? To be sure, the deity has warned the hero of the coming of the flood and has given him instructions about the ark that must be built if the flood is to be survived. But the actual saving *acts* are those of Noah, who even in his six hundredth year is build-

---

7. Cf. the account given of Genesis 1–11 by Gerhard von Rad as 'a story of God with man, the story of continuously new punishment and at the same time gracious preservation'; the Flood story itself he characterizes with the sentence, 'God transferred man...to a newly ordered world' (*Genesis: A Commentary* [Old Testament Library; London: SCM Press, revised edition, 1972], p. 153). There is no doubt in von Rad's mind who is the hero of the story.

ing the ark, collecting all the animals and stocking it with food—
singlehandedly (the verbs in 6.16-21 are all in the singular).

The ideology of the text does not contain this second reading, I
would say; the text does not authorize it, it does not encourage
us to read it that way. But then neither does it disallow it, for it
gives us all the data by which we may develop this reading
against the grain. And once we have encountered such a reading, it is hard to forget it, hard to expunge the memory of its
possibility from our consciousness, hard to adhere any longer to
the idea of a univocal meaning of the text—hard, in short, to be
sure what it is the text wants to say about God. The possibility
of reading against the grain makes for a plurality of interpretations.

b. *God and the exodus*

Here is another example of a dialectic reading of the Pentateuch.
It seems to be both a case of a reader reading against the grain
and of a tension that is immanent in the surface of the text.

In a word, the text represents the exodus from Egypt as a
great act of deliverance on God's part. The day of the exodus is
called the day when 'the LORD brought you out from there by
strength of hand' (Exod. 13.3), and the moment of victory over
the Egyptians is recalled as the time when 'horse and rider he
has thrown into the sea' (15.21). It is to be commemorated in
time to come as the day when 'By strength of hand the LORD
brought us out of Egypt, from the house of slavery' (13.14). The
text has persuaded its readers that it is telling of a mighty deed
of salvation.

What the text never says, in this connection, is that it was
Yahweh who brought them *into* Egypt in the first place. In the
book of Exodus, the presence of the Hebrews in Egypt is
regarded as a given, and the only questions are whether, how
and when Yahweh will remove them from the house of
bondage. The story of the exodus begins only at the point when
the Hebrews groan under their hard labour. Then Yahweh
remembers his covenant with Abraham, Isaac and Jacob (Exod.
2.23-24)—which is to say, the narrative of Genesis 12–36. No
one in Exodus, in other words, seems to remember the events of
Genesis 37–50, chapters that have told us how the Hebrews

happen to be in Egypt in the first place; and no one seems to remember Joseph's words to his brothers, 'So it was not you who sent me here, but God' (Gen. 45.8), and 'Even though you intended to do harm to me, God intended it for good' (50.20).[8] It is evidently not only the new Egyptian king who knows not Joseph (Exod. 1.8), but the narrator also. And his character God seems to regard the presence of the Hebrews in Egypt as nothing more than an unfortunate accident that has happened to them; he never acknowledges that it is his own deliberate design.

Now it makes a difference (does it not?) whether the deliverance from Egypt is a sheer act of divine grace in conformity with the covenant to the forefathers, or whether it is a way of undoing the damage done to the Hebrew people by engineering their descent into Egypt in the first place. Regardless of how we resolve this question, or whether we resolve it at all, we are left with an equivocal picture of 'God in the Pentateuch'. A tension immanent in the larger text of Genesis plus Exodus has led to a reading that in some respect goes against the grain of the smaller text of the opening chapters of Exodus.

c. *God and the plagues in Egypt*
In at least one place there is an evident tension, on the surface of the text, over the behaviour of God during the affair of the Egyptian plagues. There is little doubt that the general intention of the text is to represent God as the saviour of the Hebrew people from the Egyptians: in Exod. 3.17 he says, 'I declare that I will bring you up out of the misery of Egypt, to the land of the Canaanites', and in 14.13 Moses says to the people, 'Do not be afraid, stand firm, and see the deliverance that the LORD will accomplish for you today'. But the text also contains a quite contrary view of God's activity: in 5.22-23, after the Hebrews have been compelled to find their own straw to make bricks, there is a question of Moses, 'O LORD, why have you mistreated this people? Why did you ever send me? Since I first came to Pharaoh to speak in your name, he has mistreated this people,

---

8.   Though these words of Joseph's do not necessarily represent the narrator's point of view, as Yiu-Wing Fung, a graduate student at Sheffield, is pointing out in his dissertation on Joseph.

and you have done nothing at all to deliver your people'.

This is not the question of an opponent of God, and it is not rebuffed by God. Moses is not punished for asking it, and God effectively concedes the truth of it by not denying it but changing the subject in his response. Now I hardly need to observe that the text does not mean us to accept that this is how we should read the entire narrative of the plagues, as a sequence of damaging actions of God against the Hebrews; and the narrative as a whole ensures that we ultimately forget about this objection of Moses, or almost so. But what his question does is to open a window into the narrative, another angle of vision that enables the divine actions to be interpreted in another way from that of the text as a whole. This question of Moses invites us as readers to consider the whole plagues narrative from an alternative perspective; and even if we do not come to accept this perspective in the end a little note of ambiguity has been introduced into the portraiture of God.

There is another point at which the text, less overtly, introduces ambiguity into the larger picture. The casual reader remembers that after each of the plagues the Pharaoh promises to let the Hebrews leave Egypt but subsequently 'hardens his heart' and changes his mind. More observant readers know that it is *sometimes* said that the Pharaoh 'hardens his heart' (as in 8.11 [EVV 15], 28 [EVV 32]; 9.34) and *sometimes* that 'his heart is hardened' (as in 7.13, 14, 22; 8.15 [EVV 19]; 9.7, 35), but (most interestingly) that *sometimes* it is Yahweh who 'hardens the Pharaoh's heart' (as in 9.12; 10.1, 20, 27; 11.10).

The first ambiguity that arises is whether in the cases where the hardening of the Pharaoh's heart is spoken of in the passive ('his heart was hardened') we should understand it was the Pharaoh himself or God that did the hardening. If it was God, then most of the heart-hardening that was going on in the text was God's doing and not the Pharaoh's. Of course, we can never know which of these possibilities we should choose, but we can hardly help wondering about it, especially because of the second ambiguity.

The second ambiguity in the portrayal of God here is a very tantalizing one: it is the evidence in the text that God was working against his own purposes by making the Pharaoh keep the people in Egypt at the very time that he was himself trying to get them liberated from Egypt (and publicly proclaiming that as his intention). Readers of Genesis have had occasion before this to wonder at the role of the deferrals of the promise, and at God's penchant for making things difficult for himself (like choosing a childless nonagenarian to be the father of a multitude of nations),[9] but never before have we encountered such an uncompromising conflict in the divine actions. How are we to read this dissonant behaviour on God's part? Are we to say, The God of the Exodus is so powerful that he can remove every obstacle placed in his way—even those he in his omnipotence has put there himself (like an irresistible force getting rid of an immovable object)?, or, The God of the Exodus has difficulty in deciding whether he really wants these Hebrews to be out of Egypt, and defers the moment of their release as long as possible?, or, The humiliation of the Egyptian king and the transforming of him from a free agent resisting God into a mere pawn in the divine hands is more important to God than achieving the freedom of the Hebrews at the earliest possible moment?[10] Or are we to go on inventing more and more explanatory accounts of the circumstances?[11]

9. See Laurence A. Turner, *Announcements of Plot in Genesis* (Journal for the Study of the Old Testament Supplement Series, 96; Sheffield: JSOT Press, 1990); David J.A. Clines, 'What Happens in Genesis', in *What Does Eve Do to Help? And Other Readerly Questions to the Old Testament* (Journal for the Study of the Old Testament Supplement Series, 94; Sheffield: JSOT Press, 1990), pp. 49-66.

10. On this last reading, see the essay by David M. Gunn, 'The "Hardening of Pharaoh's Heart": Plot, Character and Theology in Exodus 1–14', in *Art and Meaning: Rhetoric in Biblical Literature* (ed. David J.A. Clines, David M. Gunn and Alan J. Hauser; Journal for the Study of the Old Testament Supplement Series, 19; Sheffield: JSOT Press, 1982), pp. 72-96.

11. The issue in the narrative is often cast as the problem of causality (that is, who caused the hardening of the Pharaoh's heart?), but the reader will see that I am not setting the problem up in these terms, which deflect attention from the truly critical problems in the text for the portrait of God. Nevertheless, I cannot forbear quoting some sentences from a standard work that show how badly this issue too stands in need of critical reformulation: '[T]he biblical writers speak of God hardening men's hearts...At the same time they avow men harden their own

As if aware of the oddity in God's behaviour, the text addresses the problem by offering an explanation of God's hardening the Pharaoh's heart. In Exod. 10.1-2, Yahweh says to Moses, 'I have hardened his heart and the heart of his officials, in order that I may show these signs of mine among them, and that you may tell your children and grandchildren how I have made fools of the Egyptians and what signs I have done among them—so that you may know that I am the LORD'. It is an explanation that bows under its own weight. For, in the first place, if the Pharaoh's heart had not been hardened and he had agreed to let the Hebrews go earlier, there would have been no need for 'signs' to show Yahweh playing with ('making fools of') the Egyptians; can Yahweh mean that he simply wanted to enjoy the discomfiture of the Egyptians, and that the hardening of their hearts was his ploy to give a justification for his repeated assaults on them? And, in the second place, to say that he has hardened the hearts so as to give the Hebrews something to remember in later years is to suggest that there was no justification or necessity for the hardening of the hearts at the time. Can the text really be implying that the Hebrews would otherwise not have had enough folk memories to pass on to their children, not enough evidence that 'I am the LORD'? And in the third place, we have to remember the angle of vision on this narrative opened up by Moses' earlier question, 'Why have you mistreated this people?' (5.22). That is to say, while Yahweh is having all this sport making a fool of the Pharaoh and while all these memories are being laid down in the national consciousness, the Hebrews are still at work in the brick kilns. Every day that passes in fruitless negotiations with the Pharaoh is another day

hearts...They found no apparent inconsistency in ascribing this activity both to God and to men. For men, by acting in accordance with their own self-will, were carrying out the divine purpose' (V.H. Kooy, 'Harden the Heart', in *The Interpreter's Dictionary of the Bible* [ed. George Arthur Buttrick *et al.*; Nashville: Abingdon Press, 1962], II, p. 524). On this I might comment first that it is not the end of the matter to say that 'the biblical writers...found no...inconsistency'; perhaps they should have, and perhaps we do. And in the second place, does it resolve the issue to say that humans acting freely are carrying out the divine will, unless we are prepared to say also that God acting freely is carrying out human will?

of slave labour for the people of God, even if the text does not draw our attention to the fact at this moment.

None of this is to say that we *must* read the text this way, fix our attention exclusively on the negative aspects that undermine it in some degree and ignore the larger picture, which is ungainsayably an account of God's deliverance of the Hebrews from Egypt. But whatever we do, the textual data remain, and the picture of God remains intriguing and ultimately unexplainable. If the narrator had set out to portray a deity whose purposes were not entirely clear and whose behaviour was from time to time eccentric, a deity who operated under the self-professed slogan, I will be whatever I will be, he might well have given us such a narrative as this.[12]

d. *God and the chosen people*
Fundamental to the ideology of the Pentateuch is the idea that God has chosen the people of Israel from among all the nations on earth. The idea first becomes apparent in Genesis 12, though the language of choosing is not yet used. When Yahweh tells Abram that he will make of him a great nation and that he will bless him and make his name great (12.2), he does not say in so many words that he will *not* make other men into ancestors of great nations, that he will *not* bless them or make their name great—but he implies it. The blessing to Abram has to be preferential and competitive or otherwise Abram's significance for the 'families of the earth' (12.3) is unintelligible.

Though the idea of Israel's election surfaces at various points in the Pentateuch, the language of God's 'choosing' Israel becomes prominent only in Deuteronomy.[13] In Deut. 4.37 and

12. The divine self-description in Exod. 3.14 could well be translated, 'I will be what I will be', and some commentators have rightly remarked on the note of concealment in this formulation; see, for example, Walther Zimmerli, *Old Testament Theology in Outline* (tr. David E. Green; Edinburgh: T. & T. Clark, 1978), p. 20: 'In this figure of speech resounds the sovereign freedom of Yahweh, who, even at the moment he reveals himself in his name, refuses simply to put himself at the disposal of humanity or to allow humanity to comprehend him'.

13. Cf. A.D.H. Mayes, *Deuteronomy* (New Century Bible; London: Oliphants, 1979), p. 60: 'What is really distinctive in Deuteronomy is that the whole life of the people is regulated from the point of view of its

10.15 it is tied up with God's 'love' for the ancestors and his effecting of the exodus from Egypt; in 6.7 and 14.2 it is a choosing of Israel as God's own people, out of all the peoples of the earth. The announcement of God's choice of Israel is hedged about, as the theologians do not tire of pointing out,[14] with safeguards against Israel's drawing improper implications from the fact: it was, for example, 'not because you were more numerous than any other people that the LORD set his heart on you and chose you' (7.7). We wonder, incidentally, whether any Israelites of whatever century needed to be told that they were not the most numerous people on the face of the earth; even without a state educational system or encyclopaedias, did they really imagine Israel was a greater state than Egypt, Assyria, Babylonia or Persia? Or, if they did, how does the author of Deuteronomy happen to know that they were not? And, if they did not, is there perhaps a lack of candour in denying this was a reason for God's chosing them? Nonetheless, whatever the implications, there is no doubt that the Pentateuch represents God as the God of the Hebrews—God of the Hebrews, that is, in a way he is not God of the Egyptians or Hittites, for example (even if he is God of those nations in any sense at all).

This is all right if you happen to be an Israelite and have no dealings with Hittites. You know all you need to know, which is that Yahweh is your God. But if you happen to be a Hittite, or even a twentieth-century reader of the Pentateuch, how congenial is it to encounter in its pages a deity who is bound in this way to just one nation: the nation claims that he is their peculiar deity, and he professes that he has chosen them as his own peculiar people? What is the sense in this arrangement, what rationale is offered for it—especially since the Pentateuch itself regards God as the creator of the whole world? And above all, for our present consideration of God in the Pentateuch, what does this exclusivity say about the character of the deity represented here? The Pentateuch itself sees no problem here, nothing

relationship with Yahweh, and the basic element here is that Israel was chosen by Yahweh'.

14. Cf., e.g., Edmond Jacob, *Theology of the Old Testament* (trans. Arthur W. Heathcote and Philip J. Allcock; London: Hodder & Stoughton, 1958), pp. 110-11.

to be excused or justified; if anything, it makes a point out of there being *no rationale* for the choice of Israel as the people of God. But it does not occur to it that the very idea that there should be just one nation that is the chosen people—leaving the rest of humanity unchosen—is itself problematic.

The time-honoured language, and the sense of fitness that creeps over us through long acquaintance with the idea, should not be allowed to soften the sense of shock to the modern conscience (religiously formed or otherwise) that such an example of nationalistic ideology must deliver. Nor should we blur the contours of this distinct figuration of God in the Pentateuch with some pacific harmonization or identification of this God with the universal deity of the Christian religion—or, for that matter, patronize the God of the Pentateuch by excusing the myopia of his vision as a necessary stage in the progress of religion.

The grain of the text, in short, assumes the centrality of the Jewish people and portrays a God whose attention is concentrated upon that nation. So long as we stay within the ideology of the text, we experience no discomfort with the portraiture. But the moment we position ourselves outside the text and become conscious of our own identities as non-Hebrews (which we might do even if we are Jews today), it becomes difficult not to take a more quizzical view of the character. If we do not actually *approve* of a universal deity having one favourite race, we are bound to take a different view of that deity's character from a reader who happily embraces the ideology of the text.

3. *Unifying Readings*

The readings presented above of the character God in the Pentateuch are meant only to be exemplary of the ambiguities and indeterminacy of the portrait offered by the text. They themselves, readings against the grain of the text, go against the grain also of the central tradition in biblical scholarship, which has generally striven for a harmonizing and unifying depiction of the character of the deity in the Old Testament, one indeed that maximizes the compatibility of the portrait with that of the God of the New Testament and of Christian theology. This standpoint is of course quite legitimate—provided only that it is recognized that, like all standpoints, it has to be chosen, and, when it is chosen, it restricts the range of vision.

In this section I will present some themes from the scholarly literature that treats the depiction of God in the Pentateuch, works like Gerhard von Rad's *Old Testament Theology*,[15] Walther Zimmerli's *Old Testament Theology in Outline*,[16] Claus Westermann's *Elements of Old Testament Theology*,[17] and Bernhard W. Anderson's article, 'God, OT View of', in *The Interpreter's Dictionary of the Bible*.[18] To all these authors, it should be noted, 'God' is not a character in a literary work called the Pentateuch, but is a real being concerning whom the Pentateuch is written. So far as I can tell, they do not think the Pentateuch ever says anything untrue about this 'real God' and, even as Christian theologians, they do not seem to find any inconsistency between the figure of God in the Pentateuch and the God of Christian worship and theology.[19]

1. *God is present*. The Pentateuch is not a story of human history in which God appears at the margins, making only occasional interventions like a *deus ex machina*. Even when the narrative does not foreground him,[20] he remains the story's

15. Trans. D.M.G. Stalker; Edinburgh: Oliver & Boyd, 1962. Volume 1, pp. 129-305, deals with 'The Theology of the Hexateuch'.

16. Trans. David E. Green; Edinburgh: T. and T. Clark, 1978.

17. Trans. Douglas W. Scott; Atlanta: John Knox Press, 1982.

18. *The Interpreter's Dictionary of the Bible*, II, pp. 417-30.

19. Von Rad, for example, even thinks that 'it is a bad thing for the Christian expositor completely to disregard [the cosmology of Genesis 1] as obsolete', since '[i]n the scientific ideas of the time theology had found an instrument which suited it perfectly' (*Old Testament Theology*, I, p. 148). For a case where von Rad does think that a theological view contained in the Old Testament has its defects, see his *Old Testament Theology*, I, p. 344 (on the Deuteronomist's conception of history); but somehow the motive behind this defect turns out to be the very thing that gives the Deuteronomist's work its 'theological grandeur'. Terence E. Fretheim has correctly remarked on how the portrait of God in Old Testament scholarship 'bears a striking resemblance to the quite traditional Jewish or Christian understanding of God regnant in synagogue or church' (*The Suffering of God: An Old Testament Perspective* [Overtures to Biblical Theology, 14; Philadelphia: Westminster Press, 1984], p. 17).

20. Robert L. Cohn, 'Narrative Structure and Canonical Perspective in

dominant character. Very little is said in the Pentateuch of the nature of God in himself; it is always God in relationship with humans, involved in the events of family or national history. Westermann, for example, says that '[t]he story told in the Old Testament is...not a in the sense of a series of God's salvation acts, but rather a history of God and man whose nucleus is the experience of saving'.[21] Nor is it a story of divine actions unilaterally injected into the course of human affairs, for 'all of God's acts and speaking are directed toward eliciting a response'.[22] Similarly Anderson writes: 'Just as persons are known in the context of relationship, so God's self is revealed in his historical relations with his people. He is the God of Abraham, Isaac, and Jacob, not the God of speculative thought. He is known by what he has done, is doing, and will do—i.e., in the events of history'.[23] Beyond doubt, this is a fundamental aspect of the character God in the Pentateuch.

2. *God speaks.* God is the principal speaker in the Pentateuch. Most of the central chapters of the Pentateuch, from Exodus 20 to the end of Numbers, are the speeches of God. If you write down ten of the page numbers of the Pentateuch at random, and look them up to see if God speaks or is quoted on them, you will probably find, as I did, that on 6 out of 10 pages there are words of God.

The significance of this speaking is variously understood by the theologians. Sometimes it is seen as being God's *self-revelation*. The pervasiveness of God's speech is said to establish that the text 'does not purport to be the record of human initiative in seeking for and discovering God' but rather 'testifies to God's overture, God's initiative'.[24] Sometimes the speech of

Genesis', *Journal for the Study of the Old Testament* 25 (1983), pp. 3-16, has shown how God increasingly retreats into the background throughout Genesis 12–50.

21. Westermann, *Elements of Old Testament Theology*, pp. 10-11.

22. Westermann, *Elements of Old Testament Theology*, p. 27.

23. Anderson, 'God, OT View of', p. 418.

24. Anderson, 'God, OT View of', p. 419. Anderson is speaking of the Old Testament in general, it should be noted. To take another, not uncharacteristic, example, G. von Rad deals with the speeches of God to Moses at Sinai (the 'Law') under the rubric of 'The Divine Revelation at Sinai' (*Old Testament Theology*, I, pp. 187-305).

God in the Pentateuch is seen as God's *summons* of Israel to obedience, God's announcement of his requirements. The Pentateuchal law, spoken by God to Moses, can indeed be regarded as a gift, but 'Every gift implies an element of duty',[25] and the words of God essentially impose duties upon their hearers. Sometimes the words of God are seen rather as *instruction*, the emphasis being on God's speech as guidance for life rather than as legal requirements. Sometimes it is stressed that the words of God that direct Israel's behaviour are effectively part of his *salvation* of the nation. So, it is argued, the law must not be 'separated from God's saving deed and absolutized. Because God encountered Israel as savior, he commanded to it his will.'[26] Sometimes the words of God are seen as the *provisions of the covenant* that defines the relationship between God and the people.[27] No matter what the precise significance of God's speaking is, speech is a prominent element in the characterization of God in the Pentateuch.[28]

3. *God promises*. The Old Testament as a whole has commonly been read, by Christian interpreters, as promise, to which the New Testament corresponds as fulfilment.[29] However appropriate or otherwise that may be for the Old Testament generally, the theme of promise is certainly perceived as an important thread in the Pentateuch's depiction of God. Zimmerli, for example, sees God's promise to the ancestors in Genesis as 'constitut[ing] the...subject matter of the patriarchal history',[30] so fundamental is it to the entire narrative. And I have argued myself that the theme of the threefold promise to the ancestors of progeny, land and a divine–human relationship binds the whole Pentateuch together: while Genesis develops

---

25. Zimmerli, *Old Testament Theology in Outline*, p. 109.

26. Westermann, *Elements of Old Testament Theology*, p. 176.

27. Cf. Ronald E. Clements, *Old Testament Theology: A Fresh Approach* (Atlanta: John Knox Press, 1978), p. 110: 'Tôrâh is the comprehensive list of instructions and stipulations by which Israel's covenant with God is controlled'.

28. See also Patrick, *The Rendering of God*, chapter 6 'God's Speaking' (pp. 90-100).

29. See, for example, Clements, *Old Testament Theology*, chapter 6 'The Old Testament as Promise' (pp. 131-54).

30. Zimmerli, *Old Testament Theology in Outline*, p. 29.

the element of the promise of progeny, Exodus and Leviticus concern themselves with the promise of the divine-human relationship, while Numbers and Deuteronomy focus on the promise of the land.[31] We can safely say therefore that God is viewed in the Pentateuch as the one who promises.[32]

4. *God saves*. In the work of Gerhard von Rad in particular we find the Hexateuch (the Pentateuch plus Joshua) characterized as 'salvation history' (*Heilsgeschichte*), that is, as a narrative of God's saving acts, or, as the 'biblical theology' movement put it, 'the mighty acts of God'.[33] Von Rad found the core of the Hexateuch in the confessional statement of Deut. 26.5-9, which he called Israel's Credo: 'A wandering Aramaean was my ancestor... We cried to the LORD, the God of our ancestors; the LORD heard our voice, and saw our affliction... the LORD brought us out of Egypt'. In these words are recapitulated, said von Rad, 'the main events in the saving history from the time of the patriarchs...down to the conquest'. The God of the Pentateuch is thus a God who delivers and saves.[34] To the same effect Westermann writes, 'The experience of the deliverance at the beginning [that is, at the exodus as the beginning of Israel's national history] means for Israel that Yahweh will *remain* Israel's saviour. As he was the saviour at the beginning, so his rescue continues to be expected, prayed for, and experienced. Yahweh is the saving God.'[35]

31. Clines, *The Theme of the Pentateuch*, esp. p. 29.

32. See also Walther Zimmerli, *Man and his Hope in the Old Testament* (Studies in Biblical Theology, II/20; London: SCM Press, 1971), pp. 42-69.

33. Cf. George Ernest Wright, *God Who Acts* (Studies in Biblical Theology, 8; London: SCM Press, 1952). On the 'biblical theology' movement, see Brevard S. Childs, *Biblical Theology in Crisis* (Philadelphia: Westminster, 1970), and J. Barr, 'Biblical Theology', in *The Interpreter's Dictionary of the Bible. Supplementary Volume* (ed. Keith Crim; Nashville: Abingdon, 1976), pp. 104-11.

34. For some brief criticisms of von Rad's conception of 'salvation history', see, for example, Westermann, *Elements of Old Testament Theology*, pp. 14-15, who points out that God acts for punishment as well as for salvation, and that an ongoing activity of 'blessing' also needs to be taken account of (see the next point).

35. Westermann, *Elements of Old Testament Theology*, p. 37.

5. *God blesses*. Westermann in particular has drawn attention to this aspect of the character of the God of the Pentateuch. On the first page of Genesis, God appears as the originator of blessing, that is, of a general benevolence that is 'universal and valid for all forms of life'. Blessing differs from saving, according to Westermann. God's saving is 'a special turning towards a particular group' and is experienced in 'individual events or a sequence of events'. Blessing, on the other hand, is a 'quiet, continuous, flowing, and unnoticed working of God which cannot be captured in moments or dates',[36] and which is directed toward humanity in general and not just toward Israel. The Pentateuch as a whole, though it consists for the most part of a story of salvation, that is, of the salvation of Israel, is nevertheless framed by two major statements of God's blessing: the blessing of the creator in Genesis 1–11, and 'the blessing in Deuteronomy directed toward the people in the promised land'.[37] It is hard to say, therefore, whether it is God's saving or blessing that is the more prominent in the Pentateuch; both must be given full recognition.

Here then have been five things that contemporary Old Testament theologians find the Pentateuch to be affirming about God. Without question, all these statements about God are well attested in the Pentateuch, and many students and scholars would be content to conclude their account of the God of the Pentateuch with a catalogue like the foregoing—more developed and more sophisticated, no doubt, but essentially on these lines. But each of these statements, however 'positive' or 'constructive', deserves to be probed more critically, for each statement both implies and denies far more than is evident on the surface.

4. *Conclusions*

Reading against the grain implies that there *is* a grain. It implies that texts have designs on their readers and wish to persuade them of something or other. It implies that there are ideologies inscribed in texts and that the readers implied by texts share the

---

36. Westermann, *Elements of Old Testament Theology*, pp. 102-103.
37. Westermann, *Elements of Old Testament Theology*, pp. 103-104.

texts' ideologies.[38] But, as I have suggested earlier, readers are free to resist the ideologies of texts, and, what is more, texts themselves sometimes provoke readers into resisting them by manifesting tensions immanent within the texts themselves. All the same, there is no obligation to resist, nothing wrong in adopting the ideology of one's text. All that is wrong is not knowing and admitting that that is what you are doing *or* not permitting other people to resist the ideology of the text.

I do not want to deny that the five points in the previous section represent, with whatever measure of success, the ideology of the Pentateuch on the subject of God—that is to say, the grain of the text. But so that those who wish to accede to this ideology know what they are doing, and can recognize that they are making a choice when they do so, I shall offer a few reflections that go against the grain.

None of the five themes in the figuration of God in the Pentateuch that I have outlined above can be said to be entirely true about the character. Some qualification must always be added, even though our handbooks of Old Testament theology uniformly devote themselves to exposition and refrain from critical evaluation of the portrait.

It is true that God in the Pentateuch is present, speaks and saves—but on the whole it is true only if you take the position of Israel. If you adopt the point of view of the Egyptians or the

38. This is loose anthropomorphic talk, I know (see for example Stephen Fowl, 'Texts Don't Have Ideologies', *Biblical Interpretation* 3 [1995], pp. 15-34). Strictly speaking, texts do not have grains any more than they 'have' meanings. Authors would like to put grains in their texts, of course, and readers are forever finding grains in texts, even though they are not there. But since authors do not own their own texts, not forever, authors' intentions do not constitute the reality of the texts they compose or determine their meaning. And from the readers' side, what counts as the grain of the text for them is no more than what some interpretative community or other decides to call the grain. So when I am reading against the grain, I am really reading against the practice of an interpretative community, sometimes even against myself and my own first reading. Strictly speaking, the text is not to blame for the thoughts that come into my head when I am reading it, but I am not always speaking strictly; like most people, in everyday speaking and writing I go on ascribing meaning and grain to texts.

Canaanites, God is not experienced as a saving God, and the only words you will hear addressed to you are words of reproach and threat. If you are not Israel, you do not know the presence of God, and the main reason is not some defect in you but the fact that you have not been chosen. It is perfectly true that the character God in the Pentateuch saves Israel from Egypt, but it is equally true that the same God destroys or humiliates the Egyptians, and ignores almost everyone else. The text does not wish us to think that, or, if it allows us to know it, it wants us to suppress that knowledge and concentrate on the deliverance of Israel. But when the deliverance of Israel is effected precisely through the destruction of the Egyptian soldiers, when what is deliverance from one point of view is death from another, must we succumb to the text's ideology and suppress part of the reality it bears witness to?[39]

The election of Israel is, without question, a thorny problem for the character of God in the Pentateuch. Some writers have thought to ameliorate matters by emphasizing that Israel's election is not thought to be an end in itself but for the purpose of bringing benefit to the other nations. Bernhard Anderson, for example, writes that 'the deepest insight into Israel's election or special calling is that God has chosen Israel to be the historical agent of world-wide blessing'. But he has to go on to say, 'Admittedly, Israel did not always understand her [sic] calling in this universal perspective'.[40] The fact is that Israel, or shall we say in the present context, the narrator of the Pentateuch, seems to give a very low priority to this 'deepest insight', for it is very difficult to see how the Israel of the Pentateuch brings blessing to

---

39. As an example of the prevailing agreement to regard the exodus as an 'act of God' but to ignore the fact that it did any harm to anyone, see Paul D. Hanson, *Dynamic Transcendence: The Correlation of Confessional Heritage and Contemporary Experience in a Biblical Model of Divine Activity* (Philadelphia: Fortress Press, 1978), pp. 28-35. Raphael Jospe, 'The Concept of the Chosen People: An Interpretation', *Judaism* 43 (1994), pp. 127-48, has recently undertaken to show, from a Jewish perspective, that chosenness is not a marker of privilege but 'an internally-directed Jewish responsibility to live in a certain way, based on the Torah' (p. 127)—but this too denatures the concept 'chosen'.

40. Anderson, 'God, OT View of', p. 429.

anyone at all,[41] and does not rather spell disaster for all the nations it comes into contact with. Genesis 1 and 9, indeed, speak of God's blessing upon humanity in general, and Westermann especially wants to give the idea of universal blessing parity of place with the idea of particular salvation for Israel.[42] But the Pentateuch does not support his view, for it consistently privileges Israel and marginalizes the other nations.

If we now turn our attention to the theme of God promising in the Pentateuch, again the realities in the text do not allow a clear and unambiguous statement. There is no doubt that the divine promises to the patriarchs are fundamental for the dynamic of the Pentateuchal narrative: God promises progeny, a relationship and land, and the narrative presses towards the realization of those promises. But it would be unacceptably short-sighted to depict the God of the Pentateuch as making promises without also asking whether or to what extent those promises are fulfilled. He promises to make Abram into a 'great nation' (Gen. 12.2), but has this happened in the course of the Pentateuchal narrative? The promise of the land has certainly not been realized by the end of Deuteronomy, and the divine–human relationship is decidedly less stable than we had imagined when it was first promised to the patriarchs. But perhaps this is the point at which we should question the notion of the 'Pentateuch' as an independent literary work, and invoke the entity that we can call the 'Primary History', that sequence of historiographical narrative that runs from Genesis to the end of 2 Kings.[43] Yet if the boundaries of that work are to form the horizon within which we consider the promises and their fulfilment, the news is even worse than if we restrict ourselves to the first five books. For by the end of the narrative of the Primary

41. Joseph providing food for the Egyptians is the one evident exception (cf. Gen. 47.25), but even this benefit must be set against the fact that in order to do so he deprives the Egyptians of their animals and land and 'made slaves of them from one end of Egypt to the other' (47.21). See also my essay, 'What Happens in Genesis', in *What Does Eve Do to Help?*, pp. 49-66 (58).

42. Westermann, *Elements of Old Testament Theology*, Part III 'The Blessing God and Creation' (pp. 85-117).

43. See Clines, 'The Old Testament Histories: A Reader's Guide', in *What Does Eve Do to Help?*, pp. 85-105.

History, Israel has lost the land, it has been thrown out of God's presence (2 Kgs 24.20), and the threat of Deut. 4.27 has been fulfilled, that Israel is to be scattered among the other nations and only a few of its members are to survive. Perhaps we might then reflect that even the exile is not the end of the story—though it is the end of the history-writing; perhaps the promises even now, in our own day, still await their fulfilment. But whatever historical moment we fix on to take our soundings in order to discover whether the promises have been fulfilled, we find an ambivalent situation. In short, in the Pentateuch God makes promises, indeed, but if we are to properly appreciate the character of this Pentateuchal God we need to be able to determine whether there is any truth in these promises; and the answer is far from clear.

It is the same with the speaking of God. There is no doubt that the God of the Pentateuch is not a distant, uninterested or uncommunicative God. But if we are to say anything more than bland generalities we have to flesh out what this speaking consists of. Here again there are ambivalences. For as well as the words of moral guidance he speaks to Israel in the Pentateuch there is, for example, an oracle from him about Esau and Jacob, that 'the elder shall serve the younger' (Gen. 25.23). We, for our part, find ourselves asking, Why should the traditional rights of the firstborn be overturned at this point, why should a man who cynically buys a birthright for the price of a meal be divinely authorized to keep it, is it in any case possible to 'buy' a birthright, and why in any case should one of them 'serve' the other, considering that they are brothers? Or, to take another example, what is one to make of the amazingly elaborate instructions given by the character God for the construction of the tabernacle and for the performance of sacrifice in his honour? What kind of a deity is it that wants to specify to this degree precisely how he is to be worshipped and what will count as legitimate and illegitimate expressions of reverence for him? What kind of a person is it, we might say, that is so concerned for his own honour and that lays so many constraints on the responses of others to him?

There are no straightforward answers to such questions. The God of the Pentateuch is a complex and mysterious character, passionate and dynamic but by no means conformable to human notions of right behaviour. He is not very lovable, but he must be obeyed. He has his plans, but they are not infrequently deflected. He does not do very much explaining, and he relates to people mostly by a system of threats and promises. He has his favourites, and he is fiercely loyal to them. He is hard to please. But which of all these characteristics should weigh heaviest in the scales? The Pentateuch is a machine for generating variant readings of the character of God, and the answers it gives will be shaped by the kinds of questions we allow ourselves to address to it. None of our readings will be disinterested, all will enshrine our own ideology.

10

David the Man:
The Construction of Masculinity in the Hebrew Bible[*]

There are three sets of questions underlying this study.

1. What does it mean to be a man in our own culture? What roles are available for young men to grow into, what images are there for adult men to imitate, what criteria exist for defining manliness?

2. And what was it like in the world of the Bible? Was it different, or much the same?

3. How do our answers to the first set of questions determine or influence our answers to the second set? How have our images of biblical men been shaped by our own cultural norms?

1. Being a Man in the Modern West

In the predominant culture of the West, five major themes in the construction of masculinity have been noted in one influential analysis.[1]

---

*   This essay was originally delivered as a paper in the Hebrew Bible: Gender Studies Section, Society of Biblical Literature International Meeting, Leuven, August, 1994, and at Hebrew Union College—Jewish Institute of Religion, Cincinnati, November, 1994.

1.   The typology is that of J.A. Doyle, *The Male Experience* (Dubuque, IA: William C. Brown, 2nd edn, 1989), cited by Julia T. Wood, *Gendered Lives: Communication, Gender, and Culture* (Belmont, CA: Wadsworth Publishing Company, 1994), pp. 77-81. See also Joseph H. Pleck, *The Myth of Masculinity* (Cambridge, MA: The MIT Press, 1981).

There are other important dimensions to the study of masculinity of which this essay cannot, of necessity, take account. One is that of *change* in western masculinity, and of the processes by which the prevailing norms have developed. See, for example, *Manful Assertions: Masculinities in Britain*

1. The primary rule is: Don't be female. J.A. Doyle calls this the 'negative touchstone' of men's role. Whatever women do is *ipso facto* what a real man must not do.[2]

2. The second rule is: Be successful. Men are trained to be 'success objects',[3] and their worth as husbands, friends and simply as men is determined by their successfulness. 'The object, a boy soon gathers, is not to be liked but to be envied,...not to be part of a group but to distinguish himself from the others in the group.'[4]

3. The third rule is: Be aggressive. From childhood, boys are encouraged to be tough, to fight, and not to run away. Competitive sport emphasizes these values, and in many cultures

since 1800 (ed. Michael Roper and John Tosh; London: Routledge, 1991); *Manliness and Morality: Middle-Class Masculinity in Britain and America 1800– 1940* (ed. J.A. Mangan and James Walvin; Manchester: Manchester University Press, 1987); Clyde W. Franklin, II, *The Changing Definition of Masculinity* (New York: Plenum Press, 1984); Michael S. Kimmel, *Changing Men: New Directions in Research on Men and Masculinity* (Newbury Park, CA: Sage Publications, 1987). Cf. also the reviews introduced by Michael Roper, 'Recent Books on Masculinity', *History Workshop* 29 (1990), pp. 184-93; and the review forum in *Victorian Studies* 36 (1993), pp. 207-26; James Eli Adams, 'The Banality of Transgression? Recent Works on Masculinity' (pp. 207-13); Ed Cohen, 'Mar(r)king Men' (pp. 215-210); Mary Poovey, 'Exploring Masculinities' (pp. 223-26).

Another significant dimension is *theorizing* masculinity; see especially Peter Middleton, *The Inward Gaze: Masculinity and Subjectivity in Modern Culture* (London: Routledge, 1992); and *Engendering Men: The Question of Male Feminist Criticism* (ed. Joseph A. Boone and Michael Cadden; London: Routledge, 1990).

A third dimension is the challenge to the concept of masculinity itself posed by a *deconstructive* approach to the opposition male/female. See especially Jeff Hearn, *Men in the Public Eye: The Construction and Deconstruction of Public Men and Public Patriarchies* (London: Routledge, 1992), esp. pp. 1-9.

2.   Cf. Arthur Brittan, *Masculinity and Power* (Oxford: Basil Blackwell, 1989), p. 3: 'Masculinity...does not exist in isolation from femininity—it will always be an expression of the current image that men have of themselves in relation to women'.

3.   W. Farrell, 'Men as Success Objects', *Utne Reader* (May/June, 1991), pp. 81-84.

4.   Alfie Kohn, *No Contest: The Case against Competition* (Boston: Houghton Mifflin, 1986), p. 168.

military training reinforces them.[5]

4. The fourth demand is: Be sexual. Men are supposed to be sexually experienced, and to be always interested in sex.[6] 'Sex isn't a free choice when you have to perform to be a man.'[7]

5. Fifthly, the rule for men is: Be self-reliant. 'Men are supposed to be confident, independent and autonomous... A "real man" doesn't need others, particularly women. He depends on himself, takes care of himself, and relies on nobody.'[8]

Now there is nothing natural or God-given about these roles. Masculinity, like femininity, is a social construction, the product of historical processes, as much a human construct as the pyramids or pewter, as Catharine Stimpson puts it.[9] To be masculine, as she says, is 'to have a particular psychological identity, social role, cultural script, place in the labor force, and sense of the

---

5.   See also Brittan, *Masculinity and Power*, Chapter 4 'Masculinity and Competitiveness' (pp. 77-107).

6.   Cf. W. Gaylin, *The Male Ego* (New York: Viking/Penguin, 1992).

7.   Wood, *Gendered Lives*, p. 81.

8.   Wood, *Gendered Lives*, p. 81. This is not of course the only analysis of the male role that can be and has been made. Catharine Stimpson, for example, identifies three ways in which 'real men' define themselves: they earn money in the public labour force and so support their families; they have formal power over the women and children in those families; they are heterosexual with the women they dominate and bully other men who are not heterosexual (Catharine R. Stimpson, 'Foreword' to *The Making of Masculinities: The New Men's Studies* [ed. Harry Brod; New York: Routledge, 1987], p. xiii. And here is another much-cited account of the typical male: 'Someone who: is aggressive, independent, unemotional, or hides his emotions; is objective, easily influenced, dominant, likes maths and science; is not excitable in a minor crisis; is active, competitive, logical, worldly, skilled in business, direct, knows the ways of the world; is someone whose feelings are not easily hurt; is adventurous, makes decisions easily, never cries, acts as a leader; is self-confident; is not uncomfortable about being aggressive; is ambitious, able to separate feelings from ideas; is not dependent, nor conceited about his appearance; thinks men are superior to women, and talks freely about sex with men' (Fay Fransella and Kay Frost, *On Being a Woman: A Review of Research on How Women See Themselves* [London: Tavistock, 1977, pp. 43-44], cited by Ann Oakley, *Subject Women* [Oxford: Martin Robertson, 1981], p. 64).

9.   Stimpson, 'Foreword' to *The Making of Masculinities*, p. xiii.

sacred'[10]—and all of those elements are socially constructed.

Different societies write different scripts for their men, so it is a priori likely that maleness in the modern West does not closely resemble maleness in ancient Israel. But this is at the moment a rather new question, and we have as yet no resources to tell us about Israelite masculinity. None of the Bible dictionaries, for example, broaches this fundamental cultural subject, though they are packed with trivia about the material culture of the world of the Bible. We have to start more or less from scratch.

And we had better be open to the possibility of a plurality of masculinities. Perhaps the society legitimated more than one way of being a man—though perhaps not, since social pressures tend toward uniformity rather than diversity.[11] More significant is the fact that not all males, in whatever culture, conform with the social norms. The norms may privilege young, heterosexual, strong and physical men, for example, and those who cannot be so characterized will be deviants from socially acceptable maleness. But they will still be males. We can expect, then, to find in our texts, as well as in our own society, representations of conflicting masculinities.

2. Being a Man in the David Story

My scope here is the David story (1 Samuel 16 to 1 Kings 2), which is of course not the same thing as: ancient Israel. How typical the masculinity of this story is of the Hebrew Bible as a whole I do not know, yet; and how the literary representations of masculinity in our texts relate to real men (not 'real men') in ancient Israel I shall never know. But my guess is that the myth of masculinity inscribed in the David story was a very potent

10. Stimpson, 'Foreword' to *The Making of Masculinities*, p. xii.

11. Even in a period of rapid social change such as our own, the blueprint of gender stereotypes remains remarkably constant; cf. Wood, *Gendered Lives*, p. 21; F. Cancian, 'Love and the Rise of Capitalism', in *Gender in Intimate Relationships* (ed. B. Risman and P. Schwartz; Belmont, CA: Wadsworth, 1989), pp. 12-25. Of course, it is all too easy to slip into various intellectual sins over this matter of defining masculinity; David H.J. Morgan, for example, warns against the errors of essentialism, reductionism and reification (*Discovering Men* [Critical Studies on Men and Masculinities, 3; London: Routledge, 1992], pp. 41-43).

influence upon Israelite men, and I am quite sure that the construction of masculinity in the David story was not invented by
its author—or by some historical David—but reflects the cultural
norms of men of the author's time.

In the world of the David story, then, what are the components
of masculinity? Almost the first words we read about David go a
long way, it so happens, toward answering that question. In 1
Sam. 16.18 one of Saul's servants describes him, to Saul and to
the readers: David is a mighty man of valour (גבור חיל), a warrior
(איש מלחמה), intelligent in speech (נבון דבר), a beautiful man
(איש תאר), and skilful in playing (ידע נגן).[12]

1. *The fighting male*

The essential male characteristic in the David story is to be a
warrior, a man of war (איש מלחמה) or mighty man of valour
(גבור חיל).

Throughout the story, all the principal characters are warriors
who spend a lot of their time fighting and killing. Here is a list of
references to these activities:

> David kills Goliath, 1 Sam. 17.50
> He is said to have slain ten thousands, 18.7; 29.5
> He is made the commander of a thousand, 18.13
> He is commanded by Saul to fight Yahweh's battles on Saul's
>   behalf, 18.17
> He kills 200 Philistines for their foreskins, 18.27
> He goes on fighting Philistines, 18.30
> He makes a great slaughter of the Philistines, 19.8
> Doeg kills 85 priests, 22.18
> David makes a great slaughter of the Philistines at Keilah, 23.5
> There is a battle with the Philistines at Mt Gilboa, 31.1
> The Philistines kill Jonathan and other sons of Saul, 31.2
> An Amalekite kills Saul, 2 Sam. 1.10

12. He is obviously overqualified for the job of court musician, as
Brueggemann wryly observes (Walter Brueggemann, *First and Second
Samuel* [Interpretation: A Bible Commentary for Teaching and Preaching;
Louisville: John Knox Press, 1990], p. 125). Heather McKay reminds me in
this connection of the stained-glass window in the parish church in Fairlie,
Ayrshire, in which the hyper-competent young David bows beneath the
weight of his shepherd's crook, his throwing-stone, his scrip, his lyre—and
his psalm-book.

David has the Amalekite killed, 1.15
Joab and Abishai kill Abner, 3.30
Rechab and Baanah kill Ishbosheth, 4.7
David has Rechab and Baanah killed, 4.12
He defeats Philistines, Moabites, Hadadezer, 8.1-3
He kills 22,000 Syrians, 8.5
He kills 18,000 Edomites, 8.13
Joab leads Israelites in battle against Ammonites and Syrians, 10.6-9
David leads Israelites in battle against Syrians, 10.17
David kills the Syrian general Shobach, 40,000 horsemen and the
     men of 700 chariots, 10.18
Joab besieges the Ammonites of Rabbah, 11.1; 12.26
David arranges for Uriah's death, 11.15
Absalom's servants kill Amnon, 13.28-29
David's warriors kill 20,000 of Absalom's forces, 18.7
Joab and his warriors kill Absalom, 18.14-15
Joab kills Amasa, 20.10
The men of Abel Beth Maacah behead Sheba, 20.22
David gives seven sons of Saul to the Gibeonites to be killed, 21.6-9
David fights Philistines, 21.15
Abishai kills the Philistine Ishbosheth, 21.17
There are three further battles with Philistines, 21.18-20
David's warrior Josheb-basshebeth killed 800 men at one time, 23.8
David's warriors Eleazar and Shammah killed many Philistines,
     23.10, 12
Abishai killed 300 men, 23.18
Benaiah killed an Egyptian (and perhaps two Moabites), 23.20-21
David commands the killing of Joab and Shimei, 1 Kgs 2.6, 8-9
     (2.34, 46)

David's body count, by this reckoning, is something like 140,000 men, in addition to the 15 individuals whose deaths he is said to have been personally responsible for. According to the biblical text of the David story, indeed, ancient Israel as a whole was a warrior society: in Israel there were 800,000 warriors 'who drew the sword', and in Judah 500,000 (2 Sam. 24.9). No matter whether these figures have historical value or not; they are the impression the text wants to create, they constitute the narrator's representation of his society.

It is essential for a man in the David story that he be strong—which means to say, capable of violence against other men and active in killing other men. The language of strength is pervasive; here are merely some examples:

David 'prevails' (חזק) over the Philistine Goliath, 1 Sam. 17.50

Joab speaks of the Syrians being 'too strong' for him or the Ammonites being 'too strong' for his brother Abishai, 2 Sam. 10.11

Amnon 'overpowered' (חזק) his sister Tamar and raped her, 13.14

God has girded David with strength for battle, 22.40

Saul and Jonathan are lamented by David as 'the mighty', 1.19, 21, 22, 24, 27

David is surrounded by warriors known as his 'mighty men', 10.7; 16.6; 17.8; 20.7; 23.8, 9, 16, 17, 22

David himself is described by Hushai to Absalom as a man of war and the men with him as 'hardened warriors and as a bear in the wilds robbed of her cubs', 17.8, 10

Warriors should be 'lion-hearted', 17.10

The 'hand' as the symbol of power is almost a leitmotif of the David narrative: 1 Sam. 17.37, 46, 47; 18.17, 21, 25; 20.16; 22.17; 23.4, 7, 11, 12, 14, 16, 17, 20; 24.5, 7, 11, 13, 14, 16, 19, 21; 25.26, 33; 26.8, 9, 11, 23; 27.1; 28.19; 30.15, 23; 2 Sam. 1.14; 2.7; 3.8, 12, 18, 34; 4.1; 5.19; 8.1; 10.10; 12.7; 14.19; 16.8, 21; 17.2; 18.2, 12, 19, 28; 20.21; 21.9, 22; 22.35; 23.6, 10; 24.14, 16, 17.

Physical strength and the capacity to kill other men manifests itself sometimes as what we might call courage, even to the point of recklessness. Hebrew has no words for courage or bravery as distinct from strength, but our modern versions sometimes are right to translate words from the root חזק ('be strong') as 'courage, courageous'.[13] Thus in 2 Sam. 10.12, for example, Joab says to his brother Abishai, 'Be strong (חזק), and let us show ourselves strong (ונתחזק)[14] for the sake of our people and for the sake of the cities of our God'. When Absalom commissions his servants to assassinate Amnon (2 Sam. 13.28), he tells them not to fear: חזקו והיו לבני־חיל 'be courageous and be valiant' (RSV; REB has 'be bold and resolute').

Or, to take another example, from a little outside the David story itself, in 1 Sam. 4.9 the Philistines say to one another, having learned that the ark of Yahweh has come into their camp: 'Take courage (lit. be strong), and acquit yourselves like men, O

---

13. 'Courage' also appears in RSV in a non-military context in 2 Sam. 7.27: 'therefore thy servant has found courage (lit. has found his heart) to pray this prayer to thee'.

14. RSV 'let us play the man', following AV 'let us play the men', probably borrows the idiom from 1 Sam. 4.9.

Philistines, lest you become slaves to the Hebrews as they have been to you; acquit yourselves like men and fight'. This phrase 'acquit yourselves like men', literally 'become men' (היו לאנשים, repeated as והייתם לאנשים), means, very simply, that to be a man is to fight. The whole ideology surrounding this utterance is a little more complex than that, no doubt; for the purpose of fighting is to resist slavery for oneself and to continue to keep others in slavery; and the possibility that fighting may not ensure that objective, and that the chance of being victorious can hardly be greater than fifty-fifty, is silently suppressed. But as far as the gender issue is concerned, it is simple: men fight.

2. *The persuasive male*

It is obviously also an important male role in Israel to be good with words, as David is described by Saul's servant (1 Sam. 16.18): he is 'intelligent in speech' (נבון דבר). The term נבון 'intelligent' is used elsewhere of Joseph (Gen. 41.33, 39), of tribal elders (Deut. 1.13) and of Solomon (1 Kgs 3.12), but nowhere else in the combination נבון דבר 'intelligent in speech'. Fokkelman thinks that this quality, 'so closely linked to the cares of state, the public interest, and the law', must be 'an anticipation of David's functioning as king';[15] but it is something true of David long before he is king, something that belongs rather with his masculinity than with his kingship.

Where is this characteristic of David's, intelligent speech, evident in the text? Ralph W. Klein points to 1 Sam. 17.34-36, where David persuades Saul that he is capable of withstanding Goliath, 24.10-15, where he explains to Saul why he did not kill him in the cave, and 26.18-20, where David asks Saul why he continues to pursue him, and Saul admits that he has done wrong (26.21).

15. J.P. Fokkelman, *Narrative Art and Poetry in the Books of Samuel: A Full Interpretation Based on Stylistic and Structural Analyses*. II. *The Crossing Fates (I Sam. 13–31 & II Sam. 1)* (Assen: Van Gorcum, 1986), p. 137. A.R.S. Kennedy thought that the phrase connects closely with ידע נגן 'knowing how to play (an instrument)', in reference either to the recitative that accompanied the music or to David's 'ready wit' (*Samuel: Introduction, Revised Version with Notes, Index and Maps* [Edinburgh: T.C. & E.C. Jack, n.d.], p. 119). But this requires deletion of the phrase וגבור חיל ואיש מלחמה as a secondary intrusion.

These are all effective examples of the power of words, not in any magical sense, but as instruments of control. To be master of persuasion is to have another form of power, which is not an alternative to, and far less a denatured version of, physical strength, but part of the repertory of the powerful male. We think of Odysseus too, who is before everything πολύτροπος, not merely 'much travelled' but 'versatile, ingenious, wily'.[16]

Intelligent, eloquent, persuasive speech forms part of a wider category of 'wisdom', to which Norman Whybray has drawn attention as an important motif in the 'Succession Narrative'.[17] In 2 Sam. 14.20 the woman from Tekoa says that the king 'has wisdom like the wisdom of the angel of God to know all things that are on the earth', and in 1 Kgs 2.6, 9 David assumes royal wisdom in his successor Solomon by urging him to 'act according to your wisdom' in seeing that Joab and Shimei are killed. Among the examples of 'wisdom' in the David story cited by Whybray are: David's attempts to extricate himself from the results of his adultery with Bathsheba (2 Sam. 11.14-25), Joab's use of the woman of Tekoa 'in order to change the course of affairs' (RSV), Absalom's words by which he 'stole the hearts of the men of Israel' (2 Sam. 15.1-6), and David's sending Hushai to give false advice to Absalom (2 Sam. 15.33-35).

The fact that there are also intelligent and persuasive women speakers in the David story, such as Abigail and the woman of Tekoa, by no means undercuts the assertion that this is a characteristic of masculinity.[18] It is precisely because our own culture

16. Homer, *Odyssey* 1.1. He is, according to W.B. Stanford (*The Odyssey of Homer* [London: Macmillan, 2nd edn, 1959], pp. xii-xiii), 'a symbol of the Ionic-Greek Everyman in his eloquence, cleverness, unscrupulousness, intellectual curiosity, courage, endurance, shrewdness'.

17. R.N. Whybray, *The Succession Narrative: A Study of II Sam. 9–20 and I Kings 1 and 2* (Studies in Biblical Theology, 2/9; London: SCM Press, 1968), pp. 57-60, 90.

18. It would be interesting to know if eloquence was perhaps not expected of a woman in ancient Israel. In Luther's Germany it wasn't. Praising his wife's fluency, he remarked one day at table, '[E]loquence in women shouldn't be praised; it's more fitting for them to lisp and stammer. This is more becoming to them. In men speech is a great and divine gift' (Martin Luther, in *Luther's Works. 54. Table Talk* [ed. and trans. Theodore G. Tappert; Philadelphia: Fortress Press, 1967], p. 317).

insists so strongly on defining a man as 'not a woman' that we are tempted to think that anything a woman can do cannot also be characteristically male; but that is a fallacy.

3. *The beautiful male*

One of the distinctive features noted by Saul's servant about David is that he is a beautiful man: he is a איש תאר, 'a man of (beautiful) form' (1 Sam. 16.18). Beautiful people in the Bible are both male and female: Rachel is 'beautiful of form' (יפת־תאר, Gen. 29.17), as is Abigail (1 Sam. 25.3); Esther is יפת־תאר וטובת מראה 'fair of form and beautiful in looks' in Est. 2.7,[19] and Bathsheba is 'very beautiful in appearance' (טובת מראה מאד, 2 Sam. 11.2). Among the males there is Joseph, who is 'beautiful of form and beautiful of appearance' (יפה־תאר ויפה מראה, Gen. 39.6), and Adonijah, who is 'very beautiful' (טוב־תאר מאד, 1 Kgs 1.6).[20] Saul is a 'handsome' (טוב)[21] young man (בחור) and there is none among the Israelites more handsome (טוב) than him; he is taller than any other Israelite (1 Sam. 9.2). David is 'ruddy' (אדמוני)—whatever exactly that means, it obviously refers to some aspect of physical beauty[22]—and 'fair of eyes' (יפה עינים)[23] and 'beautiful in appearance' (טוב ראי) in 1 Sam 16.12. In 17.42 he is 'ruddy' (אדמוני) 'with beauty of appearance' (עם־יפה מראה).[24] Of Absalom we hear that 'in

---

19. And Tamar is יפה 'beautiful' in 2 Sam. 13.1.

20. The same phrase may lie behind LXX's ἀγαθὸς τῷ εἴδει here; it is ὡραῖος τῇ ὄψει at 1 Kgs 1.6.

21. Moses as a child is also seen to be טוב 'beautiful' (Exod. 2.2).

22. It is generally thought to refer to the colour of the skin, but Kennedy, *Samuel*, p. 118, thinks (following Klostermann) that it may be the colour of the hair, and finds it interesting to think of David as the red-haired 'darling of the songs of Israel' (2 Sam. 23.1), 'or, as Browning has it in his *Saul*, "God's child with his dew, On thy gracious gold hair"'.

23. P. Kyle McCarter, Jr, *I Samuel: A New Translation with Introduction, Notes and Commentary* (Anchor Bible, 8; Garden City, NY: Doubleday, 1980), p. 275, emends 'with some confidence' אדמוני עם to אדם ונעים 'ruddy and attractive' (cf. אדום 'ruddy' in Cant. 5.10).

24. Some manuscripts have יפה עינים 'beautiful of eyes'; cf. LXX μετὰ κάλλους ὀφθαλμῶν. McCarter, *I Samuel*, p. 275, deletes ואדמוני עם־יפה מראה as an expansion inspired by 1 Sam. 16.12; Peter R. Ackroyd is similarly tempted (*The First Book of Samuel* [The Cambridge Bible Commentary on the New English Bible; Cambridge: Cambridge University Press, 1971], p. 145).

all Israel there was not a man so much to be praised for his beauty (lit. there was not [such] a beautiful man, איש־יפה)'; 'from the sole of his foot to the crown of his head there was no blemish in him' (2 Sam. 14.25). And there is of course the servant of Isaiah 53, who because of his disfigurement has no 'form' (תאר) or 'splendour' (הדר) that 'we' should gaze upon (ראה) him, and no 'appearance' (מראה) that 'we' should desire (חמד) him (53.2); it is implied that ordinarily one would expect a high-ranking 'servant of Yahweh' to be beautiful in form and face, and to be sexually attractive (חמד) to 'us' (? males).

Samuel is obviously impressed by male beauty. When he 'sees' Jesse's eldest son Eliab, he thinks, 'Surely here, before the LORD, is his anointed king' (1 Sam. 16.6 REB). The word 'beauty' is not there, but the word 'sees' is; what the male gaze sees attracts it, though its super-ego may feel uncomfortable about feeling attracted. Says Yahweh to Samuel, 'Pay no attention to his outward appearance and stature...The LORD does not see as a mortal sees; mortals see only appearances but the LORD sees into the heart' (v. 7 REB). But then Samuel catches sight of Saul, 'handsome, with ruddy cheeks and bright eyes' (v. 12 REB), and, with wondrous irony, as Walter Brueggemann puts it, 'Samuel and the narrator are dazzled';[25] and Yahweh, who of course does not see as a mortal sees, seizes the moment: 'This is the man; rise and anoint him' (v. 12), he commands.

Beauty is not generally a state to which a man who does not have it can aspire,[26] but obviously it is very desirable, in the world of the David story, for a man to be beautiful. Beauty is to be seen, at the least, in bodily shape, in the eyes, in the skin colour, and in the height. The language used here is not of some

25. Walter Brueggemann, *First and Second Samuel* (Interpretation: A Bible Commentary for Teaching and Preaching; Louisville: John Knox Press, 1990), pp. 122-23.

26. I should not omit the concept of 'body building', however. Rowena Chapman writes archly of those 'paragons of male aesthetics, rippling poems of perfect pectorals and shuddering quads, testimonies to current canons of male beauty...Everyone knows you don't get a body like that just by whistling[;] it requires effort, patience and commitment' ('The Great Pretender: Variations on the New Man Theme', in *Male Order: Unwrapping Masculinity* [ed. Rowena Chapman and Jonathan Rutherford; London: Lawrence & Wishart, 1988], pp. 225-48 [237]).

diffused notion of 'good looks', but reflects some quite precise and analytical thought about what makes a man beautiful. From the description of Absalom we learn that beauty is not regarded by men in Israel as a mere accident of birth that is for the most part to be shrugged off as the way the cookie crumbles. Rather, it is an aspect of 'real manhood' for which a man can expect praise and admiration.

4. *The bonding male*
A further important characteristic of maleness in the David story is friendship between males, specifically the type of friendship now known as 'male bonding'.[27] Friendship is not of course a simple category, and several typologies have been advanced that identify friendships along a continuum ranging from the 'affective' to the 'instrumental'.[28] Those friendships within the David story have strong elements of the types at both poles. Noting how little David and Jonathan seem to know one another or how few things they do together, we need to recognize that there is more than one kind of friendship, and that emotional intimacy is not necessarily part of male friendship, or at least that ideas of intimacy are not necessarily the same for men and for women. In a word, 'male bonding is not a vehicle for male–male

---

27. The term seems to have been first used by Lionel Tiger, in his *Men in Groups* (London: Thomas Nelson & Sons, 1969). Among recent studies of male bonding in literary texts may be mentioned those of Donald J. Geiner, *Women Enter the Wilderness: Male Bonding and the American Novel of the 1980s* (Columbia, SC: University of South Carolina Press, 1991), advancing the questionable theory that in the last decade the tendency in (white, male) American novels has been for male bonding to be less exclusive of women; Anne J. Cruz, 'Homo ex machina? Male Bonding in Calderón's *A secreto agravio, secreta venganza'*, *Forum for Modern Language Studies* 25 (1989), pp. 154-66.

28. Cf. Y.A. Cohen, 'Patterns of Friendship', in *Social Structure and Personality* (ed. Y.A. Cohen; New York: Holt, Rinehart & Winston, 1961); E. Wolf, 'Kinship, Friendship and Patron–Client Relationships in Complex Societies', in *The Social Anthropology of Complex Societies* (ed. M. Banton; London: Tavistock, 1966), pp. 3-27; Dorothy Hammond and Alta Jablow, 'Gilgamesh and the Sundance Kid: The Myth of Male Friendship', in *The Making of Masculinities*, pp. 241-58 (243-45).

emotional relationships, but rather is a substitute for them'.[29]

In their delightfully entitled paper, 'Gilgamesh and the Sundance Kid: The Myth of Male Friendship', Dorothy Hammond and Alta Jablow have traced a widespread myth of male friendship, which 'dramatizes the devotion between male friends, usually a dyad, forged in an agonistic setting',[30] from its classic expression in the Gilgamesh epic, through Homer and the Bible to the *Song of Roland*, bush 'mateship' in the short stories of the Australian writer Henry Lawson, comrades in arms in films of the world wars, heroes of frontier America like the Lone Ranger and Tonto, near-mythic figures like Butch Cassidy and the Sundance Kid, and even, with a gender twist, to Cagney and Lacey. In its classical formulations, as with Gilgamesh and Enkidu, David and Jonathan, Achilles and Patroclus, Orestes and Pylades, Castor and Pollux, Damon and Pythias, the friends are typically heroes: 'aristocratic, young, brave, and beautiful. In their free and wholehearted response to one another, they openly declare their affection and admiration. They engage in many adventures and battles, sharing danger, loyal to the death. Throughout life, they remain devoted and generous to each other.'[31] Such male friendship is of course not the opposite of female friendship, and I am not suggesting that the Hebrews knew of no other ways for men to be friends except on the pattern of David and Jonathan. But I am arguing that this model of heroic male bonding is one important way masculinity was constructed in ancient Israel and, as well, that the David narrative itself had a significant role in sustaining that construction.

According to Hammond and Jablow, the function of male friendship in this tradition was to provide a source of support that was freely chosen without the constraints of kinship, a support that perhaps had emotional dimensions that could not be

29. Pleck, *The Myth of Masculinity*, p. 150 (italics mine). And, while 'males measure no lower than females in sociability, they do measure lower in intimacy' (p. 149). Cf. also Drury Sherrod, 'The Bonds of Men: Problems and Possibilities in Close Male Relationships', in *The Making of Masculinities*, pp. 213-39 (217): '[w]omen seem to look for intimate confidantes, while men seek for partners for adventure'.

30. Hammond and Jablow, 'Gilgamesh and the Sundance Kid', p. 245.

31. Hammond and Jablow, 'Gilgamesh and the Sundance Kid', p. 247.

provided within a system of kinship and arranged marriages. Such male friendships operated especially in the public domain, which meant in practice in many societies, in warfare. In that context, familial support was unavailable, and warriors needed the support of likeminded and equally isolated men. At least in classical Greece, and probably also in Israel, such male friendships had no overt homosexual element; certainly in Greece, homosexual love was typically between an older lover and a younger beloved,[32] whereas male bonding friends were peers— as were Jonathan and David.

The ideology of such male friendship contains these elements: loyalty to one another, a dyadic relationship with an exclusive tendency, a commitment to a common cause, and a valuing of the friendship above all other relationships. In such a friendship there is not necessarily a strong emotional element; the bond may be more instrumental and functional than affective. Perhaps that is the nature of the bond between David and Jonathan, and that is one of the ways in which they subscribe to, and promote, the Hebrew ideology of masculinity.

5. *The womanless male*

One of the concomitants of strong male bonding is of course a relative minimizing of cross-sex relationships. It may seem strange to speak of David, a man with eight principal wives and at least ten others of secondary rank (2 Sam. 15.16), as 'womanless'. But it is a striking feature of the David story that the males are so casual about women, and that women are so marginal to the lives of the protagonists. There is in this story, on the whole, no sexual desire, no love stories, no romances, no wooing, no daring deeds for the sake of a beloved. This is not a world in which men long for women. It is rather a matter of pride for David and his men, in fact, that they have kept themselves 'clean' from women: 'Women have always been kept from us whenever I go on an expedition; the "vessels" of the young men are holy, even when it is a common journey' (1 Sam. 21.5), he avers.

There *is* sex in the story, of course, but it is perfunctory and

32. Cf. Kenneth J. Dover, *Greek Homosexuality* (Cambridge, MA: Harvard University Press, 1978).

usually politically motivated. The classic case in the David story is that of Absalom, who has sex with ten of his father's secondary wives 'in the sight of all Israel' simply in order to lay claim to the throne of his father (2 Sam. 16.21-23). Even in the Bathsheba episode, the sex is essentially an expression of royal power, and it is much more like rape than love.

In the one case where sexual desire comes into the foreground, it is accompanied by strongly negative connotations. Amnon 'loves' his sister Tamar (2 Sam. 13.2). But such love is not good for him: he is in distress (צרר) to the point of becoming ill (חלה hithpa.) 'on account of' (NIV) (בעבור) her, but perhaps rather we should translate it 'because of her'—as if it were her fault.[33] He is no longer in control of himself, but feels compelled to satisfy his lust, which he can only do by trickery, incest and rape. And the desire he experiences is unsatisfying and ephemeral: his love for her immediately turns to hatred. What is more, his desire has fearful consequences: he himself becomes hated by his brother and the object of his father's anger, and eventually he meets his death—just because of his sexual desire and experience. The message plainly is that sex can damage your health very severely, and nothing in the narrative of David goes to show that more definitively than the key episode of David and Bathsheba (2 Sam. 11).

We have to conclude that David does not actually like women very much, and certainly has no fun with them. If he can say that Jonathan's love has been 'wonderful', better than the love of women, and he has (as far as I can judge) never been to bed with Jonathan, it doesn't say a lot for his love life.

But more important than David's sexual experience is the image of masculinity that the David story promotes. It says loud and clear, if only ever implicitly, that a real man can get along fine without women; he can have several women in a casual kind of way, but he has nothing to gain from them except children, and he owes them nothing. Hanging over every woman is the spectre of fatal attraction; like the 'wily' woman of Proverbs 7, every woman is potentially a road to Sheol, a way down to the chambers of death (Prov. 7.27). A man does well to steer clear of

33. Cases where בעבור implies responsibility are, for example: Gen. 3.17; 8.21; 12.13, 16; 18.26, 29, 31, 32; 26.24.

women, a man does not need women, a man is not constituted by his relationship with women. It is a different story if we substitute 'other men' for 'women' in the previous sentence.

f. *The musical male*

A final characteristic of David, according to the glowing report of the servant of Saul, is that David is 'skilful in playing the lyre' (ידע נגן, lit. 'knowing, i.e. experienced at, playing [a stringed instrument]', 1 Sam. 16.18). I thought at first that musicianship was not an especially masculine trait in David, but just an accidental feature of his characterization, more dependent on his role in the narrative (like the notation that 'Yahweh was with him') than upon the Hebrew construction of masculinity. In any case, I would not want to lay too much weight upon this speech by a servant of Saul; it is certainly not meant by him to be a definitive summary of the characteristics of Israelite masculinity. Nevertheless, the servant of Saul certainly encourages us to ponder whether this element in the picture of David—alongside his being a warrior, a persuasive speaker and a beautiful man—may not itself be an expression of his maleness.

We ourselves are hardly inclined to distinguish between the sexes in the matter of musical ability, and would readily ascribe the predominance of males as composers of music and as orchestral conductors, for example, to more general social structures. My own modern construction of masculinity was no doubt an important reason why I did not myself immediately recognize David's musical talent as a masculine trait.[34] Is it, though? What is the evidence?

In the Hebrew Bible, women as well as men make music. But is the music-making they engage in a gendered activity? Women are singers, accompanying themselves with timbrels and tambourines and other assorted idiophones (like the שׁלשׁים, [?] 'sistrum') and membranophones (like the תף, [?] 'timbrel, tambourine, drum').[35] The playing of stringed instruments, on the

---

34. I am grateful to Francis Landy for urging me to consider David's musicality more seriously.

35. For the categories, see Ivor H. Jones, 'Music and Musical Instruments', in *The Anchor Bible Dictionary* (ed. David Noel Freedman; New York: Doubleday, 1992), IV, pp. 930-39. For the sistrum as played by

other hand, seems to have been largely a male activity. It would not be that ancient Israelite women were incapable of playing stringed instruments, of course, but rather that skill in playing— playing 'with the hand' (בידו, 1 Sam 16.16, 23), i.e. with dextrous use of the fingers, would be a male preserve. If we look at the references to the lyre (כנור, often translated as 'harp'), which is David's speciality, and is referred to more than 40 times in the Hebrew Bible, the only place where a woman plays it is in Isa. 23.16: it is Tyre as a prostitute who takes a lyre and makes sweet melody (היטיב נגן).[36] The exception proves the rule. Women never play the נבל, (?) 'lute' or the עוגב, (?) 'harp'.

Perhaps we should conclude therefore that David's kind of music, and his pre-eminence in playing it, is represented in the narrative as an essentially male trait.

g. A Conflict of Masculinities?
Now that we have reviewed what seem to be the leading male characteristics in the figure of David, there is another question that needs yet to be raised. It is, Are there are any conflicting masculinities within the David story? Focussing exclusively on David, I ask, Does David himself conform entirely to one set of models for maleness? Are there ways, for example, in which David breaks free of the role of the traditional male, are there any hints that David might be something of a 'new man'?[37]

At first sight this may seem to be so. There are several episodes in which David acts contrary to what seem to be the standards of a traditional masculinity. Joab puts it famously when he says, 'You love those who hate you and hate those who love you...Today I perceive that if Absalom were alive and all of us

women, see 1 Sam. 18.6; for the timbrel, Exod. 15.11; Judg. 11.34; 1 Sam. 18.6; Jer. 31.4.

36. In Sir. 9.4 also the reader is advised not to dally (or sleep) with מנגנת; whether they are women who play instruments or 'singing girls' (as JB, NAB) is not certain. In the LXX the term is ψάλλουσα, but in Hellenistic Greek, ψάλλω seems to mean 'sing', with or without accompaniment (in classical Greek it was 'pluck [a stringed instrument]').

37. See the brilliant essay by Rowena Chapman, 'The Great Pretender: Variations on the New Man Theme', in *Male Order: Unwrapping Masculinity*, pp. 225-48.

were dead today, then you would be pleased' (2 Sam. 19.6). We (I mean, we modern westerners) are rather attracted to this trait in David—even if it does not immediately resonate for us with Christian overtones. Many readers would agree with Cheryl Exum that the whole episode of Absalom's revolt brings before us a 'rare, intimate view of David' and that '[i]n his vulnerability the king becomes most sympathetic'.[38] At the very least, we are inclined with her to find marks of 'tragic conflict' and 'grief, so tragically excessive', and to behold a man who 'endures, broken in spirit', a man in extremity, who has 'expended all emotion'.[39]

But what if the burden of the text, reading with the grain of its gender codes, that is to say, is not that David is somehow noble and tragically heroic in this scene, but is simply a failure as a man, as a male. What reason have we to think that the narrator has any sympathy for David? On the contrary, he has Joab roundly rebuke David in terms no one has ever dared use with him before,[40] and David, for his part, does not defend himself against Joab's criticism but meekly capitulates, arising and taking his seat in the gate (19.8). In short, we ourselves may find David interesting precisely because he sometimes lapses from the ideals of traditional masculinity; but that does not mean that the text has relaxed its allegiance to those norms for an instant.[41] The text represents David as a great hero, but a fallible one; and his fallibility only serves to inscribe yet deeper the authority of the cultural norms of his time.

Reading from this direction, perhaps another unexpected

38. J. Cheryl Exum, *Tragedy and Biblical Narrative: Arrows of the Almighty* (Cambridge: Cambridge University Press, 1992), p. 130. There is an appeal in a footnote to Charles Conroy, *Absalom Absalom! Narrative and Language in 2 Sam. 13–20* (Rome: Biblical Institute Press, 1978), pp. 111-12. And cf. Walter Brueggemann, *David's Truth in Israel's Imagination and Memory* (Philadelphia: Fortress Press, 1985), p. 47: 'If there had been no interiority to David, if there were only public events, the narrative would scarcely attract us'.

39. Exum, *Tragedy and Biblical Narrative*, p. 135.

40. As Exum notes (*Tragedy and Biblical Narrative*, p. 135).

41. Brueggemann sees this when he words Joab's rebuke as a warning that 'if [David's] personal pain is allowed to erode a good public presence, the whole fragile "house of authority" will quickly collapse' (*David's Truth*, p. 72).

episode in the David story makes better sense. While the child of his union with Bathsheba is dying, David fasts and will not be roused from his identification with the child in its weakness; but the moment the child has died, David pragmatically resumes his normal activity and abandons his grieving (2 Sam. 12.15-23). Readers of David's behaviour, starting with his puzzled servants in the text, have often found something both fascinating and repellent here,[42] but none, I think, has seen it as the outworking of a gender code. If men of David's time are to be strong, David's response to the child's death is the ultimate macho act, the fitting conclusion to a narrative of aggressive masculinity that began with the rape of Bathsheba and continued with the cynical disposal of her husband. In this story, even God is treated by David in a purely instrumental way: David fasts and prays only so long as he thinks he can affect God's determination of the outcome; the moment God takes the child's life, David knows he is defeated, and abandons his weapon of a self-serving piety.[43] Whether the excessive grief over the dying child conformed with the male script of his culture or not I do not know; but if it did not, David certainly compensated very shortly for his lapse from its standards.

What of the occasions when David capitulates to fate? Are these signs of a character that is in resistance to male norms of success and indomitableness? Are they the hint of a narrator that there can be more to being a man than playing out traditional gender roles? I am thinking of the time when David hears the news that Absalom has been proclaimed king in Hebron and promptly vacates Jerusalem (2 Sam. 15.13-23). When Abiathar and Zadok volunteer to bring the ark with David into exile, David tells them to take it back: 'If I find favour in the eyes of

---

42. Though some think it 'an act of profound faith in the face of the most precious tabus of his people' (Walter Brueggemann, *In Man We Trust: The Neglected Side of Biblical Faith* [Richmond: John Knox Press, 1972], p. 36), or an affirmation of David's 'belief in Yahweh's freedom to repay as he chooses' (David M. Gunn, *The Story of King David: Genre and Interpretation* [Journal for the Study of the Old Testament Supplement Series, 6; Sheffield: JSOT, 1978], p. 110).

43. Brueggemann, *David's Truth*, p. 53, acknowledges that 'the overriding mark of David is his *self-serving*'.

Yahweh', he says, 'he will bring me back and let me see both it and his habitation; but if he says, "I have no pleasure in you", behold, here I am; let him do to me what seems good to him' (15.25-26). A little later, he is faced by Shimei, cursing and throwing stones. But David resists Abishai's offer to 'go over and take off his head' (16.9), saying, 'Let him alone, and let him curse, for Yahweh has bidden him. It may be that Yahweh will look upon my affliction, and that Yahweh will repay me with good for this cursing of me today' (16.11-12). Is David being portrayed in these incidents as 'a man of stunning faith', moved by 'more than moral courage of a tragic kind'?[44] Or is it David abandoning the soldierly norms by which he has lived, making himself more sympathetic—to pacifists at least—in the process, but not in the least inspiring the hearers of his story to a post-masculinist worldview? Is it not, from the point of view of the narrator, a weakness in David as a man (though it is perhaps a strength in him as a human being, from our point of view) that he has caved in at the first rumour of opposition to him by Absalom?

There is no 'new man' here in the David story. There is a fully fledged traditional male, who for the most part recapitulates everything scripted for him by his culture, but now and then conspicuously fails—so conspicuously that any non-feminized reader knows immediately that it is a failure that is not to be excused or imitated, but is a sorry example that serves only to reinforce the value of the traditional norms.

3. *The Conflict of Masculinities: Ours and Theirs*

There are similarities and dissimilarities between our modern western masculinity and that of the David story. The most striking, and even perhaps the most foundational, of the dissimilarities is the modern self-definition of maleness over against femininity. In David's world, evidently, the spheres of men and women are so distinct, their cultural scripts so divergent, that neither defines self over against the other. If our culture represents the 'feminization' of society, as has been argued,[45] it makes

44. Brueggemann, *David's Truth*, p. 53.
45. Such 'feminization' has been seen, historically, most clearly by its opponents, such as the Boy Scout movement. See, for example, Joseph H.

sense that males now tend to define themselves oppositionally, having lost a distinct idea of their own role.

The foundational character of this oppositional self-definition is illustrated graphically, if rather trivially, by the idea of male beauty. In a world—like David's—in which men do not have to be the opposite of women, there is no problem with men thinking of themselves and of other men as beautiful, indeed of beauty being a desirable male characteristic. But in our world, men go out of their way to avoid the idea, and have developed a language to repress it.

Perhaps another example where the oppositional self-definition has had influence is that of the persuasive male. In our culture, skill with words, especially persuasive speech, tends to be regarded as a female characteristic, and it does not figure among the typically male ideals analysed by Doyle and Wood. A characteristic male of our time is rather the strong silent type.

It is interesting to wonder how the evident lack of interest in sex in the David story, by contrast to our contemporary insistence on its near obligatoriness, fits in with the profile of masculinity in the text. Can it be that contemporary absorption in sex coheres with a masculinity that is not so sure of itself, that is troubled about self-definition and functionality? If sex is as much a way of finding oneself as finding the other, might finding oneself be a peculiarly modern desire, one that is not shared by the world of the text?[46]

There are of course also the similarities to be considered. The crucial one is the demand to be aggressive. The idea of the warrior as the ideal of maleness is instantly recognizable in both cultures, even if most of the fighting today is done either by

Pleck, 'The Theory of Male Sex-Role Identity: Its Rise and Fall, 1936 to the Present', in *The Making of Masculinities*, pp. 21-38 (23); Michael S. Kimmel, 'The Contemporary "Crisis" of Masculinity in Historical Perspective', in *The Making of Masculinities*, pp. 121-53 (143-49); Michael Messner, 'The Meaning of Success: The Athletic Experience and the Development of Male Identity', in *The Making of Masculinities*, pp. 193-209 (196).

46. Cf. Robert Nozik, 'Sexuality', in *Gender Basics: Feminist Perspectives on Women and Men* (ed. Anne Minas; Belmont, CA: Wadsworth, 1993), pp. 302-306: 'It is not only the other person who is known more deeply in sex. One knows one's own self better in experiencing what it is capable of' (p. 303).

proxy in distant wars or metaphorically on the sports field or in the boardroom. Toughness and strength are still the cultural script for boys and men, though what counts as toughness is not necessarily the same in the two cultures. David can cry, for example, without detriment to his masculinity, but a man who cries publicly today is still something of a deviant, an embarrassment at least, even if nothing worse.

The idea of success is common to both cultures too, of course. There is no point in fighting except to win, and success in the David story is measured by the body count. The idea of success in modern masculinity is very much more broadly based, however, and the modern male can easily be made to feel less than a man if he is unsuccessful in any area of his life. The problem with the criterion of success, especially when it is couched competitively, as in warfare or in sport or, often, in business, is that there are very many more failures than successes, so that the very structure of the male ideal ensures that most males will feel themselves inadequate in some way or other; the system is a 'structure of failure'. In the case of the sports world, for example, though the emphasis on competitive sports throughout the 1960s was founded on the premises that 'sports builds character' and 'a winner in sports will be a winner in life', the very opposite proves to be the case. And the criterion of success itself is self-defeating, since 'success' is almost never attainable in any absolute or permanent sense; it can only be an aspiration, so long as the message is conveyed that 'you're only as good as your last game'.[47] Whether the same intensity and comprehensiveness attaches to the idea of success in the David story is doubtful.

As for the idea of self-reliance, here too there are clear resonances between the ideals of masculinity in our culture and in David's world. But the meaning of self-reliance, and its depth, are different. The ideal of the supportive friend as part of the essence of maleness makes a lot of difference on this front.

So, even the similarities between their world and ours contain dissimilarities. What happens to those dissimilarities, I now ask, when readers from our culture read the David story?

47. See further, Michael Messner, 'The Meaning of Success: The Athletic Experience and the Development of Male Identity', in *The Making of Masculinities*, pp. 193-209 (193-95, 199).

4. *The Triumph of Modern Masculinity*

The thesis of this final section is that the profile of masculinity in the modern world has, in the literature about David, overwhelmed the quite distinctive portrait of Hebrew masculinity in the David story.

1. *Approval*

The most striking aspect of the modern scholarly response to the figure of David in the biblical narrative is the strong note of approval that is struck. Why do scholars so unanimously defend David and gloss over his faults? Have they perhaps been over-influenced by the tone of the biblical narrator, who is remarkably reticent and averse to making judgments of the characters?[48] Have they perhaps read the narrative, which rarely if ever criticizes David, as approving of David's behaviour and character, and have they adopted the narrator's standpoint, whether consciously or not? This does not seem to be a probable explanation, since biblical narrators everywhere are notoriously reticent and scholars may be expected to take critical account of that fact.

Perhaps we should consider the theological dimension of the David figure, whether or not the sentence about his being 'a man after God's own heart' is taken literally or not. Those who see David as a prefigurement of the messiah, as, for example, 'the kingly ideal...in the image of which [Israel] looked for a coming Messiah, who should deliver his people and sit upon the throne of David for ever',[49] might be inclined to minimize the negative aspects of David's character. This is no doubt a very powerful force in the interpretation of the figure of David, even up to the

48. A famous exception, so it is often said, is 2 Sam. 11.27, where the narrator writes apropos of the Bathsheba affair that 'the thing that David had done displeased Yahweh'. It is more probable, however, that this sentence is nothing more than a motivating sentence for the succeeding narrative of the death of the child of Bathsheba and David. On the matter of the narrator's reticence, cf. Robert Alter, *The Art of Biblical Narrative* (London: George Allen & Unwin, 1981), pp. 114-30.

49. T.H. Jones, 'David', in *The Illustrated Bible Dictionary* (ed. J.D. Douglas *et al.*; Leicester: Inter-Varsity Press, 1980), I, pp. 364-69 (369).

present day, as the conclusion of the article on David in the most recent of scholarly Bible encyclopaedias will show:

> Ultimately, however, David's lasting significance lay in his position as YHWH's chosen king for Israel and as the father of the royal dynasty that YHWH chose to bless. He occupied a midpoint between his great ancestor Abraham and his great descendant Jesus. The promises made to David stood in continuity with those to Abraham, and they pointed to a messianic ideal of great promise for the world, an ideal that, so Christians have affirmed, found its expression in Jesus, the Christ.[50]

If that kind of assertion of mythical and cosmic significance is to form the conclusion of one's account of David, it is understandable that the character of David is likely to have met throughout the history of interpretation with considerable approval. Yet even this angle of approach, which is of course not shared by all scholars, does not satisfactorily account for the degree of approval David is accorded at the hands of scholars generally.

What I should like to suggest is that what male scholars (most who have written on the David story are males, not surprisingly) are responding to in the character of David is his masculinity, of which they themselves approve or to which they themselves are attracted. They view his masculinity through the lens of their own, of course, but there is enough commonality for them to identify themselves and their own desire with David. This is a gender-based hero-worship. They can, and must, excuse his faults and crimes because he is at bottom a man after their own heart—which is to say, their own image of masculinity. One writer of an current encyclopaedia article puts his finger on it exactly, if rather quaintly: 'he was all that men find wholesome and admirable in man'[51]—'wholesome' meaning that they approve of David, and 'admirable' meaning that they desire to be like him.

2. *Success*

A second main characteristic of the way in which the figure of David has been shaped by the norms of modern western mas-

---

50. David M. Howard, Jr, 'David', in *The Anchor Bible Dictionary*, I, pp. 41-48 (48).

51. Jones, 'David', in *The Illustrated Bible Dictionary*, I, pp. 364-69 (369).

culinity is this: he has been aligned with the masculine model of success.[52]

Thus J.M. Myers, in *The Interpreter's Dictionary of the Bible*, concludes his article on David with an 'estimate', which displays David as wholly successful in every area of his life. David was honourable, dignified and loyal; he had a 'rare quality of diplomacy' (the choice of Jerusalem as his capital was 'another master stroke of diplomacy'); he was a great warrior and an excellent general; he was shrewd as a politician; he was a 'deeply religious man'; he was a poet and musician of note; and 'finally, David was a great organizer'.[53] That is to say, everything that David does, he does excellently and entirely successfully. What David does not do well has been totally suppressed from the 'estimate'. The commentator is comfortable with his article on David only if can show David to have been a success, for the commentator is scripted to desire success himself.

To take another example, David M. Howard, in *The Anchor Bible Dictionary*, finds David to have been 'a shrewd military strategist and motivator', a skilful politician, and a talented administrator of the military, civil and religious bureaucracies. He had renowned skills as a 'poet, musician and sponsor of music'. He displayed 'a fine religious sensitivity for the most part', as evidenced by his 'relationship with his God, his concern for others' welfare, his ready repentance when confronted with his sin, and his concern for the religious matters pertaining to the temple and the cult'.[54] Everything that David does prospers, and although there is one point at which David is not perfect—his 'sin'—somehow that too becomes a sphere of success: David,

---

52. I do not suggest that this focus entirely misconstrues the Hebrew narrative, for a sentence like 1 Sam. 18.14 encapsulates it very neatly: 'David was successful (מַשְׂכִּיל) in all his undertakings, for Yahweh was with him'. And there is no doubt that the story of David can be subsumed under the rubric of success/failure—as Exum, for example, does over some pages in her *Tragedy and Biblical Narrative*, pp. 122-26 (e.g. 'One could hardly imagine a more thoroughgoing success story' [p. 126]). The point rather is that our contemporary models of masculinity prompt us to foreground certain textual materials rather than others.

53. J.M. Myers, 'David', in *The Interpreter's Dictionary of the Bible* (ed. George Arthur Buttrick; Nashville: Abingdon, 1962), I, pp. 771-82 (781-82).

54. Howard, 'David', in *The Anchor Bible Dictionary*, I, pp. 41-48 (48).

admirably, shows 'ready repentance when confronted with his sin'. That is to say, for the commentator the sin is swallowed up in the repentance. David's success in repentance becomes more important than his failure in sin, so even his failure becomes an arena of his success.

A final example, with a more pious turn of phrase, if that were possible, comes from *The Illustrated Bible Dictionary*:

> [David's] accomplishments were many and varied; man of action, poet, tender lover, generous foe, stern dispenser of justice, loyal friend, he was all that men find wholesome and admirable in man, and this by the will of God, who shaped him for his destiny.[55]

In brief, for these commentators, everything questionable, distasteful and gross about David has been swallowed up by the modern myth of masculinity: if he is a real man, he has to be successful.

3. *Warfare*

We have seen how prominent in the construction of David's masculinity is his ability and desire for fighting and killing. Modern masculinity approves of aggression, and it is striking that our commentators never say a word against David on this score. On the other hand, since being a biblical scholar and a mafia boss at one and the same time would create an uncomfortable conflict in their own male identities, they are diffident at positively approving of David's perpetual taking of life. So they have two strategies of containment for their anxiety on this score: either they suppress the warrior David or they transform the aggression of the man of blood into the assertiveness of the decisive, problem-solving executive or tycoon.

Both strategies are evident (if you know to look for them) in the article on David by Jan Fokkelman in *Harper's Bible Dictionary*.[56] His concluding and summary paragraph begins: 'David was not only a very powerful leader and personality as both soldier and statesman, he was also a first-class poet... The court

---

55. Jones, 'David', in *The Illustrated Bible Dictionary*, I, pp. 364-69 (369).

56. Jan P. Fokkelman, 'David', in *Harper's Bible Dictionary* (ed. Paul J. Achtemeier; San Francisco: Harper & Row, 1985), pp. 208-11.

established by him...gave a tremendous spiritual and literary impulse to the literature of biblical Israel.' And so on, until it concludes, 'And the poems of David live on in the liturgy of Jewish and Christian communities, sung to this very day'. David then is what his significance is, and his significance is what endures to this very day. Of course, he was a 'soldier'—but not in the sense of killing lots of men, but in the sense of being a leader as a soldier, of being a statesman in much the same sense, and certainly in the same breath, as being a soldier. Of course he was aggressive, but only in the sense of being 'a very powerful leader and personality'—not in the sense of murdering messengers and killing Philistines for the fun of it. Elsewhere in the article also there is the same squeamishness about actual killing. There is indeed a reference to his 'courage and leadership in regular skirmishes with the Philistines', but that phrase 'regular skirmishes' makes it sound more like football fixtures than hit-and-run slayings, like good clean fun in which no one gets hurt rather than the bloody taking of human life. And there is a reference also to the fact that David 'became a war lord with his own army of outlaws and performed services of protection', as if the special function of a 'war lord' is the provision of security. The profile of David's masculinity in the text has been overlaid and obscured by Fokkelman's.

Another example is to be found in the *International Standard Bible Encyclopaedia*, where the author, David F. Payne, concludes that David was 'supremely able in the military and political spheres' and that '[h]is successes were a tribute to his personal courage, and to his ability as soldier and statesman'. 'While his adultery and murder [of Uriah] cannot be condoned, with this glaring exception he was in every way the ideal ruler.'[57] One might be forgiven for thinking that the writer not only condones but actually approves of David's slaughters and indiscriminate killings, for in every way, he says, with but one glaring exception, David is the ideal ruler.

---

57. David F. Payne, 'David', in *The International Standard Bible Encyclopaedia* (ed. Geoffrey W. Bromiley; fully revised edition, Grand Rapids: Wm B. Eerdmans, 1979), I, pp. 870-76 (876).

4. *Beauty*

There is some discomfort in the commentators over male beauty. None of the English translations or the commentators will actually bring themselves to speaking of 'beauty' in a man.[58] Their culture enables them only to think of 'good looks' or 'handsomeness' in a man, for 'beauty' is, for them, a female characteristic. To be a man is to be different in every respect from a woman, even linguistically if possible.

And there are other ways of expressing this discomfort as well. McCarter says curtly: 'The quality [of 'good looks', as he calls it] is to be interpreted as a physical symptom of divine favor'[59]—as if he can accept male beauty only as a feature of the text that stands in need of 'interpretation', only if it is a symbol for something else. It is strange too that he calls it a 'symptom', as if it were a medical condition. Ackroyd too wants to stress that 'good appearance' is seen as a divine gift[60]—as if its real significance were theological.

Another way of handling the discomfort is to make no comment on the texts that speak of male beauty. A.R.S. Kennedy, for example, says nothing about any of the texts except to suggest that David's 'ruddiness' may refer to his hair colour[61] and to curl his lip at 2 Sam. 14.25-27 as '[a] paragraph of later date eulogizing Absalom's personal beauty'.[62]

Yet another mode of commenting is to naturalize the Hebrew terminology to an acceptable code of the commentator's time. Thus Ackroyd, for example, reckons that 'handsome' (NEB) at 1 Sam. 16.1, used of David, is better translated 'a man of presence'.[63] The NEB itself actually says of Saul at 1 Sam. 9.2 that 'there was no better man among the Israelites than he', and Ackroyd remarks that 'better' 'may indicate moral quality, but

---

58. Kennedy, *Samuel*, p. 261, gives the lie to that generalization, but since his book is almost a hundred years old, perhaps it is not representative of the 'modern' West.

59. McCarter, *I Samuel*, p. 173.

60. Ackroyd, *1 Samuel*, p. 75. David's beauty is 'good appearance' also on p. 133.

61. Kennedy, *Samuel*, p. 118.

62. Kennedy, *Samuel*, p. 261.

63. Ackroyd, *1 Samuel*, p. 135.

the phrases following suggest superiority of physical appearance'.[64]

McKane is something of an exception among commentators in not only noting but also urging his readers to note 'the emphasis [in 1 Sam. 9.2] on Saul's physical attractiveness and superb physique',[65] but that is only place in his brief commentary where the subject of male beauty is allowed to raise its head. On the whole, David's beauty, and therewith the very idea of male beauty in general, is suppressed in the commentaries by the modern ideology of masculinity.

5. *Sex*

Here is the site of another set of conflicts. David has intercourse with twenty women, at least, but he is not very interested in sex. The only appreciative thing he says about love sounds homoerotic, especially because it explicitly displaces women as the object of male affection: 'I am desolate for you, Jonathan my brother. Very dear you were to me, your love more wonderful to me than the love of a woman' (NJB); 'Your love for me was wonderful, surpassing the love of women' (2 Sam. 1.26 REB); '[M]ost dear have you been to me; [m]ore precious have I held love for you than love for women' (NAB). Faced with David's sexual practice and his sexual interests, commentators find themselves in a fix. Writing for church presses and Christian sensibilities (for the most part), they feel obliged to uphold monogamous heterosexuality as the norm, while their own culture scripts them to regard sex as critical and foundational for masculinity. Given the textual evidence, how are they to construct and represent David on sex? What sort of a man is he, and how does his masculinity implictly trouble the commentators' own masculinity?

Take Kyle McCarter, and let him speak for commentators everywhere. Wherever the language of love between Jonathan and David crops up in the narrative,[66] McCarter hastens to

---

64. Ackroyd, *1 Samuel*, p. 75.

65. William McKane, *I and II Samuel: Introduction and Commentary* (Torch Bible Commentaries; London: SCM Press, 1963), p. 69.

66. I refer to 1 Sam. 18.1; 20.17; 2 Sam. 1.26 (though not 1 Sam. 19.1, where the Hebrew is חפץ, which means no more than 'deeply fond' in McCarter's translation [*I Samuel*, p. 320]; most of the rest of us think that it

assure us that it has a political connotation.[67] To be sure, it 'describes personal affection',[68] and Jonathan 'is so taken with David that he becomes vitally devoted to him in affection and loyalty',[69] and 'Jonathan's deep affection for David is a part of the close relationship that has developed between the two young men; also it is surely a sign of the irresistible charm of the man who has Yahweh's favor'.[70] Oh yes, and there was 'also' 'warm personal intimacy in the relationship between the two men'— that 'also' signifying: as well as the political implications, which were more important. What we should not forget, says McCarter, is that 'In the ancient Near East "love" terminology belonged to the language of political discourse, and many of the statements made about Jonathan's love for David are charged with political overtones'.[71] In a word, says McCarter, banish from your mind any thought of sex when you read of Jonathan's love: it is essentially political, and though there was also a warm personal 'affection', there was absolutely nothing more, honest. There is no recognition in this commentator that the David and Jonathan of 1 Samuel cannot be described as 'just good friends'; even if they are not lovers in our sense, they are certainly one another's 'significant other'—in the early days, at least. In that context, the question of sex *has* to be raised, one would have

means 'delight in', 'take pleasure in', but it's a bit ripe having men 'delight in' other men, isn't it?).

67. McCarter depends for this point upon J.A. Thompson's article, 'The Significance of the Verb *Love* in the Jonathan–David Narratives in 1 Samuel', *Vetus Testamentum* 24 (1974), pp. 34-38. But of course the meaning of 'love' in a formal treaty context (cf. also W.L. Moran, 'The Ancient Near Eastern Background of the Love of God in Deuteronomy', *Catholic Biblical Quarterly* 25 [1963], pp. 77-87 [78-79]) will hardly be relevant for the term in this narrative of personal relationships.

68. They are 'close friends', says Peter D. Miscall, charmingly (*1 Samuel: A Literary Reading* [Bloomington: Indiana University Press, 1986], p. 130).

69. McCarter, *I Samuel*, p. 305.

70. McCarter, *I Samuel*, p. 342.

71. P. Kyle McCarter, Jr, *II Samuel: A New Translation with Introduction, Notes and Commentary* (Anchor Bible, 9; Garden City, NY: Doubleday, 1984), p. 77. If love 'belonged' to the language of political discourse, readers may note, presumably wives, husbands, parents, children, courting couples and the like only ever 'borrowed' (perhaps 'stole'?) it.

thought, even if it is to be laid to rest.[72] But it is not, because the commentator's construction of masculinity has no room for the homoerotic, and David is nothing if he is not a 'real man'.[73]

How does David's polygamy fare then? Not a word from McCarter on the ten 'concubines' who are left to guard the house when David flees before Absalom (2 Sam. 15.16; 16.21) except to say that 'By claiming the royal harem Abishalom publicizes his claim to the throne'[74]—as if Absalom had put an advertisement in *The Times* announcing his royal pretensions, rather than undertaking, in a bizarre act of sexual athleticism and exhibitionism, to have sex with one after another of David's ten secondary wives in a tent pitched on the roof 'in the sight of all Israel' (2 Sam. 16.22). Polygamy and multiple rape are the unacceptable faces of heterosexuality in the modern West, so the least said about ancient males' deviation from modern norms the better. The commentator, who is no doubt a liberal intellectual, if not even a 'new man' as well, displays a quite uncanny reticence about the grotesque and the gross in this narrative, and in so doing naturalizes the biblical text. In passing no remark upon the harem system or the ethics of multiple rape the commentator affects not to have noticed something nasty in the text; or, having noticed it, judges that there is nothing to be said about it. The

72. The distinction between male friendship and homosexuality, though always problematic, has been clearly enough recognized in other ages than our own; cf. for example Alan Bray, 'Homosexuality and the Signs of Male Friendship in Elizabethan England', *History Workshop* 29 (1990), pp. 1-19.

73. Perhaps the message that 'real men' read here is that male friendship is dangerous; cf. Philip Culbertson, *New Adam: The Future of Male Spirituality* (Minneapolis: Fortress Press, 1992), p. 90. Not everyone operates with the distinction of Eve Kosofsky Sedgwick, between the homosocial, which includes all same-sex relations, and the homosexual, which denotes only that segment of the homosocial that is distinguished by genital sexuality (*Between Men: English Literature and Male Homosocial Desire* [New York: Columbia University Press, 1985]). I mean that most people are not aware how important such a distinction is; there are also those, of course, who are aware of it but do not accept it (cf. Robert K. Martin, *Hero, Captain and Stranger: Male Friendship, Social Critique, and Literary Form in the Sea Novels of Herman Melville* (Chapel Hill: University of North Carolina Press, 1986), p. 13.

74. McCarter, *II Samuel*, p. 384.

behaviour of a David or an Absalom is thereby naturalized and normalized, and the representation of masculinity in the text is harmonized to our modern consciousness.

In a word, and metacommentatingly, I conclude: Once again, we see that the function of commentary on biblical texts has been to familiarize the Bible, to normalize it to our own cultural standards, to render it as undisturbing as possible, to press it into the service of a different worldview; eventually, the effect will be to write the Bible out of existence. That is what has been happening to the Bible in the church, in my opinion,[75] and it is no doubt what happens to the Bible in any culture. I suppose it is what happens to old books anywhere, and it is the task of scholars, taking a step of critical distance as best they can from their own culture and their personal scripts, to bring back into the foreground the otherness of the familiarized.[76]

75. See my forthcoming book, *The Bible and the Modern World* (The Didsbury Lectures; Carlisle: The Paternoster Press, 1995), Chapter 4 'The Bible and the Church', where I present some empirical evidence for this claim.

76. I should like to thank my colleague Cheryl Exum for advising me that this was the next paper I should write, though I doubt that it has turned out as she would have imagined it, and Francis Landy for a typically generous and thought-provoking series of comments on a draft of the chapter (I incorporated all I could, and tried to fend off the others).

11

Psalm 2 and the MLF (Moabite Liberation Front)[*]

I stand to be corrected, but I believe that every interpretation of
and commentary on this psalm ever written adopts the viewpoint of the text, and, moreover, assumes that the readers
addressed by the scholarly commentator share the ideology of
the text and its author.[1] They take for granted that we are all of

* An earlier version of this essay was published in *The Bible in Human
Society: Essays in Honour of John Rogerson* (ed. R. Daniel Carroll R., David J.A.
Clines and Philip R. Davies; Journal for the Study of the Old Testament
Supplement Series, 200; Sheffield: Sheffield Academic Press, 1995), pp. 158-
85. The essay was earlier delivered as a Plenary Address at the Pacific Coast
Regional Meeting, Society of Biblical Literature, Redlands, California,
March, 1995, and in the Trends in Biblical Scholarship Section of the Society
of Biblical Literature International Meeting, Budapest, July, 1995.

1.   Perhaps I should reckon an article by Hans Klein ('Zur Auslegung
von Psalm 2. Ein Beitrag zum Thema: Gewalt und Gewaltlosigkeit', *Theologische Beiträge* 10 [1979], pp. 63-71) the exception that proves the rule. His
theme is the question whether Christians should use force to achieve good
ends, and he examines Psalm 2 because it apparently authorizes force in the
service of God. He concludes that historical reality shows that 'Israel very
quickly had to learn that the way of the execution of power that Psalm 2
contains is not a possibility for the people of God' (p. 67), and that 'the Bible
shows through the praxis of the interpretation of Psalm 2 that the use of
power has no place in the church' (p. 71). But I saw in the article no direct
confrontation with the claims of the text, and I was suspicious of the
attempt to 'redeem' the text by insisting that it should not be interpreted 'in
isolation' but 'within the total biblical picture' (p. 71 n. 35).
    No doubt I should also mention the occasional remarks of commentators
of an earlier age who let slip their discomfort with the psalm from their
own Christian perspective; thus Bernhard Duhm: 'This psalm can be
appropriated by Christianity only with severe alteration' (*Die Psalmen*
[Kurzer Hand-Commentar zum Alten Testament, 14; Freiburg i.B.: J.C.B.
Mohr (Paul Siebeck), 1899], p. 9), and Hermann Gunkel: 'The Christian

the same opinion—author, commentator and reader. In this essay, I want to expose the tensions that exist among these parties, tensions between author and commentators (generally suppressed) and tensions between commentators and readers (generally ignored). The text is not only about conflict; it generates conflict, a conflict of ideologies.

1. *The World of the Text*

The psalm takes its rise from a conflict, and it is wholly concerned with how that conflict is to be handled. The conflict it represents is between Yahweh, his anointed one and the poet on the one hand, and the nations and their rulers on the other hand. There is therefore more than one set of interests at stake in the world of the text. One might have thought that scholars writing on this psalm would do their utmost not to appear partisan towards one of the parties in the conflict but to evaluate the variant claims of the protagonists in the detached and objective manner that scholarship traditionally aspires to. Such is not the case.

In order to bring into the foreground the conflict, and to begin to represent the position of the party that is systematically repressed both within the text and within the scholarly tradition, I find it necessary to give a name to those who are known within the poem as the enemies, the 'nations' and the 'peoples' of v. 1, the 'kings of the earth' and the 'rulers' of v. 2 and v. 10. It is a well-known feature of polemic that opponents are denied a recognition of their own identity, as human beings in their own right.[2] Here too those on one side of the conflict bear specific names: Yahweh, his anointed, his king, his son; and they are located at a particular place on the face of the globe: on Yah-

church could base itself on this psalm only after very considerable excisions' (*Die Psalmen, übersetzt und erklärt* (Handcommentar zum Alten Testament, II/2; Göttingen: Vandenhoeck & Ruprecht, 5th edn, 1968 [original edn, 1892], p. 10). They would like to normalize the psalm to Christian standards, nevertheless.

2.   See, by way of analogy, the remarks of J. Cheryl Exum, *Fragmented Women: Feminist (Sub)versions of Biblical Narratives* (Journal for the Study of the Old Testament Supplement Series, 163; Sheffield: JSOT Press, 1993), pp. 176-77, on unnamed women in biblical narratives.

weh's holy hill of Zion. On the other hand, their opponents are called only by the most general of terms, nations, peoples, kings and rulers, and they are to be found at no particular place on earth but, indeterminately, over the earth in general. I name these opponents of Yahweh and his anointed Israelite king 'Moabites'—not that I think for a moment that the rebellious people spoken of in the psalm are actually and precisely Moabite.[3] Rather, I am using 'Moabite' as a symbolic name for people who found themselves in bondage to an Israelite king and who desired liberation from their overlord.[4]

Such are the dramatis personae of the poem. Now, what is *going on* in the psalm? Various nations of the earth have been subject to the Israelite king who sees himself as the appointee of the one universal god. These nations have now joined in a rebellion against this Jerusalem king, hoping to achieve freedom from

3.   But suppose they were. Perhaps a detached observer would find it hard to tell the difference between the religions of the two nations. No doubt Julius Wellhausen was no detached observer, but his remarks provoke thought: 'Israel and Moab had a common origin, and their early history was similar. The people of Jehovah on the one hand, and the people of Chemosh on the other, had the same idea of the Godhead as head of the nation, and a like patriotism derived from religious belief,—a patriotism capable of extraordinary efforts, and which has had no parallel in the West either in ancient or in modern times' ('Moab', in *Encyclopaedia Britannica* [ed. W. Robertson Smith; Edinburgh: A. & C. Black, 9th edn, 1878], XVI, pp. 533-36 [535]). In case a curious reader wonders, Was there then *any* difference between the two?, I continue the quotation: 'But, with all this similarity, how different were the ultimate fates of the two! The history of the one loses itself obscurely and fruitlessly in the sand; that of the other issues in eternity. One reason for the difference...is obvious. Israel received no gentle treatment at the hands of the world; it had to carry on a continual conflict with foreign influences and hostile powers; and this perpetual struggle with gods and men was not profitless, although the external catastrophe was inevitable. Moab meantime remained settled on his lees (Jer. xlviii.11), and corruption and decay were the result' (pp. 535-36). A mere accident of history, not the intrinsic quality of its religious ideas, that is to say, determined the survival of the Hebrew faith.

4.   Bernard Gosse draws special attention to the parallels between the psalm and the prophetic oracles against Edom ('Le Psaume 2 et l'usage rédactionnel des Oracles contre les Nations à l'époque post-exilique', *Biblische Notizen* 62 [1992], pp. 18-24), so perhaps it would be better to envisage an *Edomite* Liberation Front. No matter.

Israelite rule: 'Let us break their chains', they say, 'and throw off their fetters'. These non-Israelites represent themselves within the poem not simply as subject peoples or citizens of an empire not their own but as slaves, who are kept fast in bonds and fetters. Their uprising is a classic case of a national liberation movement, urging nothing but freedom from oppression. There is no word here of any desire to humiliate the Israelites, to wield power over them, to attack them or to punish them. The entire ambition of the 'nations' is to break the Israelite hold over them. Nor is there any wickedness or grossness in these nations that accounts for their flouting of Israelite rule. There is not even any heathen belief or false worship that impels their resistance to Yahweh and his king.[5] Their impulse is represented as nothing other than a desire for freedom from their bondage.

That is the situation from which the poem takes its rise—the exposition of the drama, narratologically speaking. The way in which this initial situation is 'complicated' is that on the Israelite side such a rebellion is resisted scornfully. The first indication of this Israelite point of view comes in the first sentence, where the narrator or speaking voice depicts the rebellion in an already prejudicial way. By casting the description of the conspiracy of the nations as a rhetorical 'why?'-question, he means to say, by the very first word of the poem, that their attempt is doomed to failure. The 'why?' implies a negative answer, that their effort is a waste of time. And in the last word of the first sentence, 'in vain' (רִיק), we recognize again that there is nothing remotely objective about this depiction but that a decisive judgment against the 'nations' is already built into the description of their rebellion, 'smitingly stigmatised in anticipation as "vanity"'.[6] This is the parallelism of greater precision[7] with a vengeance:

5.   As against Heinrich A. von Ewald, *Commentary on the Psalms* (trans. E. Johnson; London: Williams & Norgate, 1880), p. 148: 'The discontented at bottom merely find the dominion of the religion and law of Jahvé oppressive, and desire to return to the old rudeness and licentiousness'.

6.   Alexander Maclaren, *The Psalms* (The Expositor's Bible; London: Hodder & Stoughton, 1893), I, p. 13.

7.   See David J.A. Clines, 'The Parallelism of Greater Precision. Notes from Isaiah 40 for a Theory of Hebrew Poetry', in *New Directions in Hebrew Poetry* (ed. Elaine R. Follis; Journal for the Study of the Old Testament Supplement Series, 40; Sheffield: JSOT Press, 1987), pp. 77-100.

from the first line alone (v. 1a) we might not guess that the questions are indeed rhetorical, but the second line limits the ambiguity of the first beyond question. In the 'surplus' that line 2
offers—the ריק to which nothing in line 1 corresponds, and
which compels the reader to go back over the whole couplet and
reprocess the double question as more of a decision than a real
question—lies the essence of the poem. The rebellion of the
nations is, from the Israelite perspective, vain.

The response of the Israelites represented in the poem to the
nations' striving for liberation is, on the one hand, a depiction of
their deity's scorn at the nations' aspirations and, on the other
hand, a statement by the Israelite king of his right to their submission. He claims that his god has given him the nations as his
possession, which he may rightfully and ideally rule with a
sceptre of iron, and which he may destroy at his pleasure, like a
potter's vessel. In a word, the Israelite king as the holder of
power and the Israelite poet as his propagandist refuse to coun-
tenance for a moment the 'Moabite' claim or to acknowledge that
'Moabites' have any right to self-determination or political
autonomy.

By world standards and on a broad historical canvas, we
might well allow that there is nothing especially ugly about such
imperial resistance to nationalistic aspirations. In this case,
unlike many in imperial history, the overlord does not resort to
genocide, or to torture or cruel punishment of the leaders of the
rebellion. The Israelite response is no worse than to claim that
their deity is scornful of liberation movements, to threaten that
the Jerusalem king will intensify the severity of his rule and will
be perpetually irascible (v. 12), and to counsel submissiveness
and fear. Nonetheless, the Israelite response is unmistakably and
smugly typical of an insensitive imperial despotism.

2. *The Scholarly Tradition*

In this section, I am trying to identify some of the principal tendencies of modern scholarship on the psalm when confronted by
the conflict between Israel and the Moabite Liberation Front.

a. *A Myopic Tendency*

The most striking feature of the scholarly tradition on the Psalms is the almost total blindness of commentators to the 'Moabite' point of view, and the absence of any awareness that the text projects a situation of real conflict. The poem adopts the strategy of minimizing the importance of Israel's opponents by making them figures of ridicule, and the commentators follow suit.

I say 'almost total', for there are a few signs that the 'Moabite' critique has obtruded into the consciousness of some—though only to be no sooner uttered than immediately suppressed. Here is Artur Weiser:

> [M]ust we not persist in regarding it as the presumptuous utter-ance of an incomprehensible and intolerable arrogance when claims implying dominion over the whole world are here voiced for which no occasion can be found at any point in the history of Israel which would justify them?[8]

But he responds immediately to his own implicit critique of the psalm:

> This question will be answered in the affirmative only by those who eyes remain fixed on the visible surface of history so that they do not comprehend the hidden motive forces of historical events which are controlled by God, the Lord of universal history... The king in Zion is the anointed of God... Such a view, if pondered over deeply enough, is not to be characterized as the expression of an arrogant presumption but as a vision granted to the assurance that comes by faith.[9]

8. Artur Weiser, *The Psalms: A Commentary* (Old Testament Library; London: SCM Press, 1962), p. 111.

9. Weiser, *Psalms*, p. 111. Presumption is a terrible fault, we learn from the commentators on this psalm, and should only be ascribed to foreigners. A.A. Anderson helpfully explains how, despite appearances, the Israelite king in the poem is not himself presumptuous: his claims to universal rule signify simply that 'As God's regent (and adopted son), the King "exercised" a universal rule, even though to his contemporaries it appeared that his dominion extended only over Judah. Thus the glory of the Davidic king was a hidden one, made real only in the cult' (*The Book of Psalms. Volume I: Introduction and Psalms 1–72* [New Century Bible; London: Oliphants, 1972], pp. 64-65). So that's all right then. Quotation marks are truly *magic*, are they not? Siegfried Wagner at least raises the question whether such a representation in the cult might not perhaps be termed a

The doubt that surfaced for a moment is quickly laid to rest by the assurance that comes by (Lutheran) faith.

Again, in reference to the claim that the Israelite king will shatter the nations of the earth, Weiser allows that it 'appears to be a colossal exaggeration, if looked at from the standpoint of the purely internal history of Israel' but it is in fact 'the powerful expression of a strong faith in the miraculous might of God'.[10] The language of smashing one's enemies like earthen vessels may be paralleled in the royal inscriptions of Egypt, but

> it makes a difference whether words which bear a likeness to each other express the human lust for power, as they do in the oracles of the ancient East, or whether they bear witness to the vision of faith, as they do in the Old Testament, where man's eyes are lifted up to the power of the divine Judge of the earth...[11]

The commentator cannot conceive that there is an alternative point of view already inscribed in his text, and cannot imagine that the very existence of that Moabite point already calls into question his own easy certainties.

b. *A Moralizing/Theologizing Tendency*
A second dominant impression this reader of commentaries on Psalm 2 receives is that of a ruthless moralizing or theologizing of the poem that prevails in current readings of it.

1. *The world of the text*. Now such a reading is in sharp contrast to the very striking absence of a moral or theological dimension in the psalm itself. The psalm indeed portrays opposition to the rule of the Jerusalem king, and so, by inference, to the authority of the god of Jerusalem, but it does not characterize the foreign opponents of the Jerusalemites as evil or malign. Their only crime in the psalm is that they want to be free of the rule of the king. Thus, even in the world of the text, the conflict between the Jerusalemites and the foreigners is first and foremost a political issue, not a *moral* one.

And it is not essentially a *religious* conflict, either. It is true that

'flight from reality'—though only, of course, to deny it ('Das Reich des Messias. Zur Theologie der alttestamentlichen Königspsalmen', *Theologische Literaturzeitung* 109 [1984], cols. 865-74 [870]).
  10. Weiser, *Psalms*, p. 114.
  11. Weiser, *Psalms*, p. 114.

the poet represents the rebellion of the nations as 'against' Yahweh. But that does not mean, for the poet, that the nations deny that Yahweh is the true god, or that the Israelite cult properly prescribes the ways in which humans should offer worship to the divine, or some such theologoumenon. No doubt the foreign nations do in fact deny such things, but that is not where their rebellion lies. It is not because they cannot accept the truth of the Israelite religion or submit themselves to the worship of Yahweh that they are in rebellion; rather, it is because, finding themselves under the political hegemony of an Israelite emperor, they regard it as oppression.[12]

So, while the poet represents them as rebelling 'against Yahweh' (and against his anointed king), and as saying, 'Let us break *their* chains' (those of Yahweh and the king)—for no doubt it is *worse* to be rebelling against the god than merely against the king—when he actually describes their rebellion it is a political one, against the rule of an emperor, not a religious one, against the imposition of a religion.

We come to the same conclusion when we ask, Who is this Yahweh? What kind of a god is he? What does he do with humans and what does he expect of them? The answer within Psalm 2 must be: He authorizes and supports the Israelite king. He does not require worship, he does not lay down laws, he does not require ethical behaviour of humans, he does not, indeed, communicate with humans generally. He exists for one reason and for one reason only, in the world of this psalm—he guarantees the rights of the Israelite king over other nations. In that role, he rebukes nations for resisting the rule of the king, saying, 'I have installed the king as my king', he assures the king that he is his father, he promises the king that nations of the earth will become his property, and he authorizes him to smash them with an iron sceptre and to break them like pots. And if we wonder what it might mean in v. 11 that the kings and rulers are advised to 'serve' Yahweh with fear, v. 12 seems to make plain that their service of Yahweh will consist—not of religious wor-

12. As against Anderson, for example, who thinks that 'the universal rule of God was challenged by the worship of other gods' and that Psalm 2 is therefore 'essentially a statement of faith' (*The Book of Psalms*, p. 65).

ship, as the term עבד ('serve') might suggest,[13] but—of submission to the king. It is by kissing the king in subjection[14] that they will serve the god. In short, as far as the psalm is concerned, Yahweh's function as god is to authorize the political authority of the king.[15]

2. *The world of the commentary.* But what do we find when we read the commentaries? The *political* issue is suppressed, and the claim is made that it is essentially *moral* and *religious* issues that are at stake in the psalm. Thus, for example, one commentator writes that the psalmist 'phrases his question [in v. 1] with the prophet's scorn of creaturely presumption'[16]—and we all know that 'presumption' is a *moral* fault (at least, it is if you are a creature). But we are not dealing in this psalm with minor moral faults, of course, say the commentators; what is depicted in this psalm is the fundamental conflict between light and darkness, between cosmic good and evil: 'The theology of God's own kingship had always to reckon with the problem of rampant evil'.[17] '[T]he king is empowered by God to overcome all evil.'[18] The

13. Anderson reminds us that 'in its religious aspect [the term 'serve'] means to worship Yahweh, while politically it implies a submission to his vicegerent' (*The Book of Psalms*, p. 69). But he forbears to tell us which meaning he thinks it has here. A.F. Kirkpatrick had seen the issue clearly enough, when he wrote of v. 11 that 'political submission to Jehovah in the person of his representative is primarily intended', though the 'wider', religious sense of 'serve' and 'fear' should not be excluded (*The Book of Psalms, with Introduction and Notes* [Cambridge Bible; Cambridge: Cambridge University Press, 1891], p. 11).

14. I find no difficulty in translating v. 12a 'kiss the son', but know of no parallel to kissing the feet of Yahweh—which is what the RSV urges the nations to do. It would be hard for a non-Israelite to work out how to kiss the feet of an aniconic god (I see that this point was also made by Winfried Thiel, 'Der Weltherrschaftsanspruch des judäischen Königs nach Psalm 2', in *Theologische Versuche* 3 [1971], pp. 53-63 [59]).

15. The issue of legitimacy and filiation, so prominent both in the psalm itself and in the commentaries (cf. for example, José J. Alemany, 'Interpretación mesiánica del salmo 2', *Cultura Bíblica* 32 [1975], pp. 255-77 [268]), deserves a gender analysis all of its own.

16. John Eaton, *Psalms: Introduction and Commentary* (Torch Commentary; London: SCM Press, 1967), p. 32.

17. Eaton, *Psalms*, p. 32.

18. Eaton, *Psalms*, p. 33.

nations' rebellion is transcribed into the commentaries as an irreligious act, and the king's political authority is morphed to the god's religious authority. The poet is, on this reading, not speaking primarily of the king at all, but 'depicting the unlimited power of Yahweh over the whole earth... [T]he discontented rulers are told whom they are to fear—Yahweh, not his "anointed"'.[19] 'The outer scenes [of the psalm] describe...the attempt to break loose from the rule of God and the demand to become subject to the rule of God.'[20] And the major theological problem of the psalm for the commentators is not the ethical one of how other people are to be treated but a metaphysical one, that the psalm ascribes the title 'son of God' to a human monarch when we all know how the Old Testament insists on the incomparability and uniqueness of Yahweh.[21]

c. A Universalizing Tendency

Because a god is involved in the action of this psalm, theologians among commentators (and it is generally thought to be a strength, not a weakness, in a commentator to hold an intellectual commitment to a non-Israelite religion) think that everything they know about the God of their own theology is true of the divine character in this poem. And since they think (being historically and culturally conditioned, like all of us) that a God worth the name must be a universal god, with universal powers and universal property rights, they take it for granted that the psalm presupposes the universal dominion of Yahweh. Thus we read in the commentaries of 'Yhwh, whose property remains the earth (cf. Ps. 24.1, etc.)',[22] and are told that '[T]he psalmist proposes as a foregone conclusion that Yahweh is indeed Lord over all the earth',[23] and that behind the psalm lies 'the Israelite belief

19. John I. Durham, 'Psalms', in *The Broadman Bible Commentary* (ed. Clifton J. Allen; London: Marshall, Morgan & Scott, 1972), IV, 153-464 (174).

20. Erich Zenger, in Frank-Lothar Hossfeld and Erich Zenger, *Die Psalmen I: Psalm 1–50* (Die Neue Echter Bibel, 29; Würzburg: Echter Verlag, 1993), p. 49.

21. See James W. Watts, 'Psalm 2 in the Context of Biblical Theology', *Horizons in Biblical Theology* 12 (1990), pp. 73-91.

22. Zenger, in Hossfeld and Zenger, *Die Psalmen I*, p. 54.

23. Durham, 'Psalms', p. 174. Cf. Charles Augustus Briggs and Emilie Grace Briggs, *A Critical and Exegetical Commentary on The Book of Psalms*

that Yahweh...is the Lord of the whole world and all its history'.[24] And the whole poem is sometimes said to be essentially about the divine power; Anderson, for example, in his commentary entitles it 'Man Proposes, God Disposes'.[25] Likewise the king is said to lay claim to a universal dominion: for example, 'His remarkable claim to a world-wide office and authority is made on the grounds of a prophetic faith'.[26]

But nothing in the psalm makes any such universal claims.[27] Those who are at present subject to 'Yahweh and his anointed' are 'nations' (גוים) and 'peoples' (לאמים) who are represented by the conspiring 'kings of earth' (מלכי־ארץ) and 'rulers' (רוזנים)—that is to say, not *all* the nations and not *all* the kings of the earth.[28] Then when Yahweh promises to the Jerusalem king 'nations' (גוים) as his inheritance (נחלה) and 'ends of the earth' (אספי־ארץ) as his possession (אחזה) he does not say *all* the nations and he need not mean by 'ends of the earth' *everything contained within the earth's boundaries*. We do not even know for sure that he is talking about the 'earth' and not just about the 'land', since ארץ could mean either.[29] Moreover, his promise to 'give' these nations to the king does not mean that he, Yahweh, already 'owns' them or 'rules' them in some sense.[30] It is as the spoils of war that he is

(International Critical Commentary; Edinburgh: T. & T. Clark, 1906), I, p. 14: 'The Ps. conceives of Yahweh as sovereign of the nations'.

24. Anderson, *The Book of Psalms*, p. 64.

25. Anderson, *The Book of Psalms*, p. 63.

26. Eaton, *Psalms*, p. 31.

27. See further, David J.A. Clines, 'World Dominion in Psalm 2?' (forthcoming).

28. Bernhard Duhm is one of the very few commentators to remark that in v. 1 it cannot be all the nations who are meant, since v. 9 shows that some are still not subject to the Israelite king (*Psalmen*, p. 5).

29. T.K. Cheyne is in a minority among commentators in understanding ארץ as 'land' (*The Book of Psalms, Translated from a Revised Text with Notes and Introduction* [London: Kegan Paul, Trench, Trübner & Co., 1904], I, p. 6); most others do not even discuss which is the correct translation, but simply assume it means 'earth'. Isaiah Sonne, however, is clear that they are 'regional vassal kings' and that ארץ is 'the land of the Philistines' ('The Second Psalm', *Hebrew Union College Annual* 19 [1945–46], pp. 43-55 [45 n. 3]).

30. Cf. Peter C. Craigie, *Psalms 1–50* (Word Biblical Commentary, 19; Waco, TX: Word Books, 1983), p. 68: 'Because God is a universal God, the earthly king's jurisdiction is also represented in world-wide terms'.

promising them to the king. That is why the king must first 'ask' for them. If they were the king's right by way of patrimony, he would not need to 'ask' for them—not unless he was proposing to be a prodigal son and take his patrimony in advance. What is envisaged here is that the king will 'ask' Yahweh's assent to and assistance in foreign wars of re-conquest he will undertake,[31] and thereupon Yahweh will deliver his enemies into his hand, to coin a phrase. Likewise, when Yahweh speaks of the king shattering them like a pot, he does not have in mind the peaceful transfer of property from his own title to that of the king. This is the language of an act of war, not of dominion or simple masterfulness.[32] People do not injure their own interest by shattering their property like a pot.

In short, in the scholarly tradition the psalm is about world dominion—whether of Yahweh or of the Israelite king—whereas in the world of the text it is about the king's hopes for military victory over particular rebellious foreign nations.

d. *An Idealizing Tendency*
A recent tendency in Psalm criticism, which has the effect of deflecting criticism of its aggressiveness, has been to regard this psalm as originating, not from the royal cult of pre-exilic Israel, but from an oppressed postexilic community. Thus for Hossfeld

---

31. So, rightly, J.A. Emerton, 'The Translation of the Verbs in the Imperfect in Psalm ii. 9', *Journal of Theological Studies* ns 29 (1978), pp. 497-503 (501): '[I]t is not a matter of conquering foreign peoples for the first time, but of subduing those who have previously been subject to the king in Jerusalem'.

32. Bob Becking has made clear that, in its Mesopotamian analogues, the image of smashing pots refers to the utter subjugation of enemies (as in historical inscriptions of Tiglath-Pileser III and Sargon II) and, famously, to the destruction of the earth by the flood (Atrahasis and Gilgamesh epics). See his '"Wie Töpfe sollst du sie zerschmeißen": Mesopotamische Parallelen zu Psalm 2,9b', *Zeitschrift für die alttestamentliche Wissenschaft* 102 (1990), pp. 59-79. John T. Willis also has rightly seen that the psalm as a whole is not about lordship but about battle, observing that '[t]he affirmation that Yahweh himself had set the Judean king on his throne is important in the flow of argument in the cry of defiance, but should not be magnified out of proportion in relationship to the psalm as a whole' ('A Cry of Defiance—Psalm 2', *Journal for the Study of the Old Testament* 47 [1990], pp. 33-50 [45]).

and Zenger the admittedly 'aggressive' programme of Psalm 2 is not to be seen as the realistic and realizable ambition of a powerful state but as a hope and a vision of a threatened minority clinging to the promises of its god.[33] In similar vein Erhard Gerstenberger writes:

> The psalmist/liturgist/theologian who composed and used Psalm 2 for synagogal worship services[34] wanted to strengthen Jewish identity in a world resounding with the noise of heathen armies and with the propaganda of alien gods. The writer insists that all the apparent strength of the nations and their gods is illusory. The real master of all the world is Yahweh, who one day will reveal the participation of his Anointed and his preferred people in the administration of the world. What a dream of greatness, and what a comfort and joy for the downtrodden, suffering Jewish communities![35]

If this is the way an oppressed minority comforts itself, by aping the language and the ambitions of an oriental empire, then truly Assyria and Egypt have won the battle for hearts and minds, and it is their ideology that has triumphed. What benefit, we may ask, is it to an oppressed community to believe that the strength of the nations is illusory? On the contrary, it is the very power of their overlords that has made them the oppressed; if that power is illusory, then so too is their suffering. The

---

33. Zenger, in Hossfeld and Zenger, *Die Psalmen I*, p. 50-51. This is of course not a completely new tendency, for already Duhm, for example, was arguing that Psalm 2 represented the 'eschatological tension of the last centuries [BCE]' and was composed for the coronation of Aristobulus I or Alexander Jannaeus (*Die Psalmen*, pp. 10-11). So too more recently Marco Treves, 'Two Acrostic Psalms', *Vetus Testamentum* 15 (1965), pp. 81-85, claiming to find in it the acrostic 'Sing to Jannaeus the First and his Wife' (adequately refuted by Barnabas Lindars, 'Is Psalm ii an Acrostic Psalm?", *Vetus Testamentum* 17 [1967], pp. 60-67). But the more modern trend is to focus on the community experience rather than the political situation. Among other modern exponents of a postexilic origin is Erhard S. Gerstenberger, *Psalms: Part 1, with an Introduction to Cultic Poetry* (The Forms of the Old Testament Literature, 14; Grand Rapids: Eerdmans, 1988), p. 48.

34. Which is itself no doubt a fiction; see Heather A. McKay, *Sabbath and Synagogue: The Question of Sabbath Worship in Ancient Judaism* (Religions in the Graeco-Roman World, 122; Leiden: E.J. Brill, 1994), denying the existence of Jewish services for worship until well into the Christian era.

35. Gerstenberger, *Psalms: Part 1*, p. 49.

oppressed will never gain their freedom if their poets and religious leaders convince them that they have never lost it, that they have hidden resources and that they will 'one day' find themselves to be the real masters, administering the world from a position of power as 'preferred people'. This is nothing but an incitement to fantasize, not to engage with the real world. The psalm on this reading is not only a capitulation to the ideals of a savage imperialism but at the same time a recipe for quietism and defeatism.

On the part of commentators of our time, this approach represents an idealizing tendency, for it transmutes the violence of the psalm and its suppression of claims to national self-determination into the cry of a helpless minority who want justice more than they want power.

e. *Softening the Contours*
There are in this psalm some remarkably astringent elements, which the interpretative tradition tends to 'manage' and tone down. Among them four elements can be mentioned:

1. Yahweh's response of scorn to the nations' aspiration to independence.[36] The god of this psalm does not only deny independence to subject peoples, he pokes fun at them for suggesting they have any right to it. Commentators sometimes signal their disquiet at this divine response (a 'shrill anthropomorphism', Kraus calls it[37]), but make it their business to contain both the text and their own disquiet. The divine mockery becomes merely 'an expression of his sovereignty, majesty and loftiness'.[38] And, of course, we need to remember that 'Strictly speaking, God is not subject to anger or fury; his judgments are always tranquil; but he is metaphorically said to rage and be angry'.[39] His wrath, we are reminded, is 'not emotional irrationality, but underlines the passion with which he wants to restore the disturbed

36. No matter whether the laugh of Yahweh is 'a poetic expression for a peal of thunder' (Cheyne, *Psalms*, I, p. 5).

37. Hans-Joachim Kraus, *Psalms 1–59: A Continental Commentary* (trans. Hilton C. Oswald; Minneapolis: Fortress Press, 1993), p. 128.

38. Kraus, *Psalms 1–59*, p. 129.

39. R. Bellarmine [d. 1621], *A Commentary on the Book of Psalms* [trans. John O'Sullivan; Dublin: James Duffy, 1866], p. 3.

order'.[40] One commentator is reduced to remarking that at least
God's reaction shows that 'the Almighty is able to share in
human feelings'.[41] And another analyses punctiliously how this
is not an outburst of laughter as a thoughtless reflex, nor wild
laughter that releases tension, nor ironic laughter that is mali-
cious and disrespectful—but simple laughter, which,
'imaginative and optimistic, underlines the comical side of individuals, encounters and the circumstances of life and which
leads those who laugh to dissociate themselves from that at
which they laugh while at the same time drawing to themselves
those who surround them'.[42] It is good to know that the divine
laughter is so circumspect. Looked at from the right point of
view, indeed, one commentator opines, 'the laughter of the
psalm is consistent with the tears of Jesus as he stood on
Olivet';[43] the only problem is, like that of Archimedes, finding
the place to stand in order to take such a point of view. On the
whole, though, what we find is that commentators have rather
little to say about the divine mockery—which is the most effective way of 'managing' it, of course.

2. The king's claim to a right to pulverize the nations. Mostly
this savage language is 'managed' by transcribing it as a mere
right to dominion or by insisting that it is nothing other than a
picture—of the ease, for example, with which the king will
reduce his opponents.[44] For Kraus it is no more than the statement of 'universal, judiciary absolute power'.[45] Alternatively, the
language can be read as an expression of mere possibility. Long
ago, Cardinal Bellarmine commented: '"Break them in pieces"
does not imply that Christ will actually do so, but that he can do
so if he wills; breaking their sins and infidelities in pieces,
through his mercy...or breaking them in pieces in everlasting
fire'.[46] Clearly this is a containment strategy with great staying

40. Zenger, in Hossfeld and Zenger, *Die Psalmen I*, p. 53.

41. Anderson, *Psalms*, I, p. 66.

42. Louis Jacquet, *Les Psaumes et le coeur de l'homme: Etude textuelle, littéraire et doctrinale* (Gembloux: Duculot, 1975), I, pp. 230-31.

43. Maclaren, *Psalms*, I, p. 16.

44. Jacquet, *Les Psaumes*, p. 236.

45. Kraus, *Psalms 1–59*, p. 133.

46. Bellarmine, *Psalms*, p. 4.

power, for, much more recently, Anderson takes the same line: *'if need be*, the King will defeat all his enemies',[47] and so too J.A. Emerton: 'A king may need to shatter his vassals if they rebel, even though he will hope that he will not have to resort to such action'.[48]

3. The rule of terror sanctioned by the deity. Yahweh rebukes the nations in his wrath and terrifies them in his anger, the king threatens them with crushing, and they are advised by the poet to serve Yahweh with fear and 'rejoice' (?) with trembling, to pay homage to the king lest he be angry, because his wrath can flare up in a moment. There is a lot of anger about in this poem, but it too is 'managed' by the commentators. Either the subject is not mentioned (the favourite method), or else it is argued that the air of irascibility that the psalm breathes does not tell the whole story. For example, 'By long-drawn-out, gentle patience He has sought to win to obedience (though that side of His dealings is not presented in this psalm), but the moment arrives when...sleeping retribution wakes at the right moment, determined by considerations inappreciable by us'.[49] 'The quick anger may sound like the touchiness of a despot', allows Derek Kidner, 'but the true comparison is with Christ, whose wrath (like his compassion) blazed up at wrongs which left His contemporaries quite unruffled. This fiery picture is needed alongside that of the one who is "slow to anger".'[50] The anger that fills the psalm may be one-sided, that is to say, but it is necessary to a more whole and harmonious view of the divine.

4. The professed concern for the nations in vv. 10-12, coupled with the callous disregard of their own desires in the rest of the psalm. There is something unsavoury about a pedagogy that professes to teach wisdom and offer advice (v. 10) but is based upon contempt for its pupils (v. 1) and accompanied by threats of bullying (v. 9) and even capital punishment (v. 12). The threats are serious enough, so it is hard to see any genuine altruism in the appeal to reason in v. 10.

47. Anderson, *Psalms*, I, p. 68 (my italics).
48. Emerton, 'The Translation of the Verbs', p. 503.
49. Maclaren, *Psalms*, I, p. 16.
50. Derek Kidner, *Psalms 1–72* (Tyndale Old Testament Commentaries; London: Inter-Varsity Press, 1973), p. 53.

The commentators, however, want to swallow up the threats in the advice, the wrath in the love:

> This Psalm opens the Psalter with a proclamation of God's love and a denunciation of God's wrath against those who reject it... God's mercy is not impaired by the declaration of His wrath, but if the awful reality of that wrath were withdrawn, the bright truth of God's Love would fade away into a twilight of moral indifference.[51]

What kind of love is it that brings denunciation if it is rejected? What sort of love is it that fades to moral indifference if it does not include wrath? Hell obviously hath no fury like a deity scorned. The tension between the protestations of concern and the threats of violence remains, and the poem will always begin where it begins, with scorn, and end where it ends, with death for all those who do not 'take refuge' in the God who rules from Zion.

A softening of the contours is especially notable in Christianizing ('messianic') interpretations of the psalm, which want to maximize the degree of fit between the king of Jerusalem and Jesus but, on the other hand, resist blurring the cleancut lines of the Christian Jesus with alien figurations. In such readings, the violence of the Israelite king is usually passed over in silence, the ideas of compulsion and subjugation are transcribed as divine sovereignty, the claims of the king are swallowed up in the universal lordship of Yahweh, and the king is messianized and transformed into a wisdom teacher and evangelist:

> the Messiah calls the kings and rulers of earth to become servants of the reign of YHWH. He teaches the nations the fear of the Lord just as he teaches people obedience to the Torah of the Lord (in Psalm 1). To both he offers a better way than the way that offends the divine sovereignty.[52]

Or, more sophisticatedly,

> In the view of the final redaction the (messianic) king in Zion lays hold, not of weapons, but of words, in order to move the kings of the nations on to the path towards the kingdom of God... The

---

51. R.M. Benson, *The War-Songs of the Prince of Peace: A Devotional Commentary on the Psalms* (London: John Murray, 1901), I, pp. 70-71.

52. James Luther Mays, '"In a Vision": The Portrayal of the Messiah in the Psalms', *Ex Auditu* 7 (1991), pp. 1-8 (3).

'messianic' king here brings to realization, as 'teacher of the Torah', the eschatological vision of Isa. 42.1, 6; 49.6; 51.4.[53]

The commentators are encouraging us to forget the unpleasantness of the scornful laughter and the aggressive language of shattering, are they not? If we can end our experience of the poem with a nice taste in the mouth, of eschatological mission and conversion and an evangelical kingdom of God, all is well, and the text is more positive, more Christian and more humane than it sounded.

Of course, if the going gets too hard, it is always possible to jettison the offending element in the text in a 'critical' mode, by that very means heightening the authority of what has not been 'critically' excised. Thus for example, in an essay on 'Preparing to Preach on a Royal Psalm',[54] Delmar L. Jacobson writes that in the New Testament use of Psalm 2 there is

> a startling turn of events: a new and contrary way which leads, not to the smashing of Messiah's enemies as announced in Psalm 2, but to the astonishment of Israel's enemies as announced in Isaiah 52:14-15.

This new and contrary way is a better way, naturally; and the Israelite king is textually punished by the commentator for not having been the messiah Jesus:

> In reality, however, things did not turn out as pictured in Psalm 2... Indeed, the day came when the Davidic king himself was broken 'with a rod of iron' and the Davidic kingdom dashed 'in pieces like a potter's vessel'.

But at the same time it is not just for not living 'down' (we might say) to the meek self-sacrifice of the Suffering Servant for which the Davidic kings are to be blamed, but also for their not having lived 'up' to the fearsome and domineering splendour portrayed in Psalm 2: 'None of the successive Davidic kings achieved the greatness envisioned by the temple songs such as Psalms 2, 45, 72, and 110'. Coming down hard on the Israelite kings for not really achieving world dominion is perhaps the ultimate capitulation to the ideology of the psalm. Not only is there nothing

---

53. Zenger, in Hossfeld and Zenger, *Die Psalmen I*, p. 54.
54. Delmar L. Jacobson, 'The Royal Psalms and Jesus Messiah: Preparing to Preach on a Royal Psalm', *Word and World* 5 (1985), pp. 192-98 (197, 198).

wrong—if you're an Israelite—with being brutal, the real fault is not being brutal enough.

f. *Hardening the Edges*

A contrary move on the part of commentators is to align themselves wholeheartedly with the savagery of the psalm, and to find justification for their totalitarian instincts in its wording. Whereas my complaint, when I find the contours of the psalm softened, is against the commentator for denaturing the psalm, here it is more against the psalm for authorizing and encouraging the commentator. Does the psalm bear no responsibility for the interpretations it licenses?

Here is one such hardening of the edges of the vision of Psalm 2, still firmly in the political sphere:

> [H]istory is nothing else than a prolonged exhibition of the scorn of God for human pride... Three hundred years ago the king of Spain equipped a huge fleet and despatched it against England, to chastise that heretical land and bring her under the papal yoke... Trusting in their strength the Spaniards reckoned on victory; but there were two factors of which they had taken no account: one, the valour of the English seamen...and the other, and by far the greater, the scorn of Him who sate in the heavens. He blew upon them, and they were scattered; He sent forth a mighty wind into the sea and drove them along the Channel and up into the cold North Sea... [O]f all that vast Armada only fifty-three...got home to Spain, with but a poor remnant of broken and dispirited men to tell how He that is enthroned in the heavens had laughed and mocked at them.[55]

This jingoistic rendering of the psalm, it should be noted, is not the private interpretation of some marginal author of a more uncouth age, but belongs to the mainstream of British biblical interpretation in this century. It is to be found in *The Speaker's Bible*, a compilation by the James Hastings who edited *The*

---

55. David Smith, 'Biblical Laughter', *The Expository Times* 12 (1900–1901), pp. 546-49 (548-49), quoted in *The Speaker's Bible. The Book of Job. Psalms I* (ed. James Hastings; Aberdeen: The 'Speaker's Bible' Offices, 1924), pp. 285-86. I should add that the 'Speaker's Bible' was so called because it was commissioned by the Speaker of the House of Commons; this commentary series was therefore not simply a churchly production of a bygone age but had a certain place, and an authority, in British political life.

Expository Times, The Dictionary of the Bible, and *The Encyclopaedia of Religion and Ethics.* The aim of *The Speaker's Bible,* according to its distinguished editor, was 'to preserve all that is worth preserving of the modern interpretation of the Bible'—a sobering thought.

And here is another instance of a hardening of the edges:

> The second Psalm is one of the best Psalms. I love that Psalm with my heart. It strikes and flashes valiantly amongst kings, princes, counsellors, judges, etc. If what this Psalm says be true, then are the allegations and aims of the papists stark lies and folly. If I were as our Lord God, and had committed the government to my son, as he to his Son, and these vile people were as disobedient as they now be, I would knock the world to pieces.[56]

Luther, of course. It is a classic example of the pernicious influence of the psalm's violence, as well as of the use of the psalm as a vehicle for the interpreter's own anger.

g. *Refusal to Draw the Implications of Ancient Near Eastern Parallels*
There is a considerable literature pointing out the detailed parallels between the wording of this psalm and ancient Near Eastern literatures.[57] But it is not recognized that the closer the analogy

56. I have a notation that this is from Martin Luther's *Table Talk*, but I cannot now find the source. I searched *Luther's Works.* 54. *Table Talk* (ed. and trans. Theodore G. Tappert; Philadelphia: Fortress Press, 1967), the six volumes of *Tischreden* in the Weimar edition of Luther's works, and the extra *Tischreden* in vol. XLVIII, pp. 365-719, all to no avail. Nor is the passage to be found in Luther's voluminous writings on Psalm 2 in his *Lectures on the Psalms* (*Luther's Works,* XII [ed. Jaroslav Pelikan: St Louis: Concordia, 1958], pp. 4-93, and XIV [ed. Jaroslav Pelikan: St Louis: Concordia, 1955], pp. 313-49. But no one can doubt that the passage is from Luther! For another example of the influence of this psalm, see the Koran, Sura 2.14.
57. See for example Gerhard von Rad, 'The Royal Ritual in Judah', in his *The Problem of the Hexateuch and Other Essays* (trans. E.W. Trueman Dicken; Edinburgh: Oliver & Boyd, 1966), pp. 222-31 [original, 'Das judäische Köingsritual', *Theologische Literaturzeitung* 72 (1947), cols. 211-16 (= his *Gesammelte Studien zum Alten Testament* [Munich: Kaiser Verlag, 1958], pp. 205-13)]; Thiel, 'Der Weltherrschaftsanspruch'; Victor Sasson, 'The Language of Rebellion in Psalm 2 and the Plaster Texts from Deir 'Alla', *Andrews University Seminary Studies* 24 (1986), pp. 147-54; Albert Kleber, 'Ps. 2:9 in the Light of an Ancient Oriental Ceremony', *Catholic Biblical Quarterly* 5 (1943), pp. 63-67. Oriental analogies to kissing the feet of a ruler (not otherwise attested

between the Hebrew text and the ancient Near Eastern texts, the stronger the case for believing that this psalm represents the ideologies of world empires like Babylonia and Egypt that are, by most accounts, inimical to the theology of the Hebrew Bible.

Artur Weiser, for example, recognizes that the setting of the psalm (which he identifies as that of a world-wide rule of the Israelite king) 'copie[s] a foreign pattern...[,] that of the court etiquette of the great empires of the ancient Orient and of its royal cult'[58] and 'borrow[s] the setting...of victories over the other nations and of dominion over the whole world, from foreign prototypes'.[59] But he wants to insist that

> If two people say the very same thing, it is nevertheless not the same thing. The oracles of the ancient East impart to the historical aspirations of the kings for power a greater energy by the promise of divine help; the emphasis is, however, on the internal affairs of the nation in question. In the Old Testament, on the other hand, the internal historical events—in our present context the kingship in Zion—are recognized as bearers of a divine will which transcends history and for that reason encompasses it totally—both as regards space and time—and that divine will bursts the narrow bounds which limit the internal historical events...and makes these events the blueprint of and the signal for that divine judgment which in terms of space is universal and in terms of time is final (eschatological).[60]

It goes without saying that from a Moabite point of view—or indeed from any point of view that does not identify with the world of the text—this is special pleading. If such language as we encounter in the psalm signifies in its ancient Near Eastern analogues a lust for royal power, a disinterested observer will need a lot of convincing that it means something totally different in the psalm.[61]

---

in the Hebrew Bible) are conveniently summarized by Gunkel, *Die Psalmen*, p. 8.

58. Weiser, *Psalms*, p. 110.

59. Weiser, *Psalms*, p. 113. Similarly Zenger, in Hossfeld and Zenger, whose first sentence on Psalm 2 is: 'In the background stands the ancient Near Eastern and Egyptian view of world order' (*Die Psalmen I*, p. 53).

60. Weiser, *Psalms*, p. 114.

61. A similar observation is also made by Thiel, 'Der Weltherrschaftsanspruch', p. 58.

Here is another example, this time from a learned and eloquent preacher rather than a professional scholar:

> The lower half of the picture is all eager motion and strained effort; the upper is full of Divine calm… He needs not to rise from His throned tranquillity, but regards undisturbed the disturbances of earth. The thought embodied is like that expressed in the Egyptian statues of gods carved out of the side of a mountain, 'moulded in colossal calm', with their mighty hands laid in their laps and their wide-opened eyes gazing down on the little ways of the men creeping about their feet.[62]

So, we must conclude, for the Christian interpreter the theology of Egypt was in the right after all, and we may be grateful that the Hebrew poet had the breadth of vision to lay under tribute the wisdom of his erstwhile national oppressor. Or, to abandon the irony, is it not amazing that so many can see the parallels with the ancient Near East, and so few can see their significance?[63]

h. *Sweeping Politics under the Aesthetic Rug*
The 'beauty' and dramatic force of the psalm have often been remarked on. For example:

> This song is a noble outburst of these truly great reflections, these sublime sentiments… This is the type of a perfect song, blending in itself rest and unrest, contemplation and sensibility in the finest manner… This beautiful song must necessarily proceed from the most splendid period of the kingdom…[64]

> …this splendid but commonly misunderstood psalm…[65]

> …this magnificent lyric…[66]

---

62. Maclaren, *Psalms*, I, p. 15.
63. It is to the credit of Winfried Thiel ('Der Weltherrschaftsanspruch') that he raises the issue at all, that he critiques both Weiser's and Kraus's attempts to deal with it, and that he proposes his own. I must say, however, that the claim that the Old Testament itself offers 'corrections' to the theology of Psalm 2 ('Der Weltherrschaftsanspruch', p. 59) does not for me remove the scandal of the text (any more than in the essay by Klein, in note 1 above).
64. Ewald, *Commentary on the Psalms*, pp. 148, 149.
65. Gunkel, *Die Psalmen*, p. 5.
66. Maclaren, *Psalms*, I, p. 11.

...this beautiful poem...[67]

[Verses] 1-3 place us, in masterly fashion, immediately into the situation... For its power, its vividness and its precise language, Psalm 2 has few equals.[68]

In sublime language, and with great dramatic power, [the nations] are rebuked for their folly...[69]

Its author, a master of words full of great poetical power and bold ideas ...[70]

The psalm is effective and dramatic in its literary style.[71]

The four sections/scenes form an artistic composition.[72]

The poetry in v 9 presents this regal authority in a dramatic manner...[73]

There comes a point, however, when one wonders whether this chorus of approval for the psalm's aesthetic qualities is not a systematic deflection of attention from its political intention and its ethical shortcomings. I do not mean to dissent from the critics' universal praise, but simply to ask: If we may make aesthetic judgments about this text, may we not also make ethical ones?[74]

i. *The Inscription of Ideology in Modern Translations*
There must be very few biblical scholars[75] who did not first read this psalm in Hebrew but in a modern translation in their own language. But no one ever seems to notice that their interpretation of the psalm must have been in important respects con-

---

67. Hans Schmidt, *Die Psalmen* (Handbuch zum Alten Testament, I/15; Tübingen: J.C.B. Mohr [Paul Siebeck], 1934), p. 6.
68. Duhm, *Psalmen*, pp. 5, 10.
69. W.T. Davison, *The Psalms, I–LXXII* (Century Bible; Edinburgh: T.C. & E.C. Jack, n.d.), p. 50.
70. Weiser, *Psalms*, p. 109.
71. Craigie, *Psalms 1–50*, p. 65.
72. Zenger, in Hossfeld and Zenger, *Die Psalmen I*, p. 49.
73. Craigie, *Psalms 1–50*, p. 67.
74. In this I am entirely at one with Wayne C. Booth's vigorous attempt to restore 'ethical criticism' to our literary agenda; see his *The Company We Keep: An Ethics of Fiction* (Berkeley: University of California Press, 1988).
75. I am obviously leaving out of account at this point those for whom Hebrew is a native language.

trolled and determined by the ideology of the modern versions they grew up with.

1. We have already seen how the use of the definite article in vv. 1, 2 and 8 (the nations, the peoples, the kings of the earth, the rulers, the nations, the ends of the earth) universalize the psalm. Can it be that scholars do not question the idea of universal dominion in this psalm because they have always 'known' that it is about 'the' nations and 'the' peoples?

2. I have also already noted how translating the term אֶרֶץ as 'world, earth' rather than 'land' likewise predetermines the reader, and even the scholar familiar with Hebrew, to see in the psalm an unambiguous reference to world dominion.

3. Another ideological decision that has been imported into translations of the psalm is that it concerns Yahweh's universal lordship and the delegation of his dominion to the king (the NAB, for example, heads the psalm 'The Universal Reign of the Messiah'). Thus תְּרֹעֵם (v. 9), which is unmistakably 'you will break' (from רעע), and which suits the parallelism of תְּנַפְּצֵם ('you will shatter', from נפץ), is emended to תִּרְעֵם and translated 'you will rule' in the NIV and the NAB[76]—though 'break' in AV, RV, RSV, JB, NJB, NEB, REB, GNB and 'smash' in NJPS. This is evidently a Christianizing rendering, given contemporary currency both by an evangelical Protestant and by a Roman Catholic translation.

4. Perhaps the most conspicuous example of how theological and ideological interpretations of the psalm have been inscribed and enshrined in modern English translations is the capitalizations of the NIV. The 'Anointed One', the 'King' and the 'Son' are not names for an Israelite king (in Ps. 45.1 [NIV], for example, the poet recites his verses for 'the king', with a lowercase 'k'). This is

---

76. On the basis of the Septuagint ποιμανεῖς and the Vulgate *reges* (cf. also Rev. 2.27 ποιμανεῖ), Briggs and Briggs, *Psalms*, I, p. 22, among others, think 'rule' is 'more suited to the context of the sceptre, even if it be of iron'. And it is more recently defended by G. Wilhelmi, 'Der Hirt mit dem eisernen Szepter. Überlegungen zu Psalm ii 9', *Vetus Testamentum* 27 (1977), pp. 196-204, and by Emerton, 'The Translation of the Verbs', p. 502; but see, to the contrary, J. Alberto Soggin, 'Zum zweiten Psalm', in *Wort–Gebot–Glaube: Beiträge zur Theologie des Alten Testaments. Walther Eichrodt zum 80. Geburtstag* (ed. Hans Joachim Stoebe *et al.*; Abhandlungen zur Theologie des Alten und Neuen Testaments, 59; Zürich: Zwingli Verlag, 1970), pp. 191-207.

a blatant Christianization of the psalm. and yet another example of the ideology of the scholarly tradition.

3. *The Question of Ethics*

The tendency of this paper is toward showing that there is a question of ethics—hitherto largely unrecognized—both in the world of the text of Psalm 2 itself and also in the scholarly commentary on it, where the ethical problems raised by the psalm are only further compounded.

a. *In the World of the Text*

The primary ethical question raised by the psalm is, What is an appropriate response to assertions of national independence and claims to national self-determination? Any answers we give to this question, indeed any thoughts we have on the subject whatsoever, are subjectively ours, and more or less conditioned by our own historical and social location and experience. But if we are serious and autonomous people, they are ours, and therefore the only views we should, in my opinion, hold.

Now the text of Psalm 2 says that, when the nations seeking independence are non-Israelite and are seeking it from Israel, they should not have it. The poet is against it, the king is against it, and the god is against it. Psalm 2 is not in two minds on the matter. Any nation contemplating a liberation movement had better know that it will be resisted and that it will be scorned. If its leaders have any sense, they will bow in humble submission to the Israelite king and not risk his wrath.[77]

I myself, living in a post-imperialist culture, do not think very highly of this attitude. Moreover, I think it important, as a scholar engaged professionally with this psalm, to make my unease with it very plain—if for no other reason, because I should hate for anyone to construe my silence as consent or to take my neutral or 'objective' remarks about the text to signify any refusal or incapacity on my part to form ethical judgments.

---

77. I am understanding נשקו־בר as 'kiss the son', though of course the reading and interpretation are much debated. See, for example, A.A. Macintosh, 'A Consideration of the Problems Presented by Psalm ii. 11 and 12', *Journal of Theological Studies* ns 27 (1976), pp. 1-14.

But my unease with the psalm goes deeper, I believe, than my own 'instinctive' (which is to say, culturally conditioned but also 'owned' by myself) disagreement with its programme. For it is not just that the ideology of the psalm is in conflict with mine (and that of people I approve of): it is in conflict also with other streams of thought in its own culture—in ways that make its ideology questionable. In a word, while Israel is very happy to have been liberated itself, this psalm does not want anyone else to be liberated—and that seems to undermine the value Israel put on national freedom, and to render its attitude to freedom ambivalent and incoherent. It was apparently fundamental to Israelite national self-perception to remember itself as originating as a body of slaves escaped from Egypt. Whether or not it had historically been the case that Israel had come into being by way of liberation from imperial overlords, that is how Israel chose to construct its own history. Now Psalm 2 is not explicitly denying that construction of the past, but, in refusing a similar history to others, it implicitly does so, and thus denies the value of its own liberation.

It would not be so bad if Psalm 2 happened to promote a view that was simply in opposition to another view expressed in the Hebrew Bible. If it did, it would have a perfect right to do so, and it would not be for us to insist that the Hebrew Bible should display a uniform ideology. And it would not be so bad if it were just a question of our preferring another Hebrew Bible view about national autonomy to that expressed in this psalm, for we would have a perfect right to do that, and there is no obligation on any of us to approve of everything that is in the Hebrew Bible. What is so bad for me about Psalm 2's ideology is, as I have just now suggested, not only that I do not approve of it but that it cannot sustain itself or justify itself in terms of Israel's own self-awareness.

And that is the ethical problem of the text: the text is an act of bad faith, an attempt to deceive itself about the nature of reality.[78]

78. This condition of bad faith (*mauvaise foi*) is classically described in Jean-Paul Sartre's *Being and Nothingness: An Essay on Phenomenological Ontology* (trans. Hazel E. Barnes; London: Routledge, 1991 [original edition, 1943]), pp. 47-70. The worst form of bad faith, as Roger Poole notes (in *The*

b. *In the World of the Commentator*
What happens in the world of the commentator on Psalm 2 is
that its ideology of the repression of national liberation movements is affirmed and perpetuated. I call this a compounding of
the ethical dubiety of the text itself in that the commentators
should know better, since they, as scholars, should have no particular unrecognized and undeclared investment in a text they
happening to be commenting on (for one thing, they will probably be commenting on a quite different and quite possibly dis-
crepant text next week) and they should be able to relativize
their text by situating it within a wider cultural and intellectual
context. It is no great crime, perhaps, that the poet of Psalm 2
should do his own thing, make his own statement, utter his own
prejudices, be as opinionated and one-sided and passionate as
he likes. But it is a shocking thing that scholars of these texts
should only be able to comment on how insightful and (in one
sense or another) 'true' this text is, without ever embarking on a
critical evaluation of it. They compound the moral dubiety of the
text by perpetuating its claims and by lending them their own
moral authority.

Any commentator worth his or her salt knows how important
in Old Testament theology the theme of national freedom is,
whether it is in the announcements of the mission of the
Deutero-Isaianic servant (e.g. Isa. 61.1), or in the piety of the
psalmists (e.g. Ps. 44.2; 69.18) or in the historical narratives (e.g.
Exod. 3.8; Judg. 10.11; Neh. 9.28).[79] But they all suppress what

Harper Dictionary of Modern Thought [ed. Alan Bullock and Stephen Tromb-
ley; New York: Harper & Row, 1988], p. 67) is 'that self-deception which
allows a subject to believe that he [*sic*] is not free to change things, or that
things could not be otherwise'; this is the form of bad faith to which commentators are most susceptible.

79. Curiously, though, the writers of articles in our standard Bible encyclopaedias do not know this, but almost invariably know only about personal freedom or captivity. So for example J. Marsh, 'Liberty', in *The Interpreter's Dictionary of the Bible* (ed. George Arthur Buttrick; Nashville: Abingdon Press, 1962), III, pp. 122-23; F. Stanley Jones, 'Freedom', in *The Anchor
Bible Dictionary* (ed. David Noel Freedman: New York: Doubleday, 1992), II,
pp. 855-59 ('[T]he OT does not develop a theology of freedom on the basis
of the Exodus. Rather, Israel was ransomed in order to be God's servants...and the language used to describe this event is primarily that of

they know about liberation, deliverance and freedom when it comes to non-Israelite peoples—and so are complicit in the unlovely ethnocentricity of the text. They know that the Hebrew Bible is supposed to favour the poor, the weak, the under-privileged and the oppressed, but they forget that orientation when it is a matter of foreigners. And they know that the language of this psalm echoes the language of the brutal oriental empires, but they 'manage' that fact out of their consciousness.

Some are pointing out these days how Psalm 2 functions as part of a preface to the Psalms, setting a tone and an orientation to the Psalter as a whole.[80] They do not notice that this position of the psalm makes the ethical problem it raises only more acute. If it is problematic that the psalm resists national claims to self-determination, and represents the Jerusalem king as a ruler in the pattern of oriental tyrants, a serious question is raised about the piety of the Psalter as a whole—namely, whether what is represented in it is a universally valid and desirable type of piety, or whether its theological opinions stand in need of critique from the standpoints of its readers (whatever they may be).[81]

"redemption," not of "freedom"' [p. 855]—which does not seem at all true to me). Contrast F.F. Bruce, 'Liberty', in *The International Standard Bible Encyclopedia* [ed. Geoffrey W. Bromiley; Grand Rapids: Eerdmans, 1986], III, pp. 119-22: 'The paradigm of liberty in the OT...is the deliverance of the Israelites from their servitude in Egypt' [p. 119]). Slavery, too, is generally recognized in the textbooks as purely a personal matter. So I. Mendelsohn, 'Slavery in the OT', in *The Interpreter's Dictionary of the Bible*, IV, pp. 383-41, and Muhammad A. Dandamayev, 'Slavery', in *The Anchor Bible Dictionary*, VI, pp. 58-62, concluding that 'The institution of slavery was taken for granted not only by the free persons but also by the slaves themselves, who never demanded its abolition' (p. 61). How would we know? And why should 'literal', personal slavery be privileged by dictionary-article authors over the slavery of whole nations?

80. Cf. Erich Zenger, 'Der Psalter als Wegweiser und Wegbegleiter: Ps 1–2 als Proömium des Psalmenbuchs', in *Sie wandern von Kraft zu Kraft: Aufbrüche, Wege, Begegnungen. Festgabe für Bischof Reinhard Lettmann* (ed. Arnold Angenendt and Herbert Vorgrimler; Kevelaer: Butzon & Bercker, 1993), pp. 29-47 (I am grateful to Erich Zenger for sending me a copy of this article); A. Deissler, 'Die Stellung von Psalm 2 im Psalter. Folgen für die Auslegung', in *Beiträge zur Psalmenforschung* (Forschung zur Bibel, 60; Würzburg: Echter Verlag, 1988), pp. 73-83.

81. And if, as Gosse argues ('Le Psaume 2 et l'usage rédactionnel'), the

There is also the fact, which must be taken into account at this point, that Psalm 2 is among the most frequently quoted psalms in the New Testament. From an ethical point of view, this fact should not be taken to exculpate the ideology of the psalm but rather should call into question the New Testament itself—a text that draws its authority, in part, from the violence and repressiveness of Psalm 2. It does not matter that the intertexts of Psalm 2 do not take the psalm 'literally', for from an ethical point of view it is all one whether the violence is literal or metaphorical. If the reign of the messiah is to be founded on violence and the suppression of what we would today call the legitimate interests of others, that constitutes a problem for Christianity.[82] In short, the quotation of Psalm 2 in the New Testament by no means legitimates the ethics of the psalm, but rather problematizes the New Testament.

4. *A Bible Readers' Liberation Movement*

So far in this essay, it has been the freedom of 'Moabites' and their rights to self-determination that have been the subject of discussion. But they are not the only ones to have their interests and rights suppressed by the psalm. There are also the readers.

There is no denying that the psalm has its own kind of dramatic and aesthetic power, and, since it professes to speak about God, and moreover to extol his lordship, it is a rare reader who

psalm represents inner conflicts in the postexilic community projected onto the outside world, the ethical problem of the psalm takes on yet another dimension: it is whether it is right to use the language of political suppression to deal with conflicts in the realm of ideas—whether, to put it concretely, you do not have an ethical problem with your beliefs if you find yourself wanting to smash those who disagree with them like a potter's vessel.

82. Here, for example, is the language of violence masquerading as the language of piety: 'When [Christ] burst the bands of the grave... He purchased for Himself an universal dominion. Henceforth His kingdom has been established in Zion, and all people of the earth will be subdued either to His love or to His wrath. What remains for us but to yield ourselves reverently to His sway...?' (Peter Young, 'The Book of Psalms', in *The Old Testament according to the Authorised Version: Poetical Books* (London: Society for Promoting Christian Knowledge, 1878), *in loc.*

is not intimidated by this psalm into thinking that it offers rewarding insights into spiritual realities. Whether or not such intimidation goes under the name of 'the authority of the Bible', there can be little doubt that most readers feel no freedom to resist the power and authority of the psalm—and thus, its ideology. It is not only fictional 'Moabites' who have fetters upon them but real people at the end of the twentieth century also who are constrained by the psalm to believe that God has favourites among the peoples of the earth, has no time for the idea of toleration, and resorts to violence to solve his problems.

But there is another kind of power to which Bible readers are subject—at least Bible readers of the kind who read essays like this. It is the power of the academic community, who control what may be said about psalms. The scholars who write commentaries and learned papers on the psalm do not merely give us information about the backgrounds to the text or offer us exegeses for our consideration. They also control—it is not too strong a word—the reading and interpretation of the text.[83] It is too late in the day for anyone to claim the innocence of texts, whether Bible texts or scholarly commentaries; all have their own interest to serve, and they serve it with their whole being. The commentaries are written precisely to tell us how we should read Psalm 2, and what they say with a single voice is that the psalm is good and true and admirable and uplifting. They have

---

83. For this reason, I am at present teaching a course on the Psalms in which I forbid students to read books (other than the Psalms). I mean: I require them in their essays to show no evidence that they have read anything but the text, for I know all too well that if they do, they will believe the books and not the evidence of the text. Needless to say, they find this an oppressive regime, telling me every day that they know no other way of writing essays but to read books. This rebellion only encourages me the more, and I laugh them to scorn, taking a leaf out of the Psalter. One day soon, however, when they are firm and confident in their own ability to read psalms, I shall demand that they turn to the commentaries, and discover for themselves the difference between the texts and the scholarly tradition. They will praise me then (I fondly believe) for enabling their freedom from the tyranny of the tradition. It may be of interest to mention that in our departmental statement of goals for each graduating student in Biblical Studies the first of the goals is 'that he or she can handle the Bible confidently, and is not intimidated by it or the scholarship about it'.

no fault to find with it. Compared with this insistent and united message, often conveyed subliminally and therefore all the more effectively, their dissent from one another over details of exegesis or questions like the date of the psalm are trivial. Indeed, in the very act of evaluating the differences among commentators—which is the substance of most scholarly work—the reader is systematically deflected from considering what it is that they have in common: a complicity with the text.

In such a situation, what is called for, in my opinion, is a readers' liberation movement.[84] Too many readers are in bondage either to the text or to the approved interpretations of the text—or to both. With one bound—as the saying goes—they could be free. Like the freedom fighters of the Moabite Liberation Front, they have nothing to lose but their chains, but unlike them they do not even need to unite to find their freedom—everyone can do it for themselves.

Being free from the authority of the text and of its professional interpreters does not mean denying or rejecting everything they say. It is not obligatory to deny the psalm's claim that it is foolish to resist God or that God wants humanity to be obedient to his will. But it does mean being free to decide for oneself whether one will accept that these are appropriate terms in which to speak of the divine. It is a sad day for theism if the only language its adherents can find to express their sense of the divine is the language of oriental despotism, with its scornful deity who offers comfort to petty kings in their grandiose ambitions and authorizes state violence and a regime of terror against those who want nothing more gross than self-determination.

Have I been *fair* to this text?, I wonder finally, re-reading this essay. What have these few scratchings of ink on leather (or whatever) that we call Psalm 2—a mere 365 letters in all, occupying no more than four or five lines of printed footnote text[85]—

84. Terry Eagleton has guyed the idea of readers' liberation in his *Against the Grain: Essays 1975–1985* (London: Verso, 1986). But for all his charisma, Eagleton probably does not know what life is really like out here in the wastelands where the Bible is still being read as if it were gospel truth.

85. Here is the *whole* of the text of Psalm 2 (printed, for authenticity's sake, without the usual typographical and reading conventions like space

done to deserve this disproportionate scrutiny, this excessive interrogation by an alien and apparently hostile critic? And have I not, with my dreadful hermeneutic of suspicion, offended against what Wayne Booth calls the 'golden rule' of reading, 'Read as you would have others read you'? I console myself with reflection on the disparity between us, between the text and me. If we were partners, on more or less the same footing, I would do as I would be done by. But this text has a power so incommensurable with mine that my voice is no more than a whimper. The text is a ocean liner (the S.S. Authority) bearing down on me out of the fog, me in my leaky dinghy trying to navigate the chartless sea of meaning. This text has been chanted by millions of the faithful over two millennia, subliminally supporting, *inter alia*, papal authority, the divine right of kings and the British empire too—and its force will not abate even if the institutions it supports may change from time to time; my hope of (this-worldly) immortality, on the other hand, is nothing more than an entry in the ATLA database. Do I *need* to be *fair*?

between words, verse numbers, poetic lines, and Masoretic vocalization):

למהרגשוגוימולאמימיהגוריקיתיצבובומלכיארצורוזנימנוסדועליהוהועלמשחוננתקהאתמוסרותימוונשלכהממנע
בתימויושבבשממימישחקאדנייילעגלמואזידבראלימובאפובחרונויבהלמואניסכתימלכיעלציונהרקדשיאספרה
אלחקיהוהאמראליבניאתהאניהיומילדתיהשאלממניואתנהגוימנחלתכואחזתכאפסיארצתרעמבשבטברזלככלייו
צרתנפצמועתהמלכימהשכילוהוסרולוהשכיארצועבדואתיהוהביראהוגילוברעדהנשקוברפניאנפותהאבדודרככיי
בערכמעטאפואשריכלחוסיבוי

INDEXES

INDEX OF REFERENCES

HEBREW BIBLE

NEW TESTAMENT

OTHER JEWISH WORKS

INDEX OF AUTHORS

INDEX OF SUBJECTS